Chicken Soup for the Soul: My Crazy Family
101 Stories about the Wacky, Lovable People in Our Lives
Amy Newmark

Published by Chicken Soup for the Soul, LLC www.chickensoup.com
Copyright ©2018 by Chicken Soup for the Soul, LLC. All Rights Reserved.

The publisher gratefully acknowledges the many publishers and individuals who granted Chicken Soup for the Soul permission to reprint the cited material.

Front cover photos: Old man DJ courtesy of iStockphoto.com/dubassy (©dubassy), cleaning woman courtesy of iStockphoto.com/SrdicPhoto (©SrdicPhoto), woman with hat courtesy of iStockphoto.com/MilicaStankovic (©MilicaStankovic) and yoga guy courtesy of iStockphoto.com/Yuri_Arcurs (©Yuri_Arcurs)
Back cover and Interior artwork courtesy of iStockphoto.com/Ann_Mei(©Ann_Mei)
Photo of Amy Newmark courtesy of Susan Morrow at SwickPix

Cover and Interior by Daniel Zaccari

Distributed to the booktrade by Simon & Schuster. SAN: 200-2442

Publisher's Cataloging-In-Publication Data
(Prepared by The Donohue Group, Inc.)

Names: Newmark, Amy, compiler.
Title: Chicken soup for the soul : my crazy family : 101 stories about the
      wacky, lovable people in our lives / [compiled by] Amy Newmark.
Other Titles: My crazy family : 101 stories about the wacky, lovable
      people in our lives
Description: [Cos Cob, Connecticut] : Chicken Soup for the Soul, LLC,
      [2018]
Identifiers: ISBN 9781611599770 (print) | ISBN 9781611592771 (ebook)
Subjects: LCSH: Families--Literary collections. | Families--Anecdotes. |
      LCGFT: Anecdotes.
Classification: LCC HQ734 .C45 2018 (print) | LCC HQ734 (ebook) | DDC
      306.85--dc23

Library of Congress Control Number 2018933622

PRINTED IN THE UNITED STATES OF AMERICA
on acid∞free paper

25 24 23 22 21 20 19 18   01 02 03 04 05 06 07 08 09 10 11

My Crazy Family

101 Stories about the Wacky, Lovable People in Our Lives

Amy Newmark

Chicken Soup for the Soul, LLC
Cos Cob, CT

Chicken Soup for the Soul

Changing lives one story at a time®
www.chickensoup.com

Table of Contents

❶
~Eccentrics R Us~

❷
~Mom Did What?~

❸
~Happily Ever Laughter~

❹
~We're All Nuts Here~

❺
~Childhood Hijinks~

❻

~Grand and Great~

❼

~Sometimes You Just Have to Laugh~

Chapter 1

My Crazy Family

Eccentrics R Us

That Crazy Squirrel Lady

*Things aren't often what they appear to be
at first blush. But embarrassment is.*
~Jarod Kintz

"**M**om, look at this." My daughter opened her hand, exposing a tiny ball of gray fur. "I found it on the road sitting beside its dead mother. When I went to walk away, it ran up my leg and across my arm into my hand." Her face was a study of wonderment and delight. Although it was a heartwarming incident, there was the immediate question of what to do with a baby squirrel.

Our home had seen its share of babies over the years. We had five children, a Persian cat, a Samoyed dog, two chickens and a rabbit — all thriving under one roof.

Our youngest child was six months old, so I always had a small emergency bottle of formula in the fridge. We retrieved the bottle for the squirrel and warmed it a little in the microwave. The children gathered close to see what would happen. That fuzzy, little thing curled up on his back, clutched the nipple with both paws and sucked it dry. Amazing! Before I could warn the kids, they had already named him and made him a bed in a shoebox. Our fate was sealed, and Peanuts became a new member of the family.

For some reason, Peanuts liked to sleep in warm, dark places. Many times, we would be looking for him everywhere, and then see a slight bulge under the covers on our waterbed where he had snuggled down for the night. The other place he particularly loved to be was in my housecoat pocket. That way, he could run up my arm and sit on my head to watch the activity in our busy household.

With five kids, mornings were filled with changing diapers, eating breakfast, doing hair and packing lunches. The kids often left for school before I was out of my housecoat, and this provided Peanuts with a few hours of entertainment, as he ventured in and out of my pocket to check out what we were doing.

One particular morning, we had a new van being delivered. A delivery service dropped off the new van with the keys and left. It was lovely — dark red with a delightfully clean interior. In the middle of morning mayhem and still in my housecoat, I decided to try out the new car. Grabbing the keys, Peanuts and I headed to the garage. No matter how I tried to get those keys in the ignition, they would not go. I was frustrated and feeling short on patience. Marching back to the kitchen, I snatched up the phone and dialed the dealership. Some unfortunate soul answered as I explained that the wrong keys had been dropped off. I asked if someone could please bring the right ones immediately.

I must have sounded a little cranky as, minutes later, the doorbell rang. Opening the door to a gentleman, I was about to explain the situation again when Peanuts decided to see what caused the commotion. He scooted out of my pocket and nimbly climbed to his position on top of my head. Unlike other times, however, he managed to get perched in the wrong direction. With his head facing backwards, his tail dangled over my face, like a raccoon hat on backwards.

I was in the middle of a serious discussion with the man from the dealership and, without thinking, I pulled the squirrel from my head and stuffed him in my pocket. Within seconds, Peanuts had scampered back up to his lookout perch, backwards once again. Continuing my diatribe as to how they had left me the wrong keys, it just seemed easier at this point to hold the tail to the side and continue the conversation.

I realized mid-sentence that the man was no longer looking at me. His eyes were wide and fixated on the squirrel. He wasn't listening to me at all and probably hadn't heard a word I'd said. Had this man never seen a squirrel before? Quickly, I whisked the squirrel off my head and stuffed him in my pocket again.

"Come with me," I told the man, and turned to lead the way to the garage. We marched past the passel of kids eating breakfast in various stages of dress, the toddler in the Tupperware cupboard, the dog cleaning the cat's ears, and the piles of laundry waiting to be done, and then sidestepped the lunchboxes and rain boots lined up in the back hall. We still had to climb over a few bikes in the garage before standing in front of the new vehicle.

As I dangled the keys in front of him, the man's eyes slowly slid from the squirming little mass in my pocket to the key ring. He stared for a moment or two, and I saw his mouth twitch in a peculiar way.

"Madam," he said, "these aren't the keys we brought. I think those must be the ones to your old van."

I looked at them again, realizing my error. By now, the squirrel had scrambled back on my head, at least sitting in the right direction, and peering with beady little eyes at the man from the dealership.

"Oh, my," I stammered. "I'm terribly sorry. I don't know how I could have made that mistake."

His glance took in my worn housecoat, the squirrel perched on my head, the dangling wrong keys, and my embarrassment. He smiled with every inch of his face and mumbled something about not worrying; it happened all the time. We found the new keys stuffed in a drawer. Within minutes, he was in his car and speeding away.

After the kids had left and with Peanuts back in my pocket, I sat at the now quiet kitchen table sipping a steaming cup of coffee and replaying the entire incident in my mind. Slowly, it dawned on my obviously overworked brain what that man must have been thinking of this bizarre, chaotic home and the crazy squirrel lady. Though it was a little embarrassing, I supposed if we caused even one man to go home that night with a new appreciation for his wife and children, all was not lost.

Peanuts stayed with us throughout that cold Quebec winter until the spring, when we released him again to the wild. The dog and the cat missed him most, and the kids watched for him out the window daily, but I was ever so glad to have my waterbed and housecoat to myself again.

~Heather Rodin

Now That's Cheap

Often, it's tied to family tradition.
~Jack Dolan

"There's a Christmas card from A.F. in the mail today," said Mom. "I saved it so we could open it together."

A.F. was our family's abbreviation for our Great-Aunt Flora. Technically, she was Mom's aunt and my great-aunt, but everyone just called her A.F.

Mom took the letter opener, slit open the envelope very carefully and retrieved the card. She placed the card on the table without opening it while we hovered over the envelope, something we did whenever we received a card or letter from our dear aunt.

"How does she do that?" I asked.

"She uses a pencil eraser," Mom replied. "I've watched her do it."

Great-Aunt Flora was one of the original "recyclers." She turned every envelope inside-out, wrote a new address on the previous inside panel, and reclosed it with a small dab or two of clear stationery glue — the kind that came in an hourglass bottle with a pink rubber dauber on the end of it.

"She got this one from Cousin Pearl," said Mom, squinting to read the handwriting on the new inside corner of the envelope. "I can't quite make out the postmark, though."

We finished marveling at the envelope and turned our attention to the card.

The Santa with the bulging bag of toys on the front panel looked a little haggard, but was otherwise intact. Inside, where someone, most likely Cousin Pearl, had signed her name, the bottom had been neatly cut off the card with a pair of pinking shears, leaving a jagged bottom above which Great-Aunt Flora had scrawled her name.

I laughed while Mom sighed. "I've given her boxes of new cards," she said, "twenty-five to a box. But as far as I know, she saves them for God-only-knows-what-reason!"

When I left to attend college, I started receiving my own cards from A.F. Sometimes, she enclosed two well-worn, one-dollar bills, folded and smoothed numerous times, but I never received them inside a "new" card.

As A.F.'s health began to fail, she moved into assisted living, and Mom and Aunt Jo took on the onerous task of cleaning out the house where she'd lived for nearly eighty years.

"How are you set for greeting cards?" Mom asked me during one of our weekly phone chats.

"Let me guess," I replied. "You found a dozen boxes of brand-new cards?"

"More like three dozen." Mom sighed. "I just don't know what we're going to do with all the things she's 'saved' over the years."

"Umm…" I hesitated, but decided it was now or never. "Could I put in my bid for the pinking shears?"

There was a short pause. "Most of the black paint is worn off the hand grips," Mom replied. "You'd probably be better off buying a new pair."

"I don't care about the paint."

I waited through another short pause and another sigh. Finally, Mom said, "You'll have to get in line. Aunt Jo and I are going to arm wrestle for them."

Great-Aunt Flora was ninety-eight when she passed. Mom must have won the arm-wrestling contest because, right after A.F.'s funeral, I got a brand-new card from Mom with the inside bottom cut off with a jagged edge.

"Mom!" I gasped in disbelief. "You don't need to cut the bottom off the card if it hasn't ever been signed!"

"Family tradition," explained Mom. "I wouldn't want you to forget your roots."

Mom was right. Roots are important. That's why, when Mom passed nearly thirty years after A.F., the pinking shears were the first thing I claimed for my own. Today, they hold a place of honor on my desk, reminding me forever and always that I come from a long line of amazing women.

~Jan Bono

Secret Family Language

*The family — that dear octopus from whose tentacles
we never quite escape, nor, in our inmost
hearts, ever quite wish to.*
~Dodie Smith

ost families have nicknames for each other. Little Billy is "Snoogles" or Grandpa is "Walleye King." It's an accepted practice and outsiders accept these monikers and know they likely have a charming backstory.

But some families take this shorthand beyond nicknames and also have a secret language that only their clan understands. Frankly, they don't want the rest of us to become fluent anytime soon. At least that's how my family sees it when it comes to our own secret language. It's all about private family communication.

For us, it all started with a "bookenheimer." You read that right: a bookenheimer. Your family never used bookenheimers? Are you sure? Even when your children were babies? Our private dictionary of words started with the lowly pacifier, when my oldest (now in her mid-twenties) had a health scare as an infant. At an ultrasound appointment, her father and I wanted to help calm her. We were instructed that she could not have a bottle, but pacifiers were allowed.

"Do you have the bookenheimer?" I asked him as our baby girl began to fuss.

"No, but I'm pretty sure it's in the diaper bag. I thought I put an extra bookenheimer in there. Maybe check your purse, too."

We searched through my purse and the diaper bag. The ultrasound technician and the doctor exchanged glances when the item was triumphantly produced. The technician cleared her throat and stated the obvious. "We hear a lot of names for pacies in here but bookenheimer might take the cake." She raised an eyebrow.

We scoffed, "Pacies! What a goofy name for a bookenheimer!" A classic secret family language moment if ever there was one. But why stop there? We began, as I am confident many families do, to adopt words and phrases that had specific meaning to our family.

If you are ever with us and happen to hear any of us casually refer to cheesecake, just know it has nothing to do with cheesecake. It is that most sacred of family shorthand: emergency gastrointestinal alert. Many years ago, someone in the family had a dire emergency after an outing to the Cheesecake Factory. The person in question didn't even *have* cheesecake, but cheesecake is taking the fall. Now, you'll hear us say, "I forgot to tell you that Aunt Ethel needs us to bring a cheesecake to the picnic." Or, "Did you happen to take that cheesecake out to thaw?" The point we all understand is: "I've got an emergency! Cover me!"

Our secret family language is often called into service at social gatherings. I suspect that many secret family languages are used at work parties, neighborhood gatherings, and school functions. We will now have to find some new secret substitutes because I am revealing our current favorites. Again, I have no idea how it started, but "Low Temp Alert" means, "I'm not having a good time and I want you to know." This is not to be confused with one of us saying, "I could really use a glass of water," which means, "We need to leave right now. Like this minute."

Even though we like to think that we are fluent in our own family language, there can be some miscommunications. Last summer, we were at a gathering that was an obligation rather than a fun party. It was very hot, and when my husband said, "I could really use a glass of water," I thought I was being a pal by going and getting him a glass of water. When he gave me the Stare Of Death (part of the Secret Family Body Language), I realized that he wasn't thirsty. He was sending an SOS and I had motored right past him in a speedboat. Lesson learned and language remembered.

My now adult children have seamlessly gone with the flow, too. We were talking politics over the holidays (will we never learn) and my son said, "Remember the slide." Our immediate family knew that he was saying, "Take it down a notch." We have photographic evidence of the time he hurled himself down a multi-story waterslide. His tiny careening body is forever captured against the vertical drop of that mammoth structure. It's a cautionary picture and phrase.

The bookenheimer has traveled the nation now. My daughter took the word with her from our home in the north to the East Coast. I was visiting her and we were walking around Brooklyn. On the sidewalk lay a tiny object. My daughter bent to pick it up.

"Someone lost their bookenheimer!" she exclaimed as she put it up on the corner of the nearest stoop.

"I hope they have a few backups," I said. "Bedtime for babies is absolutely no good without a bookenheimer." We walked a few steps and she added, "Not everyone believes in bookenheimers, Mom. Apparently they aren't that great for your teeth."

The bookenheimer is a controversial thing for sure.

~Lucia Paul

Clean Living

Laundry… the never-ending story.
~Author Unknown

My great-aunt's house, with clothes draped everywhere, made the Goodwill store look like Saks Fifth Avenue. We would visit her once a year, "often enough," according to my father. It was a significant road trip from our Eastern Iowa farmstead across the mighty Mississippi River to Illinois, and what we found when we arrived, every year, was chaos.

The amazing thing about this aunt is that she never put away things she had laundered. Towels, bed linens, underwear, overalls — anything that had passed through the washing machine — were folded and draped over chairs and tables in her house. Her living room looked like the January white sale at JCPenney.

It wasn't that we objected to drying laundry in full view. Although my mother would normally hang our clothes outside to dry, she would occasionally dry them indoors during the worst part of winter. But when they were dry, they were folded and sent to the proper drawer or closet.

So Mom was completely flabbergasted by her aunt's laundry exhibit. No one, as far as I know, ever said a word about this mess to my great-aunt. Hence, every summer visit there would be the same. We were greeted by vast quantities of folded laundry, displayed as to render every piece of furniture useless. There were no chairs you could sit in, no tables you could dine at, and no sofas on which to lounge.

It seemed our summertime visits always coincided with favorable weather, allowing drinking and eating to occur outside. I think my dad prayed for a sunny day whenever we went to my great-aunt's house. Before one trip, I heard him tell my mom, "I sure hope it's a nice day so we can sit outside."

He never elaborated on what would happen if it were a rainy day, but we youngsters always imagined that he was tormented by the prospect of squeezing himself onto the couch between various pieces of our great-aunt's unmentionables.

~Dale Kueter

It's All About the Dogs

*You can usually tell that a man is good if
he has a dog who loves him.*
~W. Bruce Cameron, A Dog's Journey

"If anything ever happened to your mom, I'd be devastated," my dad confessed. "But if something ever happened to Sadie Mae, I don't think I could survive."

"Dad, never tell Mom that!" I shrieked.

Sadie Mae was his German Shorthaired Pointer. I grew up knowing that it was all about the dogs. There was Pixie, Chrissy, Seymour, Brandy, Charlie, and, of course, Sadie Mae.

And somewhere behind the list of dogs were the kids: Sherrie, Connie, and David. Dad could never remember our names, but why should he? He knew all the dogs' names. We knew where we stood — our pedigrees couldn't measure up to those of our housemates. Our human plans were often altered to accommodate the "doglings" because they always came first.

According to my father, kennels were no place for "human" dogs. And pet sitters never lasted very long because the dogs made sure they trashed the house to remind all of us who was really in charge.

I remember when my parents drove me to Whitworth University — my freshman year — and dropped me off at my dorm at 5:00 a.m.

so Dad could get home to his dogs. I knew then I was not my dad's favorite "child." After taking a few psych classes, I understood that my family was a "little" crazy, particularly my dad.

I married and had children, and it wasn't all about the dogs. In fact, we never had a dog while our two boys were growing up. They had our full and undivided attention. And they bemoaned the fact that all their friends had dogs and cats and other pets (hamsters, rabbits, and goldfish).

When our older son graduated from Donegal High School in Mount Joy, Pennsylvania, in the year 2000, we sent out save-the-date invitations to our entire family. Since we lived on the East Coast and everyone else lived on the West Coast, it took some planning. We rented a venue, had the event catered, and all the family from my husband's side and my side planned on attending. I could hardly believe it when I heard that my mom and dad were coming and leaving Sadie Mae in a kennel.

Due to a scheduling conflict, we had to have the party the day before graduation. It was going to be a combined family reunion/high school graduation. Everything went as planned: The food was delicious and everyone raved about the leather photo album that I put together of Jeremy's childhood through high school years.

The next day, we planned a lovely brunch before we headed to the graduation, where Jeremy was to receive a scholarship award. That morning, I received a call from my mom. She said, "Dad won't be attending the graduation."

"What?" I questioned. "Is Dad sick or something?"

"No, nothing like that," Mom explained. "Your dad needs to fly home to be with his dog."

"But *you'll* be staying for graduation, won't you?"

"No, dear. I'll be flying home with your father. I hope you understand," Mom said apologetically.

I hung up the phone and sobbed until I realized there was no reason to cry. It had always been about the dogs, so what was my problem? I had grown up with this.

We said our goodbyes, Mom and Dad got on the plane, and Jeremy graduated with honors. And we had a great time anyway.

There are things in every family that one has to either accept or reject. I chose to accept the fact that my dad would never change, and I had to make a decision to accept his behavior as crazy, but normal for him.

It's been seventeen years since Jeremy's graduation. We have another family reunion coming up and, again, it's all about my father's dog — Charlie — who doesn't like children.

So we've arranged for my other son and his wife and toddler to stay at a nearby hotel. That way Dad won't have to kennel his beloved "Charlie Girl." At eighty-seven, that's out of the question for him.

It will always be about the dogs.

~Connie K. Pombo

Classically Driven

*I don't care how much money you have, free
stuff is always a good thing.*
~Queen Latifah

unt Dorothy's penny-pinching may have set a new standard for thriftiness. Yet while she was tight with her cash, she was generous in her willingness to spend time, creativity, and persistence in the pursuit of something she highly valued. And what she valued most was good music.

She had been a schoolteacher, and although she was retired and in her eighties, her passion for music education had not diminished, particularly when it came to classical composers and the artists who performed their works. I was always impressed with her astounding ability to attend dozens of concerts a year on a fixed income, and even fund her friends' experiences. After all, culture isn't cheap. I once asked her how she did it.

"To attend the really good concerts," she answered professorially, "you have to use your imagination."

Aunt Dorothy was imaginative, no doubt about it. As I discovered, her level of invention raised the pursuit of the musical freebie to an art form in itself. Her methods ranged from the intuitive to the outlandish. She joined the arts organizations in her city, at least the ones whose benefits included cut-rate concerts with big-name conductors and soloists. Moreover, she diligently watched her mailbox. Having her name on the subscription lists of countless musical newsletters reaped almost limitless rewards when it came to finding classical shows for a song. She got in on members-only performances, dress rehearsals, even presentations for school groups.

"Why not?" she reasoned. "I was a teacher for more than forty years."

But Aunt Dorothy had even more innovative methods. "Stalking" is probably too strong a word for it, but she did volunteer at the nursing home where the mother of the local symphony's first violinist lived. Extreme perhaps, but it was good for a couple of complimentary center-section passes now and then.

I once confronted her. "The idea of free music is really a compulsion with you, isn't it, Aunt Dorothy?"

She was indignant. "I merely take advantage of opportunities as they present themselves," she retorted.

Some opportunities posed more of a challenge than others, however, even for such a maestro of marked-down music. For example, one day an advertisement from a local car dealership came in the mail. It contained a coupon for two free tickets to an upcoming symphony concert for anyone coming in to test-drive a new Mercedes-Benz. *Anyone*, it read.

Aunt Dorothy drove a car, a big Oldsmobile. But she never drove it far and rarely at night. Somehow she managed to get a friend to drive when they attended the evening concerts. As a result, her automobile stayed in immaculate condition. The original tires were hardly worn. The speedometer never ventured above fifty. She had her oil changed every six months or every two hundred miles, whichever came first.

Aunt Dorothy admitted that the thought of test-driving a new Mercedes was a little scary for an octogenarian, even one as independent as she. "But I just can't take my mind off those symphony tickets," she confessed.

The thought of that no-cost concert continued to intensify, until finally a crescendo of mounting bravery reached fever pitch. It happened while the two of us were running errands at the shopping center a few blocks from her home. Aunt Dorothy had just been to the hairdresser and was feeling a little reckless. She checked her purse.

Yes, the coupon was still there. The Mercedes dealership was not far. "One more stop to make," she said decisively, as she pushed down the accelerator halfway.

Inside the dealership, a grinning salesman greeted us. "What can I do for you today?" he chimed.

Before I could speak, Aunt Dorothy blurted out breathlessly, "I'd like to test-drive a Mercedes. I'm here for the symphony tickets." She thrust the document at the salesman.

"Oh," he said, taken aback. Glancing suspiciously at the coupon, then at the like-new Olds she had parked outside, and then down at its gray-haired driver, he finally turned to me and asked, "Do you plan on buying a new car in the near future?"

"Actually, she's the one in for the test drive," I explained feebly, pointing to Aunt Dorothy.

"I see," the salesman said, even more feebly. He looked at the flyer. "Is this promotion still going on? I thought that ended already."

"No, not for a few days," Aunt Dorothy insisted, purposefully pointing to the expiration date.

The salesman looked worried. "Could you wait just a moment, please? I need to show this to my manager. Can I get you anything? Coffee? Tea?"

"No, thank you," Aunt Dorothy replied, her thin frame sinking into a cushioned leather chair.

While we waited, I could sense Aunt Dorothy's boldness begin to wane. "How far do you think I'll have to drive the car?" she asked me. "Do you think I'll have to drive it on a busy street?" Suddenly, she looked horrified. "What if it has a clutch?"

I assured her that the car probably didn't have a clutch.

"Are there any age limits for test-driving a luxury car?" she asked to no one in particular. "Oh, I wish I had checked with AAA."

"It's going to be okay," I said, trying to calm her, while at the same time trying to convince myself.

Suddenly, Aunt Dorothy steeled herself, and with renewed courage, she declared, "You're right. I've come this far; I'm going to see this through."

Just then, the salesman returned. He looked relieved.

"Ma'am," he said to Aunt Dorothy almost apologetically, "it won't be necessary for you to test-drive a car unless you really want to. You'll receive the tickets in the mail in about a week. Is that all right?"

Aunt Dorothy stood and beamed with an air of confident satisfaction. "That would be fine, young man."

On the slow drive home, I asked Aunt Dorothy, "Would you really have driven that car to get those tickets?"

Aunt Dorothy chuckled. "You know the answer to that," she said.

"You simply take advantage of opportunities as they present themselves, right?" I laughed.

Aunt Dorothy just smiled, never taking her eyes off the road.

~Barbara Walker

The Sighting

Families are like fudge —
mostly sweet, with a few nuts.
~Les Dawson

om's voice was at such a frenzied pitch that I barely recognized who was calling. "Cindy, run outside and look up into the sky toward our house. There's a flying saucer!" *Click.*

I froze in place, staring into the receiver.

"Mom? Are you there?" The line was dead.

The kids and I were stirring up a batch of fudge in the kitchen, which was our tradition on quiet Sunday evenings when their dad was away working. It was good bonding time with Holly and Brian, ages eight and six respectively.

"That was Grandma Betty on the phone. She says there's a flying saucer going over their house," I said to the kids, trying to remain calm.

Both kids shrugged their shoulders and exchanged what's-the-big-deal glances with each other. Neither of them seemed to think there was anything odd about a flying saucer hovering overhead.

"Let's pour the fudge into the pan. While it's setting, we'll go outside to see if anything looks unusual in the sky," I said.

It was a rare evening in the Pacific Northwest. The stars hung low in a semi-darkened blue sky. The kids asked me to point out the Big and Little Dippers.

"Do you see anything that resembles a flying saucer?" I asked the kids.

"Not a thing," Holly said flatly, showing little interest in a possible UFO sighting.

"I can't wait to tell Dad that we saw the Big Dipper!" Brian remarked.

"If you're ready, let's go back in the house. I need to call Grandma," I said, directing them inside.

Our house sat on a hill overlooking the valley where Mom and Dad lived, which was about nine miles southwest of us. A small, local airport was situated in the valley midway between our homes, so we often heard the sound of small, private planes and the *wop, wop, wop* of helicopters. If anything significant flew over, it would be easily distinguishable by sight and sound.

"Mom, we couldn't see anything out of the ordinary up in the sky, just lots of twinkling stars," I chuckled, trying to lighten the subject.

"Don't bother me now. Your dad's on the roof with his rifle," she screeched into the phone. *Click!*

Once again, I stared into the receiver as if to find an answer to the craziness. She'd hung up on me again. I didn't know what to think other than my down-to-earth parents had suddenly gone stark raving mad.

We went outside again and scoured the evening sky. I reasoned that maybe a falling star could resemble a flying saucer, but surely my parents would know the difference.

I tried to speak slowly and clearly when I called Mom again. "Mom, tell Dad to get off the roof and not to fire his rifle!"

She squealed into the phone, "Go back outside and look again. They have slowed their speed, so you might get a glimpse. You can't miss it." *Click!*

I loaded the kids into my Volkswagen Beetle and headed down the hill. I fully expected to see my parents' house surrounded by flashing emergency vehicles. I also feared that I would see Dad handcuffed and taken to the police station for booking. Mom would be secured in a straitjacket screaming, "But we all saw it! We can't all be nuts!" My imagination had gone as crazy as my parents had.

The scene was quiet when we arrived. A few neighbors had gathered on the front lawn and were discussing the UFO. Apparently, they'd all seen it.

Much to my relief, I learned my dad wasn't trying to shoot the alien craft out of the sky. He wanted to use the scope to get a closer look, but by the time he found his gun and climbed onto the roof, the saucer had flown out of sight. Couldn't Mom have told me that over the phone so I wouldn't think they'd gone completely berserk?

Several hours later, the kids and I were back home, enjoying some fudge and talking about Grandma and Grandpa seeing a UFO. Although we made light of the sighting, I secretly feared Mom and Dad's recent retirement was making them a bit wacky. What was it going to take to convince them their sighting was somehow explainable, especially considering that the neighbors backed up the entire incident?

After the kids went off to bed, I sat in the living room scanning the clear, inky sky, which was much darker than it had been earlier during the sighting. Suddenly, I saw the glimmer of a narrow strip of twinkling lights. They floated like a ribbon through the gentle breeze. The lights became clearer as they drew closer, and a side view of the ribbon formed what appeared to be a perfect saucer shape. It was trailing behind a low-flying, light aircraft to announce "GRAND OPENING... TOM'S TIRES!"

~Cynthia Briggs

Give an Inch, Get a Mile

Never compete with someone who has nothing to lose.
~Baltasar Gracian

It all started with the candy bar. Kristen, my husband's young cousin, brought a box of candy bars to a family gathering. She explained that her school choir was having a fundraiser. I have quite a sweet tooth, so I handed her a dollar and chose a chocolate bar. Aunt June, standing behind her daughter, beamed.

Soon after, our son came home with an order sheet for wrapping paper. His baseball team was trying to earn money for new equipment.

"Ask the relatives at Grandpa's birthday party next week," I told him. "Maybe you'll get some orders."

I didn't think about it again until a week later when it was time for Brian to turn in his order sheet to the coach. I scanned it quickly, smiling at the small orders from Grandma and Uncle Don. Then I saw June's name. She had ordered seven rolls. At eight dollars per roll, that was quite a hefty order.

At the Fourth of July picnic, Kristen was selling potholders she had made. They were very nice quality. I complimented her and chose two that would match my kitchen. Aunt June came over and thanked me for my purchase.

Two weeks later, it was our daughter Amy's birthday. Aunt June arrived with an enormous present — a two-story dollhouse. Amy was thrilled. For the next twenty minutes, she gushed to Aunt June about how much she loved it. I felt guilty, remembering the small art set we had given Kristen as a birthday gift.

When Kristen rang our bell and asked if we'd like to buy some Girl Scout cookies, I only ordered three boxes since my daughter was also selling them. When Amy called Aunt June to inquire if she would like to order any, she hung up the phone with a big smile. "Aunt June ordered ten boxes!" she announced as I cringed.

This went on for almost two years. For some reason, Aunt June was being extremely kind and generous to our family. When I tried to repay the kindness, she would "up the ante." If we gave Kristen a gift card, our children would receive one for double the amount. We sent Aunt June a card for Mother's Day. She had flowers delivered to me.

The last straw was the enormous box of candy that was delivered on Labor Day. "A little back-to-school treat!" was written on the enclosed note. "Why is she doing this?" I asked my husband in despair. "This is crazy! Who sends Labor Day gifts? She's not fighting fair!"

My husband threw back his head in laughter. "It's our turn, I guess. Aunt June does this to everybody. If you do something nice for her, she becomes obsessed with paying you back. When my sister lent their family a tent, Aunt June returned the tent along with a camping stove and three new sleeping bags. It's just a weird quirk she has. Don't worry, she'll move on to another family soon. The key is to let her win."

I was puzzled but took my husband's advice. We started buying nice but affordable gifts for June's family again. We sponsored Kristen in her school's Fun Run, but kept our donation reasonable. It took a while, but slowly the competition and stress faded away.

On Christmas Eve, I breathed much easier as our children each unwrapped a game from Aunt June. One game. One simple, delightful game. My husband caught my eye and nodded his head toward Grandpa, who was scratching his head as he studied an enormous package with his name on it. On the side was written "All my love, Aunt June." My husband leaned over and whispered in my ear, "Grandpa fixed her sink…."

~Marianne Fosnow

Starstruck

A cousin is a little bit of childhood
that can never be lost.
~Marion C. Garretty

My cousin was absolutely starstruck. If she saw a movie star or rock star in person, she would go bonkers. The bigger the star, the more bonkers she went. She was already an adult, not some impressionable teenager, but she lived in a small town in the middle of Kansas so the probability of seeing a major star — or even a minor one, for that matter — was slim to none. On the other hand, I grew up in Los Angeles. Seeing stars wherever we went was no big deal. I went all through school with some stars or the kids of stars. My father worked for some of the major studios in Hollywood, and he was always taking me "on the lot" for one reason or another. A pretty major recording star lived a few doors away from us, and another lived a few blocks away. Seeing stars was no big deal for me. I mean, it was interesting, but not earth shattering.

But for my cousin, it was the biggest deal of her life. If she saw a star, she didn't just look at him or her and then go on with whatever she was doing. Oh, no. She would point and gasp, and then start squealing like a pig, jumping up and down. How embarrassing. The people who lived in Los Angeles knew not to act like that because we saw stars all the time — at the market, picking their kids up from the same schools we went to, at the doctor's office, etc. — but my cousin didn't have a clue. She thought that seeing a star could change her life.

My cousin was older than me by more than a few years, pretty opinionated and obnoxious, and she liked to boss me around. But when she visited me in Los Angeles, I was the one she looked up to. I was the one who had all the information she wanted. I was the one in charge. She would ask to go for drives into the different neighborhoods where the stars lived, so that I could point out their houses.

"See that house?" I would say.

"The big one with the iron gate?"

"Yes. Do you know who lives there?"

"Who?" And I would tell her. She would almost faint with excitement. Then we would drive on. When it was time for lunch, I always took her to a restaurant where I knew at least one star might be dining. And if no stars happened to be there, I would point to some poor, unsuspecting person who had never been in a movie or on the stage and tell my cousin that he was a star—a very minor star and one whom she probably didn't recognize—but a star nonetheless. It was a harmless lie, but it made her day.

The best star sighting that ever happened was when we went to a black-tie charity event. The room was full of stars. Although I told my cousin she couldn't make any of those squealing noises and jump up and down, she was in her glory. She did try to behave for the most part.

My husband and I, along with my cousin and some of our friends, were seated at one table, and my parents were at an adjoining table. Because my parents were directly involved with the charity putting on the event, they were at an important table that included a few stars. My cousin was gaga with excitement!

One star in particular got my cousin's attention right away. He was seated right next to my father. My cousin was facing that table while my husband and I had our backs to it. I heard some gasping noises coming from my cousin, so I gave her the look that meant "stop that and behave!" She looked at me and swallowed… hard. Once, twice, three times. She was sputtering and stuttering and flustered. She looked like she wanted to talk, and her mouth was moving, but no words came out. A blessing, for sure! Then my father called me over to his table. He and the gentleman he was seated next to stood up as I walked over.

My father introduced me to his friend. His introduction went like this: "Paul, I would like you to meet my daughter, Barbara. Barbara, this is my friend, Paul Newman." We shook hands.

Paul Newman! You had to tell me who he was? Really, Dad? Like his blue eyes wouldn't have given away his identity? Duh! (And, oh my, they were so blue!) Like I said, my father worked at the major studios and was friendly with many stars. He had worked with Paul Newman on different occasions, and he just wanted to introduce his daughter to his friend. It was as simple as that. How nice for me! Now I am not starstruck, but I must admit that meeting Paul Newman made my heart beat just a little bit faster. The three of us talked for a few minutes and shook hands again, and then I went back to my seat.

My cousin was paralyzed. Her eyes were as big as saucers. She couldn't move. She couldn't talk. Dinner was served. She could hardly eat. She just sat there with her mouth open, staring at my father's friend Paul. She wanted to hold my hand—the hand that had held the hand of Paul Newman. She told me I could never, ever wash my hands again. Before dessert was served, she got up and walked around in back of his chair so she could say she had been within three feet of Paul Newman. Later, after he had left the event, she jumped up and ran back to his table to steal the napkin he had used. Too late—someone else had already taken it. His glass was gone, too. I think she would have tried to take the tablecloth or his chair if she could have figured out how to do that without making a scene.

My cousin never forgot that evening, and she told many people about the night she had dinner with Paul Newman. I guess you could say she did, technically, have dinner with him because she was in the same room. But maybe I'm being too critical. Just recently, we went to dinner at a little restaurant in town. The hostess seated us, and when I looked around, I saw that Rod Stewart was sitting at the next table. *Rod Stewart! Right next to me!* I could have reached out and touched him—we were that close to each other. I was having dinner with Rod

Stewart! Well, technically, we weren't having dinner together — or maybe we were. My cousin got *some* things right.

~Barbara LoMonaco

A Honey of a Christmas

The manner of giving is worth more than the gift.
Pierre Corneille, Le Menteur

As a young bride, I learned that I was in big trouble if I showed up at Aunt Honey's without a bag of trash. We're not talking about the coffee-grounds-and-eggshells variety, but the kind made up of boxes, bags and labels from name brand products. Honey, who never shopped, managed to obtain gifts for the family by clipping and mailing product "qualifiers" from the packages to turn this rubbish into mounds of Christmas gifts.

Aunt Honey and Uncle Joe were quite a pair. I don't know how to describe them. How can I make all the love, pettiness, squabbling, originality, meanness, kindness and humor shine through without making them into either a pair of cranks or an affable Mr. and Mrs. Claus? They drove everyone a little crazy.

Our family party took place on Christmas Eve at the home of Honey's brother, our Uncle Harry. Once we were all assembled, we were led into the basement, blinded by the lights from Uncle Wayne's omnipresent movie camera. There, amid the washer, dryer, water pipes and furnace, was Honey's little workshop. She had once again worked her yearly magic on the family trash, turning discarded packaging into free products and cool gifts.

Honey lived for Christmas Eve, and she began clipping and mailing labels every December 26th. She'd keep it up for an entire year until everyone could count on a newspaper-wrapped stack of crazy, sometimes useful, gifts. We'd sit in our little family clusters tearing at the wrapping to discover toothpaste, laundry detergent, shaving cream, macaroni and cheese, shoe polish, and more.

In 1974, for example, she provided the first two babies in the family with stacks of disposable diapers in a variety of sizes. Each box had the product stamp carefully removed, saved for some future magic. As struggling young teachers, we found her gifts a godsend.

Since Honey was aunt to seven nieces and nephews and their families, she tried to be evenhanded about her gifts, making sure that everything was equal. If she couldn't get enough of a particular gift, she would hold what she had until the next Christmas when she might have obtained more. One year, she had a huge fiberboard playhouse for each family with kids. At the time, there were four of us. She forced Uncle Joe to assemble them — right there in the game room. As if that were not enough, she topped each house with a little doll in a crocheted dress with its legs neatly tucked into a full roll of toilet paper. The doll held the reins to a huge, inflatable dog the size of a Volkswagen. We could barely move to open our other gifts — and there were other gifts!

Each of us remembers a favorite silly gift, like the Sprout dolls from Green Giant, or the Lucky Charms T-shirts in sizes infant to XXL. There were radio hats advertising beer, nightshirts proclaiming the cleaning power of Tide, toys of every imaginable product mascot, and cookbooks featuring everything from creamed corn to crème de menthe. Not every gift was silly; there were Timex watches and silver napkin rings, tea towels, ornaments, cereal bowls, golf balls, jewelry and games. If it had an advertising slogan or product name emblazoned across it, there was a good chance it was under our tree.

We always brought stacks of gifts for Honey and Uncle Joe, but nothing we ever gave them could equal the pleasure they derived from watching us and our children open the presents they had been gathering all year long. We tried, though. We bought them TV sets and nativity sets, clothes and food. We lovingly made things for them:

blankets and potholders, crayon pictures and embroidered pillowslips, homemade jam and nut bread. Honey and Uncle Joe were the heart and soul of our family Christmases, and we wanted them to feel as loved as we did year after year.

I'd like to say that they stayed in the bosom of their loving family until they died at a ripe old age, but it didn't quite happen that way. Uncle Joe, always suspicious of everyone who had the children he did not, quit coming to the family parties after an imagined slight. We tried to bring him back into the fold, to no avail.

Honey continued to enjoy opening gifts on Christmas or any morning — one morning became like another to her in her final days. I put a tube of toothpaste in my grownup children's Christmas stockings every year to remind them of Christmases past, when she and Uncle Joe were the cornerstone of our family Christmas Eves.

~Rosemary McLaughlin

Chapter 2

My Crazy Family

Mom Did What?

Swipe, Don't Tap

I realized something on the ride. I realized if I wait
until I'm not scared to try new things, then I'll
never get to try them at all.
~Marie Sexton

My phone buzzes. "I have something to tell you," she texts, "but it's a secret."

She knows I am powerless against clickbait.

"What kind of secret?" I ask.

Moments later, I hear clunking on the stairs.

She shuffles to my door and pokes in her head. Her face glows with mischief, and she is unable to mask her glee. Mom makes a show of checking for eavesdroppers, though we both know it's only us.

"I'm going to drive for youber!" she exclaims.

Her smile is practically wrapped around her head.

"Oh… you mean Uber?"

I am bemused. My mother is great at making sales, packing snacks and cussing out retail managers. But driving competently and using technology? Not so much.

I am half-expecting her to abandon this idea before it fully percolates, like her foray into jewelry sales or the time she tried to make a scrapbook. But then she asks me to help her download the app.

Mom has sworn me to secrecy because she thinks my dad and sister will judge her. She is probably right. Under the cover of midday, while the rest of the family works, we download the app, watch the training videos, and talk about how to pronounce the "U" in Uber.

We practice driving on Tuesday morning. I order the ride to our house while we sit in the car one block away. We go through the motions of picking up a rider and dropping her off in our neighbourhood. It does not go smoothly.

The navigation system is too quiet. The screen is distracting. The GPS doesn't know the best route. The destination requires a U-turn. The button is a slide instead of a tap. It is confusing. It is stressful. The ride ends in tears.

"Don't worry," I say. "We can try again tomorrow." Mom decides one hour later that she is ready for the road.

On her way home from grocery shopping, she turns on the app, which matches her quickly with a rider named Matthew. As she makes her way toward him, the panic from the morning creeps in. The silent navigation. The screen confusion. The swipe/tap debacle. It is just too much.

Naturally, she turns off her phone. She does not cancel the ride. She does not contact him to explain. She does, however, feel an imminent need for acupuncture. Mom spins her Lexus 180 degrees and races toward her practitioner.

A few minutes later, Mom turns on her phone to check her text messages. She has several missed calls from Matthew, who has been watching her on his screen and has seen her drive in the opposite direction for the past five minutes.

A word to the wise: Turning off your cellphone does not cancel an Uber ride.

Matthew calls again. She hesitates, and then picks up the phone.

"Why are you driving in the opposite direction?" he asks.

"Listen," she pleads. "This is my first time with youber, and I don't know how to use it. Please cancel the ride."

Matthew is late for work and doesn't want to foot the cancellation fee. Somehow, he coaxes her into picking him up. Mom finds the destination, trolls the parking lot for a while, and eventually he waves her down and hops in.

Matthew is a handsome man in his early thirties with a kind face and a crisp suit. A GoodLife duffel is slung across one shoulder, and a messenger bag hangs off the other. He is overseeing a grand opening event at the mall. Mom realizes how unprofessional it would be to show up late.

She mutters an expletive and gets ready to gun it, telling Matthew he'll need to manage the technology if he wants to arrive on time.

"So, start the trip," she barks and tosses her iPhone to the back seat in what is surely a breach of protocol. He obliges.

As Matthew co-pilots the ride, Mom gathers intel. They chat about his career, education, home life, and aspirations. She jokes about how incompetent she feels and about how embarrassed her daughter will be once she finds out about this. They laugh, talk and eventually arrive at Yorkdale — albeit at the wrong entrance.

"Crap, I'm sorry," she says.

"It's okay, Paddy," laughs Matthew. "Everyone is a beginner at some point."

He ends the trip, returns her phone, and starts to climb out of the car.

"Hold on," she says. "Will you show me how to do that?"

So Matthew explains, with the time that he doesn't have, how to use features on the Uber driver app.

"Matthew," she calls from her window, "you better not rate me one star."

"I'm rating you five right now!" he says, and he really does.

Matthew disappears into the mall, smiling. She smiles, too, proud that her first ride was such a success.

~Bronwyn McIntyre

12

Thanksgiving Dressing

Most turkeys taste better the day after; my mother's
tasted better the day before.
~Rita Rudner

I gave my mother her wake-up call, as requested, and she assured me that she had been up since six and everything was fine. The giblets were boiling on the stove and the turkey was in the pan, ready to go.

Despite her confidence, I had an uneasy feeling something was amiss, although I wasn't sure what. I was only certain of one thing: My quirky, independent mother had insisted on making the Thanksgiving turkey this particular year.

Mom said, "I have to find something to cover the turkey breast, or it'll be dry. I need cheesecloth. But the oven's already hot, and I hate to go running out last-minute to the market. Besides, it's probably a madhouse. Well, I'll figure out something. Lemme get off the phone."

I heard a click as she hung up. Actually, I shouldn't have been concerned. Improvisation was second nature to Mother. After all, she was a former nightclub singer, and a rather creative thinker, too.

The nutty thing about my mother was that she heard music where the rest of us didn't. Music for Mom could be anyplace. Even a watercolor painting in the living room might serenade her. To me, you, or anyone else, it was merely a picture of a branch. To Mother, it was a line of musical staff. The drawing on the wall showed three small birds sitting in a tree. A larger bird (their parent) perched slightly below to the right. I knew from its colorful beak that the fourth bird was a toucan. For the longest time, Mother walked by the picture without giving it so much as a blink. Then one day she suddenly stopped and froze, staring at it intently.

"Reminds me of Beethoven," she muttered.

"Who?"

"You know. Beethoven. The composer."

A week later, she walked past it again. Only this time…

"Now I get it!" she exclaimed. "Beethoven!"

"Ma-RONE, Mom. What's with you and Beethoven?"

Rolling her eyes, she pointed to the birds. As she did so, with infinite patience she sang each note slowly. One after the other.

"Da-Da-Da-DUM! See?"

I did. Sort of. Those four birds represented to her the opening notes of Beethoven's Fifth Symphony.

My mother definitely thought outside the box, and she was continually surprising me. My uneasy feeling about our Thanksgiving dinner continued to bother me. Later that day, I called her again. "Hey, Mom, it's me again. Everything all right?"

"Terrific." She sounded happy, almost elated.

"Did you get the cheesecloth?"

"Ah, no. But I found something else. Don't know why I didn't think of it before."

"What'd you use?"

"You'll see when you get here. Oh, be sure and bring some more butter."

Relieved to learn things were on track, I began wrapping the foods I had prepared to accompany the turkey: cranberries with grated orange zest, bourbon yams, and green beans sautéed in broth. My sister was bringing a pie. It was going to be a great Thanksgiving! I grabbed the canvas tote bags, tossed in my keys and wallet, and walked out the door.

Hurrying down the hall in Mom's building, I could hear sounds of dishes clanking and happy voices in conversation coming from behind apartment doors. I was anticipating a warm, delightful family celebration with no surprises. Mom greeted me with a hug. I caught the aroma of cinnamon as our cheeks touched. I put the butter in the fridge and unpacked the food. Then I turned my attention to the turkey.

"Can I baste it?" I asked.

"Sure," Mom smiled, handing me a large spoon. "You know," she added, "I was right. The covering I used for the turkey worked great!"

Slowly, I opened the oven. A blast of hot air hit me, mingled with the heady scent of roast poultry. The oven had no light so I peered in, took a mitt, and slid the enamel pan toward me. There it lay. Brown and fragrant, the ten-pound bird reclined, flanked by glazed onion slices. Its ankles were tied with string. But my brain needed a few seconds to fully comprehend what I was seeing. The turkey was wearing a pair of white cotton underpants.

I started to giggle and couldn't stop.

"Mom, this is too weird!" I gasped between chuckles. "You've outdone yourself this time!"

"What's the matter?" she snapped. "I used a new pair that was in the back of the drawer. Jeez, it's not like I wore them or anything!"

With the help of trusty kitchen scissors, we snipped away the undies and eased them down, effectively disrobing the turkey. It was done to perfection. Moist, not dry as Mother feared it might be.

I had just dropped the fabric shreds into the wastebasket when the intercom shrilled. Our guests had arrived.

Soon, we were carving off the slabs of meat, and all of us tucked into a splendid holiday meal. Our neighbor, his mouth full of food, noted a stripe across the turkey's breastbone. The panty's elastic waistband had left a mark.

"Oh, that," Mom said casually. "I tied an extra string nice and tight. Can't let the stuffing spill out."

"Good thinking," he nodded. With that, he tossed another dollop of yams onto his plate. Mom shot me a quick sidelong glance. I decided to keep quiet and eat.

~Cindy Legorreta

13

Chinese Takeout

Keep on knocking 'til the joy inside opens a window
look to see who's there.
~Rumi

t night, I think about my mother and hope she's asleep. She lives in the little town of Golden, Colorado, in a house high up on a hill. She and my father had it custom-built after my brother died. It was supposed to be their dream home, a place for the two of them to fill with new, happy memories. Now my mom lives there alone.

I'm out in L.A., so there's not much I can do — except worry. She won't move here, and I can't visit her as often as I'd like. During the day, I worry that she's out jogging on the winding country road on the other side of Highway 93 and that some crazy guy in a pickup will drive by and kidnap all 102 pounds of her. At night, I worry that she's awake and lonely, thinking about the people she has lost.

I called a little while ago. She said it had been snowing all day, and her nose was running non-stop. I kept thinking of her, sick and alone in that empty house. I had this little fantasy about how, if I lived there, I'd run out to get her some chicken noodle soup. Then I came up with a great idea. I'd surprise her with some hot-and-sour Chinese soup, just the thing for her sinuses.

There's this southwestern restaurant on Main Street where my parents always took me when I came to town, and I remembered seeing a little Chinese restaurant right across the street. So I dialed

Information and asked the operator to search the Golden listings for Chinese restaurants. But the operator explained the directory search didn't work like that. He told me he needed an actual name. I kept that operator on the line, inventing dozens of listings for him to check: Lotus Blossom, Cherry Blossom, Forbidden Garden, Forbidden City, Jade Garden, Jade Palace, Golden Palace, Golden Dragon. It's incredible that operator didn't disconnect me. When I finally hit on the right name, I felt kind of silly for not guessing it right away: Golden Peach, named for the town of Golden and the official state fruit.

I went ahead and paid the extra charge for the operator to connect me, and I ordered the soup, plus egg rolls, moo shu chicken, stir-fried vegetables and beef in oyster sauce. It was an entire Chinese banquet for one tiny lady. With the snow piling up, I figured she could use the leftovers, plus at that point I guess I was sort of hungry myself. I charged the whole order to my credit card, including a tip. Then I just sat back, feeling pleased with myself, and waited for my phone to ring.

I glanced at my watch. I worried Mom might decide to turn in early. I worried about the roads, especially that last steep part before the turn for her street. I hoped the delivery guy had snow tires and four-wheel drive. Maybe even chains. But then I thought about how surprised my mom was going to be. I wished I could see the look on her face.

Sure enough, about an hour later, my phone rang. Mom was laughing and making kissing sounds into the phone, telling me I was the best daughter. She told me she had a fire going, and everything was cozy. She was enjoying the food.

Mom told me her side of the story between bites. Turns out my great idea didn't go exactly the way I'd envisioned. According to her, when the delivery guy showed up, he started pounding on her door. I bet she was blasting one of her old belly-dance albums and didn't hear the bell. Poor guy was probably freezing. Anyway, Mom got scared. It was night, some man was pounding on her door, and she was afraid to open it. But the guy refused to go away.

So Mom went to the kitchen, picked up the phone and dialed 911. The dispatcher told her to hold tight; she'd notify the police. But just as Mom hung up, the delivery guy came around to the kitchen back door, which has a window. When he saw my mother, he held up the takeout bag and pointed at it. "Your daughter in Los Angeles!" the guy hollered. I could just picture Mom standing there wide-eyed in her blue terrycloth bathrobe, mouth agape.

Mom unlocked the kitchen door, grabbed the bag of food, and cried, "You better go right now! The police are on their way!" Good thing I paid his tip up front.

At least Mom's still welcome at the southwestern restaurant. And if either one of us wakes up in the night, we'll have something funny to think about for a change.

~Mara A. Cohen

14

My First Board Meeting

Always laugh when you can. It is cheap medicine.
~Lord Byron

Tuesday, January 18, 10:50 a.m. 7th Floor — Corporate Board Room. "Hi, I'm Karen Ekstrom. I'm here for the 11:00 a.m. board meeting," I said nervously.

Without looking up, Mrs. Henry, the publisher's personal assistant — a plump, prematurely gray woman — opened a folder, found my name and checked it. "You're fourth on the agenda. Go inside, find the seat with your name on it and sit there. We'll start shortly."

"Great. Thanks." I pasted a big, fake smile on my face, just in case she looked up. She didn't.

A lightning bolt of terror ricocheted through me — my fifty-seventh for the day. And it was still early.

I couldn't believe it. With just one day's advance notice, I'd been ordered to report on the Special Projects Division, at least my part of it, to the corporate bigwigs. So I'd scrambled. I'd stayed up all night. But I'd gotten it done. Now I just had to present it. This was my moment to shine.

Deep breath. Stay calm.

I hoped I'd done everything right. This was, after all, my first presentation to the board. Ever. And my boss had been unavailable to answer questions yesterday, so I was flying blind.

I entered the conference room. Impressive. Very Old World. Elegant. Gleaming mahogany walls, red velvet curtains, a ginormous Oriental rug and two colossal chandeliers. Twenty-two leather chairs surrounded the conference table.

My heart stopped. I had prepared twenty copies, not twenty-two. *Be calm. Breathe in. Breathe out. You'll be fine.* My boss and I would do without copies.

I found my name on the far side of the room, three-fourths of the way down the table. My boss's name was on the seat beside me. I unloaded graphs, sales reports, contracts and previous copies of the newspaper's special sections. Then I gathered my notes and placed them on top as people filtered in.

It was easy to tell who belonged and who didn't. The big brass entered, talking in loud, jovial voices. The other peons and I whispered.

11:02 a.m. The meeting was called to order.

Twenty long, agonizing minutes passed as I watched the first two of my fellow peons get shot down. Using the correct business vernacular, of course. But it was bloody awful, just the same. The third was holding his own — just barely.

I reached over, took a sip of water and tried not to look nervous. My boss mouthed, "You'll be fine." This might have made me feel better except he had an unconscious habit of spinning his wedding ring when he was nervous. And it was spinning like a Ferris wheel.

11:26 a.m. "Karen, your report on… ahh…" The Vice President of Advertising shifted through some notes. "The Special Projects Division." He pulled up his head, and his eyes met mine.

I felt a drop of sweat trickle down. I stood and started talking as I passed copies to each of the Vice Presidents.

"These are the line-item expenses along with the sales figures as of last Friday."

A soft knock sounded on the door. I didn't turn. I didn't look. I kept talking.

"As you can see…"

I heard the door open. Someone whispered something. I heard

my name.

"Excuse me," Mrs. Henry said.

I stopped.

Mrs. Henry, the publisher's secretary, crept in the door. "Forgive me, but Mrs. Ekstrom has a phone call."

All eyes swung my way.

What the… Mortified, my blood rushed to my face. Desperate to sound professional, I responded, "Would you take a message?"

"It's your… mother." Mrs. Henry's face radiated sympathy. "She says it's a medical emergency."

Oh, God. Please. My mother was a lovely person, but she was also the world's biggest hypochondriac. But I couldn't tell that to this room of VPs. They would think I was a horrible daughter.

I struggled to sound normal. "Would you tell her I'll call her back in about an hour?"

"She sounds quite upset," Mrs. Henry insisted.

I stood there, humiliated. Calling me at work with some imaginary emergency was one thing, but this was a board meeting full of bigwigs. And it could be important for my career… Of course, this was my mother. She wouldn't stop… And everyone would think I was awful if I ignored her.

"Karen," Mrs. Henry shifted, pleading and glancing around the room. "I really think you should take the call."

My boss reached over and grabbed my report. "I'll take over, Karen. Go."

Everyone in the room nodded, sure someone had died. But, knowing my mother, I doubted it.

"Excuse me," I said to the big bosses and fled the room.

11:32 a.m. I grabbed the phone. "Mom, are you okay?"

Suddenly, four people discovered they had business within feet of the phone. Plus, the door to the conference room stood open. My mother now had everyone's attention.

"I just left the emergency room. The doctor said… Well, you need to drop everything and…" my mother gasped into the phone, "go to the grocery store. Get me some bran flakes."

"What?"

"Bran flakes… Bran flakes…" Mother's voice skyrocketed from frail and dying to hysterical. "Can't you hear me?"

Oh, geez, here we go. I lowered my voice. "Mom, slow down. Who's in the hospital?" I enunciated each word with care.

"I was," Mother's voice screeched in my ear. "Can't you hear me? I was in the hospital. And now I need bran flakes. Do you hear me? Bran flakes."

"Like the cereal?"

"Yes, damn it." And the world's biggest hypochondriac let loose.

While she vented in my ear, I turned and mouthed "I've got to go" to the listening crowd. Not that I wanted to. But if I didn't, she would just get more hysterical.

Mrs. Henry's face crumbled into sweetness. "Of course. Don't you give it another thought."

I shot Mrs. Henry a look of sincere gratitude, and then turned to appease my mom.

"Mom, I understand, and I'm coming."

11:37 a.m. I hung up the phone and dashed out.

12:02 p.m. I ran into my mother's house just in time to hear her say, "May I speak to the publisher?"

Panting, I raced down the hall. I grabbed the phone, ripped it out of her hands and slammed down the receiver.

"Mother," I shoved the grocery bag at her, "here's your box of bran flakes."

Her face lit up. "Why, thank you, dear." She pulled out the box and then looked up.

"Oh, no…" Her lips pursed into frustration. "I called Mrs. Henry back and told her to tell you not to forget the milk. Didn't she call you?"

~Karen Ekstrom

15

Lucille Ball Junior

I'd rather regret the things I've done than
regret the things I haven't done.
~Lucille Ball

My mother had a knack for getting herself into some pretty strange and funny situations without even trying! Hence her nickname — Lucille Ball Junior. We always knew something had happened when our mother began a sentence with, "Well, Lucy has struck again!" Very often, however, we were firsthand witnesses, such as the day when we visited the White House in Washington, D.C.

It was a dream of my mother's to tour the White House, and she was beyond "excited." Since D.C. is a little difficult to drive in if one is not familiar with the area, my father decided that we should make a "test drive" the evening prior. I think he was hoping to alleviate any of my mother's worries about being on time. Well, we got lost both getting there and getting back to the hotel. A premonition of things to come!

However, the next morning dawned bright and beautiful, and my father had figured out the best way to get us there and on time. Everything was off to a great start.

Our group began the tour, and my mother was in heaven. It really was beautiful and there was so much history. And then it happened… my younger sister started to feel ill. So my mother interrupted the guide to ask where the restrooms were. Since the guides are instructed to keep everyone together, he was reluctant to tell her until my mother exclaimed, "She is going to be sick right here, right now!" So, off they went.

As my mother tells it, she was in the ladies' restroom with my sister when, all of a sudden, my father walked in.

"What are you doing here? You can't be in here. This is the ladies' room!" she exclaimed. He explained that he wasn't all that interested in seeing the White House, so he would take care of my sister while my mother finished the tour.

Enter Lucille Ball Junior. My mother ventured off on her own, trying to find our group, wandering from one room to another. At one point, she opened a door, only to be met by what we later decided were Secret Service agents who, of course, questioned her at length as to who she was and what was she doing there. After apparently explaining successfully, they pointed her to a tour group and told her to stay with them.

Of course, that was not her original group, and the guide (who was trained to keep track of these things) stopped the tour to ask her who she was and where she came from. She explained and he said okay, but she was to stay with his group until the end of the tour.

Now, we know that didn't happen! After all, Lucy Junior was in charge. As her "new" group was going into one room, my mother spotted my brother and me, in her original group, going into another. So, of course, she began to follow us until she heard a loud voice say, "Where are you going?" It was her new guide.

"I just saw my children and my original group," my mother answered.

The tour guide gave a huge sigh as he said, "Go. But if I catch you wandering again, I will have you arrested!"

Of course, our family did not know any of this had happened until we had finished the wonderful tour and met up with my father and sister outside. My father asked my mother, "Did you enjoy it?" And my mother answered, "You are not going to believe what happened to me!"

Lucy Junior had struck again — a story we have since laughingly referred to as "The Time Our Mother Almost Got Arrested by the Secret Service!"

~Helen A. Scieszka

16

Saturated Patience

A little nonsense now and then is
cherished by the wisest men.
~Roald Dahl

s children, my brothers and I constantly terrorized our mother. When we combined forces, we had the power to make that sweet, loving woman go mad.

One day, I had just arrived home from school feeling overheated, exhausted, and furious with my brothers for kicking me out of the car and making me walk home. Taking a few steps inside, I dropped my books and realized the house was a little too quiet. Looking around, my anger turned to weariness, and suddenly I felt a fierce stream of water glide across my shirt. Before I realized what was happening, another blasted me directly in the face. I dove behind the couch as I heard my brothers yell, "Water fight!"

Scrambling to the other side of the room where my own water gun was hidden beneath a loose floorboard, loaded and ready to go, I grabbed it and congratulated myself for preparing in advance. Instantly, my anger with my brothers disappeared, and I eagerly joined in the water spraying.

We didn't stop until we were nearly soaked and out of water. Calling a truce, we decided to team up and take on a larger, more dangerous enemy. While taking turns reloading our weaponry, we hatched our devious plan.

Our mother was outside watering the garden, blissfully unaware of the three menaces approaching her from behind. We silently counted to three and began showering her with water. She turned around and stood eerily still as we finished the last of our supply. Only when she thought our guns were empty did she dare speak a word. However, when she began to lecture us, a stray round shot from my gun, landing smack dab in her right eye, and she lost it.

We sprinted for the house with our mother close behind and barely reached the door in time to shut her out. She began pounding on it and shouting for us to let her in, but we had no idea that this was all an act. She actually had a key to the door in her pocket, but she had decided to hatch her own devious plan.

Once she went back to watering the garden, we refilled our guns and decided to keep the prank going. We would take turns slightly opening the door, spraying her, and then quickly shutting and relocking it. Every time, she would play the furious mother role, but inside she was calmly waiting for an opening.

Our confidence grew as we successfully sprayed her and saw her increasing flustered state. We would leave the door open for longer periods each time, laughing at her until we left it open a little too long. With the water hose in hand, she swiftly flew through the door and demolished us — and the entire living room — with water.

Impeccably timed, our father appeared in the doorway and absorbed the scene. Furious, he shouted, "Clean this place up! You're all grounded!" Then, looking directly at Mom, he clarified, "*All* of you!"

~Madeline Evans

17

The Holiday Merger

Love is no assignment for cowards.
~Ovid

Mom jumped up from the dinner table and said, "I have an announcement to make!" My petite Italian mother hovered over the yams, part of the first holiday meal that I was hosting to introduce my fiancé Jim's conservative Catholic parents to one-half of my non-practicing kind.

Mom glanced at me and then at Jim, excited about something neither of us knew about. As her smile widened, I squeezed the stem of my wineglass. Mom, who'd been divorced for seventeen years, turned to the rest of the people she'd just met: my future in-laws who had recently celebrated forty years of marriage.

"I'm married again!" she proclaimed, hugging her chest.

I'd spent my twenties dating one toad after another and had resigned myself to the fact that I was going to be a thirty-something cat lady. Then, on St. Patrick's Day in 2008, I met Jim. It was chaos, hardly a time to meet someone worthwhile, but we quickly connected as we stood outside an overcrowded bar in Manhattan and started talking, realizing we went to the same high school in the neighboring borough of Staten Island.

Jim, thirty-one, was divorced with no kids, and yet he understood the repercussions of coming from a divorced home. He mentioned, however, that his church-going family rarely spoke of the "D-word," even when he was in the midst of his own.

Despite his solid upbringing, Jim was pretty rebellious. He forfeited a scholarship after high school to join the military, and later bought a motorcycle — both decisions made against his parents' wishes. After a yearlong relationship, Jim proposed to me in Las Vegas, and we planned a wedding that didn't include the Catholic Church. Although I wasn't a favorite of theirs, his parents did like that I had a successful career, owned my condo, and was thriving on my own. I didn't need their son's money, car or townhouse. They were formal yet friendly when we visited them and gradually grew comfortable with our arrangement. That's when Jim and I decided to host this holiday meal where both families would finally break bread over our engagement.

Because my mother lived in Florida, she had to travel by plane to the event. Everyone else was within driving distance. And because this was my first time playing Martha Stewart for real — stressing about menus (who had a food allergy?), the ambiance (should I stick with traditional harvest colors or spice up the theme?), seating arrangements (if I put my family on one side of the table and his on the other, was that insinuating "us versus them"?) — I became neurotic, and Mom knew it. She had arrived a few days early to help me prep.

So when her outburst came on the heels of a "Welcome to our family!" toast to me from Jim's father, I was stunned. I presume she thought the evening was going well, which it was, up until her proclamation. Picture a reserved senior standing proper and talking calmly when a rather vocal woman who was enjoying her wine suddenly interrupted him.

I glanced down at my full plate as everyone else sat around the table nervously smiling and blinking at one another. Not sure what to do, I immediately took a swig of the Cabernet Sauvignon. I wasn't upset over Mom's announcement, but rather the timing of it.

"That's wonderful news!" Jim said, jumping up and wrapping his arms around her. He saw the corners of my mouth do a funny dip, so he reached out and patted my knee. Right away, I knew that my soon-to-be-hubby, a full-time firefighter with the FDNY, was going to somehow save us from these smoldering embers.

Jim's mother slowly stood and straightened her perfectly pressed slacks.

"Congratulations on your nuptials," she said, and motioned for a hug.

Jim's dad, ever the gentleman, got to his feet and raised his cup.

"It's an honor to have learned that our family is growing already," he said, and winked at me.

I smiled and turned to Mom. "We're both brides! Who woulda thunk it?"

She gave me a firm squeeze. "Sometimes it takes another shot at finding true love. Jim gets it."

I, too, knew what she was getting at. I think we all did. What matters most is our happiness, regardless of the path we have to travel to get there.

~Dawn Turzio

18

A Table with a View

A smile starts on the lips, a grin spreads to the eyes, a
chuckle comes from the belly; but a good laugh bursts
forth from the soul, overflows, and bubbles all around.
~Carolyn Birmingham

My mother and I traveled to the beautiful city of San Francisco, a place that Mom had never been before. We decided to have lunch one day at the top of a hotel with a circular, revolving restaurant, giving one a 360-degree view of the city.

The restaurant was set up with two circles of diners. On the lower level, rectangular tables were arranged perpendicular to the windows. The upper level, which made up the inner circle, was a couple of steps up and contained smaller tables, mostly for parties of two. The tables were arranged so that both people sat next to each other facing out. It was at one of these tables that my mother and I were seated.

The day couldn't have been more beautiful with a clear blue sky and fluffy white clouds. We felt we could see forever.

After a long, leisurely and delicious lunch, we got up to leave. As my mother was putting on her coat, she bumped up against the wall of mirrors on the one side of our table. Not realizing at first that it was her own reflection, she said, "Oh, excuse me!" Of course, we both started laughing. And, as a result, she didn't notice the step down to the lower level, lost her balance and literally went "flying" across the long rectangular table at the bottom of the stairs, heading right for the windows.

If only there was a way to share the expressions on the faces of the young businessmen whose table she "flew" across! Their drinks spilling and salads flying, they were paralyzed with their forks mid-air!

At first, we were afraid she would go straight out the window, but she "stopped" about mid-table. Of course, everyone from everywhere came running to help her up.

Being the dutiful daughter that I am, once I knew she was okay, I walked away. I had to as I had started to laugh uncontrollably. Once she joined me, she did the same. And it continued not only the rest of the day, but for years every time we recalled the event.

~Helen A. Scieszka

19

Dog Gone Clean

Visits always give pleasure — if not the arrival,
the departure.
~Portuguese Proverb

Money was tight in our household, but my mother always shared what we could, as long as there was a genuine need. But that generosity had limits, limits which Mom handled in her own inimitable fashion.

We had some neighbors who finally pushed Mom over the edge. One day, they stopped by just as Mom was finishing dinner preparations, so she invited them to stay. But then it happened again a few days later — and then again after that! It actually became a regular thing. They would come knocking just before dinner and stay for a free meal. One thing I should mention is that they were in the same financial situation as we were. They could afford the same food we could. So, it was often frustrating to us kids. We knew these neighbors were taking advantage of us.

But Mom took care of the situation one night.

Right on schedule, the neighbors showed up for dinner again. Mom served it the same as always. When the meal was finished, the neighbors offered to wash dishes (a first for them). My mom said, "No, I can take care of it." Without missing a beat, she took all the dirty dishes and put them on the floor. Our dogs came rushing into the kitchen and happily lapped the plates clean, after which my mom put them back in the cupboard. Then she smiled at the neighbors and told them they were "ready for tomorrow."

Of course, tomorrow never came as far as our neighbors' dinner raid was concerned. For some strange reason, they stayed away after that!

~Betty Maloney

20

The Endless Summer

In family relationships, love is really spelled T.I.M.E.
~Dieter F. Uchtdorf

My four kids couldn't wait for school to be out for the summer. On the last day of school, they used poster paint to paint our station wagon with "Schools Out! FREEDOM at Last!" They tied balloons and streamers to my car, and we had a one-vehicle parade to the school. When I picked them up later that day, we came home and had a bonfire in the back yard where they burned all their school papers. While the kids were roasting marshmallows over the fire, I washed the poster paint off my car.

Unfortunately, it didn't come off. The next day, I took my car to a place that detailed cars, and they told me I would need to have the car repainted. Okay, we weren't off to a great start for the summer, but the new paint job looked great. It was only a small setback.

My son Troy, who was ten, said he wished he could stop time and that summer would never end. My other three children — ages nine, eight and seven — agreed that summer should last forever. I told them we couldn't stop time, but we could ignore it for three months. I took the calendars off the wall and put them in a drawer. I took off my watch and put every clock in the house in the drawer with the calendars. I turned off the ringer on the phone and decided I would check the missed calls only twice a day, only returning the important ones. I was surprised that I never received any "important" calls, and eventually I started checking my calls only once a week. Then the battery on my phone ran down, and I just threw the phone into the drawer with the calendars and clocks. I discovered it was easy to live without a phone glued to my ear, and that none of the calls that formerly ate up my time and peace of mind were important.

We had stopped time and silenced the outside world. The feeling was incredible.

Every night, we hauled quilts and a basket of snacks up onto the roof and lay up there and watched the stars.

In July, we celebrated the Fourth of July. We decided to celebrate Halloween on July fifteenth. We carved watermelons like they were pumpkins, made costumes, and ran around the yard pretending to be ghosts, witches and pirates. On July twenty-fifth, we decided to celebrate Christmas. We set up our artificial tree, decorated it, baked Christmas cookies and watched a marathon of Christmas movies.

We watched old, silent movies with Harold Lloyd and Charlie Chaplin on TV. They always seemed to end in a pie fight, which looked like great fun. I filled fifty paper plates with whipped cream, and we had a pie fight in the yard. We were all completely covered with whipped cream, so we used the garden hose to wash off.

We learned we could rent any musical instrument for ten days for five dollars. We discovered we couldn't play the trumpet, violin, flute, guitar, banjo or bagpipes. Our family had no musical talent at all. That's a good thing to know.

We learned that if we drew a chalk line on the sidewalk it would hypnotize a chicken.

Our neighbors were often amused and confused by our antics. We were called "weird, eccentric and odd."

It was freedom. We ate when we were hungry, slept when we were tired, and got up when we felt like it. My daughter made a twelve-layer chocolate cake that looked like the Leaning Tower of Pisa, but it was delicious.

It was our summer to explore, invent and do amazing things. There was a Renaissance Fair, and we dressed up in costumes. We rode an elephant and a camel at the fair. My sons engaged in mock swordfights with knights, while my eight-year-old daughter got to be a princess and was rescued from a dragon (two men in a dragon costume).

Every afternoon, I'd throw a quilt under a shade tree, and bring a picnic basket and a book. The kids would lie on the quilt and eat while I read classics like *How to Eat Fried Worms, The Secret Garden,* and *Lord of the Rings.*

Then one day, I was hanging my laundry on the clothesline when I saw the school bus drive by. I wondered if the bus driver was making a trial run on his route before school started. If he wasn't making a trial run, that would mean school had started — and my kids had missed the first day.

I dashed into the house and called my neighbor, who informed me that school had started. Her two children had just caught the bus.

I woke up the kids and told them that, if we scrambled, they could be at school by noon and only miss half the first day. Or we could just forget about the first day, and they could start tomorrow morning. I told them we could make a fast trip to the mall and buy all the things they needed to start school.

They thought about it, and then Troy said, "Or we could just wear our old clothes, use our old notebooks and supplies from last year, and have one more day of summer. We can go shopping on the weekend."

They agreed they'd start school a day late so they could have one more day of our endless summer.

And that day was the best day of all. We packed a lunch and went hiking in the woods. We sat by a little creek and ate our lunch. A deer watched us take off our shoes and wade in the creek.

We had a campfire and roasted hot dogs for dinner. We hauled quilts and a basket of snacks up onto the roof, and lay there watching the stars and talking about what school was going to be like. The next day, we'd get up and eat breakfast, and the kids would go to school. I'd miss them terribly.

"This was the best summer ever, Mom. We'll never forget it," Peter said.

He was right. We never forgot our perfect, endless summer.

We had spent three months without going to the mall, using the phone, or knowing what time or day it was. We'd had the best three months of our lives, and except for renting the musical instruments and paying to ride an elephant and a camel, we'd spent less than $200 on entertainment.

When the kids were finally back in school, and the teachers asked how they spent their summer vacation, my kids would say they fought dragons, rode elephants and camels, celebrated Christmas, threw fifty pies at each other in a pie fight, hypnotized a chicken, and saw billions of stars.

It was the summer of absolute freedom, and there was never another summer so wonderful.

~April Knight

Chapter 3

My Crazy Family

Happily Ever Laughter

21

Everything's Going South

*Some relationships are like Tom and Jerry, they argue
and disagree all the time, but they still can't live
without each other.*
~Author Unknown

The alarm rang at 6:12 a.m., just as it rings every week-day morning. I know exactly how long it will take me, down to the minute, to get out of bed, take a bath, eat my breakfast, figure out what I am going to wear, feed the dogs, let them out so they can run next door and scare poor Mrs. Carlson's cat to death, find my keys, and head out the door. I walk out the door each morning at 7:43 a.m. It takes exactly seventeen minutes for me to get to work. No more, no less. I am very precise with time. It is a control mechanism for me.

So, you can see how anything out of the ordinary would completely throw the entire process out of whack. For instance — my mother calling.

Before I start that whole sorry business, let me explain something. I am from the South; my entire family is from the South. For those of you who have never known someone from the South, you will probably not understand this story. My husband is from Michigan, where I currently live. We have been married ten years, and my parents still call him "The Yankee." I explained to my father that he isn't a Yankee, and I wasn't even sure Michigan had participated in the Civil War, to which my father replied, "He's a Yankee. You can't get much farther north than Michigan."

You see what I am dealing with here. As a rule, Southerners tend to be controlling, judgmental and faithless. The myth about Southern hospitality is just that — a myth. Some of the meanest women I've ever met wear pearls with everything and attend meetings of the Junior League.

I digress. As I was saying, my mother called this morning at 6:36 a.m., which is about the time I am getting into the bathtub. I almost let it go to voicemail, but I thought someone might be dead, so I answered it. Another thing you should know about Southern people is that there is always some sort of crisis going on within the family. No one ever calls just to say "hi." There is always a "situation."

"Your father hasn't been home in four days," she said. "I think he's probably lying dead in a ditch somewhere."

Okay, a little history on my parents. There was a period in my life between eleven and fifteen years of age when my parents did not speak to each other. Not a word. I was the go-between. My mother would say things like, "Tell your father the car is making that funny noise again," or "I thought I smelled something electrical burning this morning while I was on my way to the grocery store." I would relay the message like my father had not just heard it, and he would reply, "I don't know how she could hear anything over that hoochie-coochie music she listens to," or "How could she smell anything over that toilet water she wears?" Then my mother would reply, "Well, we'll see how he feels when I end up lying dead in a ditch somewhere."

You get the picture. I was never entirely sure why they stopped speaking, but when I was in the tenth grade, I came home from school, and they were sitting at the kitchen table talking about what color to paint the den like nothing had ever happened. I asked my father years later how the disagreement started, and he told me there was never a disagreement; he just didn't feel like talking to her. Then he woke up one day and realized I would be going away to college soon, so he felt he better make peace. That is about the time he started disappearing for days at a time without telling anyone where he was going.

"What happened the last time you saw him, Mom?"

"Well, he told me he wanted pork chops for dinner, and then he left to go fishing. I haven't seen him since. I hope the sorry old son of a bitch fell in the river and drowned."

"Mother, you don't mean that. Have you called Nick Jr. to see if he can look around for him? There's not much I can do from up here."

"Yes, I called your brother, and he thinks we should just wait and see if he shows back up. He didn't take his truck, so he must be somewhere close unless he has a girlfriend and she picked him up."

"Mother, Dad doesn't have a girlfriend. I agree with NJ. Let's give it one more day and see if he shows up."

"I need you to come home and find your father."

"Mother, I have a job. I can't just leave because Daddy picked this week to go off the rails."

"Christie Ann, it's been four days. He's never been gone more than three days. I just have a bad feeling he's dead in a ditch somewhere."

I let out a long sigh. "Fine, Mother. If he isn't back by bedtime tonight, I will fly down there tomorrow."

"Thanks, baby girl. I will call you tonight."

She hung up. That's another thing about my mother. She never says bye; she just hangs up when she finishes talking. *This is not what I need this week,* I told myself. *I have a big presentation on Friday, and I'm not remotely prepared. Luckily, my boss's wife is from Tennessee, so he understands. Crap, now I'm late for work.*

Later that morning, I called my brother to get his take on the situation.

"Hey, little brother. What's up?"

"Not much. Just hanging out, working on my newest project. It's a 1956 Ford truck. Got it for $500."

My brother restores old cars and trucks. He is talented, too. He has a waiting list of people who want him to work on their vehicles. It suits him. My brother isn't very good with time constraints and rules.

"So, where do you think Dad is?"

"Hard to tell. He's been drinking a lot more hooch than he used to. I think it's screwed up something in his head."

For those who don't know, hooch is moonshine. It is about 180 proof and highly illegal.

"That's just great. He's probably passed out in one of the fishing shacks down on the river."

"Could be."

My brother never uses three words when two will do, and I have never seen any emotion from him at all. How that is possible with our parents is a mystery to me.

"Well, if he's not back tomorrow, I'm flying down there. I'll call you if I decide to come."

"Okay, sis."

He hung up. *What is it with my family? Can't anyone say goodbye?*

I called my mom around 5:30 p.m., and my dad was still not back. There is a 7:45 p.m. flight from Detroit to New Orleans, so I booked a seat. I had exactly two days to find my father and get back to Michigan to deliver my presentation at work. All I knew was that if he *wasn't* dead in a ditch, he *would* be when I got finished with him.

The flight was delayed, so I arrived in New Orleans around 1:00 a.m. Then I had to pick up my rental car and drive two hours to my parents' house. They live out in the middle of nowhere in an old antebellum home they have been restoring my entire life. My mother swears it's haunted. I've never seen a ghost, but according to my mother, you must believe in them before they will make their presence known. She says when she is in the kitchen with the windows open, she can hear children laughing.

When I arrived at the house, every window was lit — not a good sign. I grabbed my bag from the back seat and walked in the side door into the kitchen. The front door is for company; the kitchen door is for family. As I took in the scene in front of me, I saw my brother and my two aunts, Derenda and Earline, making sandwiches — even though food was covering every surface. That's another thing about Southerners: When something bad happens, they bring food.

My brother came and hugged me.

"Welcome to the loony bin."

"Where's Mother?"

"Lying on the fainting couch in the formal living room."

I walked down the hall into the living room and saw my mother lying on a chaise lounge in the semi-darkness with a washcloth on her head.

"Mama?"

She lifted the cloth and looked at me, and then proceeded to burst into tears.

"Oh, Christie, where is he?"

I walked over to my mother and wrapped my arms around her. I always forget how small she is.

"We'll find him, Mama. It's going to be fine. I'm here now."

I went to her bedroom and looked in the bottom of her jewelry box. I took out one of the sleeping pills she had hidden there. I walked back into the living room with a glass of water and made her take the pill. I led her into her bedroom and put her under the covers. She was asleep before I walked out of the room. I happened to glance at my father's nightstand. There was a picture of the four of us in a frame. NJ must have been twelve or thirteen, and I was fifteen or sixteen. We were all laughing with our mouths wide open. I had never seen the picture before. Quietly, I walked out and shut the door. I grabbed my bag from the hall, went to my room and went to bed. The next day was going to be long.

I woke up to the sound of the coffee grinder. I rolled over and looked at the clock: 6:10 a.m. Ugh! I got dressed and walked into the kitchen. I wore my oldest pair of jeans and an LSU T-shirt. Ernestine, my mother's cleaning lady/cook, was making breakfast. She engulfed me in a warm hug that smelled like chocolate-chip cookies and magnolia. I loved that smell; it meant safety to me. Ernestine had been a part of my life for as long as I could remember. She had cut my hair to get out the gum, tended many scrapes and cuts, brought homemade ice cream to the hospital when I had my tonsils out, and held me many times when I cried over some boy who had dumped me. She was like a mother to me. My mother had always been jealous of my relationship with Ernestine, even threatening to fire her, but my dad put his foot down. Ernestine was staying until she made the decision to leave.

"How you holding up, baby girl?"

"I'm fine. I have racked my brain, and I can't figure out where he could be. Has anyone checked the fishing shack?"

"They checked it yesterday, but he wasn't there. He's also not on the bayou, at your grandma's old home place or Sam's bar. They've checked all his usual haunts, and no one has seen him. It just doesn't make sense. He left on foot, so he couldn't have gotten too far."

"Unless he had someone helping him."

"Well, yeah, there's that."

About that time, my mother breezed into the kitchen in crisp khaki linen shorts and a button-up shirt with a sweater tied around her neck. She looked like she was headed to the country club for lunch.

"Ernestine, some coffee please."

"Yes'm."

"Good God, Christie Ann. Is that what you're wearing today? The local news is supposed to be here to tape us asking your daddy to come home, and you look like you just walked out of a cotton field."

"Good morning to you too, Mother. I had actually planned to change, but since you like this outfit so much, I'll just keep it on."

"Don't sass me today of all days. I don't think you grasp the fact that your father is *missing*."

"I'll go change."

I went into my childhood bedroom with the pink canopy bed, dresser with a matching vanity and an upholstered chair that matched the duvet. My mother had decorated the room when I was nine and the biggest tomboy on the street. My dad had wanted a boy so I did everything I could to prove I was just as tough. I refused to sleep in the room for a month until my dad took me deer hunting and asked me to use the room to "keep the peace." I hated the room when I was nine, and I still hated it. It went against everything I stood for. My mother always asks me "where she went wrong." A feminist, pouty-mouthed, take-no-crap daughter was not what she wanted. She wanted me to join the Junior League, wear pearls with my sweater sets, and use my everyday china and my fine china separately. I just grabbed whatever was closest and put my food on it. China did not excite me.

I had brought one decent dress with me, so I put it on and headed back down the hall. A lot of noise was coming from the living room, so the camera crew must be setting up. As far back as I could remember, Judy Wagoner had been the anchor on Channel Four news. She hadn't aged a day. I don't know who her plastic surgeon was, but he was good. My mother revered Judy Wagoner, calling her a class act. How she came to this conclusion is beyond me. She'd never met the woman until then.

I heard my mother speaking to someone in her "company voice" — the voice she uses when the preacher comes over for Sunday dinner.

"Christie? Christie, honey, is that you?"

I walked into the living room, and my mother was sitting on the sofa while a woman with a ton of make-up brushes fussed over her. This was my mother's nirvana.

"Christie, come over here and let me introduce you to Judy."

I held out my hand and said hello. Judy grasped both of my hands in hers and started shaking them up and down.

"I'm so sorry you are going through this horrible ordeal. Your mother said you flew down from Michigan. That must be quite the trip. Did it just take forever?"

I had forgotten that anything north of the Mason-Dixon line was not in these people's realm of imagination. If they couldn't drive there in six hours or less, it wasn't worth going. Slowly, I removed my hands.

"I only had to change planes three times, cross the Mississippi once, and then ride some farmer's jackass for about twenty miles to get here. It wasn't too bad."

My mother jumped up and asked Judy if she would like some coffee. I wanted to be anywhere else but there. It was going to be a long day.

The television crew finally left around noon. The taping went well. I sat on one side of mother, and my brother sat on the other. We each held one of her hands. She even managed to work up some tears. She told Judy my dad had been forgetting things recently, and she was afraid he might be somewhere and not know how to get home. This was news to me. He would tell me the same things over and over, but I just assumed it was because my mother had finally driven him crazy.

"Mother, why didn't you tell me that Dad had been forgetting things?"

"Because he didn't want anyone to know, especially you. You've always been a daddy's girl."

I was about to launch into one of my speeches about family and how we need to share things with each other, and how just because I'm 1700 miles away didn't mean I didn't care, when the telephone rang.

My mother answered.

"Hello?"

"Hello?"

"Is anyone there?"

"Oh my God, Nick, is that you? Where are you? We've been worried sick. Yes, she's right here. Hold on."

She turned to me. "He wants to talk to you."

I picked up the phone.

"Daddy?"

"Hey, baby girl. When did you get in?"

"About 1:00 this morning. Dad, where are you?"

"The casino in Cottonport."

"How did you get there? You left your truck here."

"Well, that's where things get a little fuzzy. A few days ago, I walked down to Delmar's fishing shack, and he had some 180 proof he wanted me to try. The next thing I remember, I'm watching your mama on the gosh-darn TV, begging me to come home."

"Daddy, you stay right there. Don't go anywhere. I'm on my way."

I hung up and looked at my mother. She looked as if she'd aged twenty years since I saw her at Christmas. It dawned on me at that moment that she was truly worried about my father. They had been married forty-two years. I honestly didn't know what they would do without each other. They have bickered my entire life, but my dad also brought her yellow roses each year for their anniversary and Chanel No.

5 perfume for every birthday. I realized at that instant that my parents loved each other. My mother's eyes met mine, and I could see her tears.

"C'mon, Mom. Let's go get your husband."

~Christie Collins Lypka

22

The Mysterious Package

A happy marriage is the union of two good forgivers.
~Fawn Weaver

It had gone on for years and years, and it always seemed to be about the same issue. Dad would receive some letter or package with a postmark from an exotic location, and Mom immediately wanted to know what he received. As a child of nine years of age, I remember some good-natured wrestling between the two of them. If it was a letter with a postmark from somewhere in Africa — although it was obviously from an acquaintance of Dad's from one of his far-flung forays into God-knows-where — Mom had to see what it was, who it was from, and what it said. She couldn't help herself. In hindsight, I think she may have been a little jealous or insecure. Perhaps she thought Dad was having an affair with the Queen of Sheba or some goddess from the Nile basin.

If the postman made a delivery while Dad was at work, he would invariably come home to find that whatever had been delivered had been opened and read. I personally loved the things Dad received from everywhere because my stamp collection was growing by leaps and bounds.

"What's that?" or "Who's that from?" Mom would ask every time one of those letters or packages arrived.

"None of your beeswax" would be Dad's standard reply.

So, this went on year after year. Letters and packages were received and would be opened by the time he walked in from work, or there would be a wrestling match to see who could maintain control of the thing.

One day, I saw the postman's red lorry turning off South Road and into our circular pebble driveway. He drove counterclockwise around the driveway and stopped in front of the house. He carried several letters in his hands, as well as a box covered with heavy brown paper and tied with string.

Since I was outside already, I took the items and carried them inside. Mom didn't come on the run, but as I placed the items on the coffee table in the television room and was eying all the exotic stamps from India that had been affixed to the brown paper covering on the box, Mom appeared quietly at my side. She picked up the box, shook it next to her ear, sniffed it, and then put it back down. She then looked at the letters, walked over to Dad's little study next to the enormous bay window, and placed the letters carefully on top of the green felt writing surface. Walking back to me, she picked up the box again and hurried off upstairs.

I didn't think too much about it and knew that Dad would be setting aside those great Indian stamps for me anyway. It was nearly 7:00, and we were getting ready to sit down for dinner when Dad finally arrived home from work. He greeted everyone and hurriedly made his way into the little first-floor bathroom before walking into the study. A couple of moments later, he came into the dining room and was uncharacteristically quiet.

Dinner went along pretty much as normal, with two or three conversations going on simultaneously. By 8:30, we were getting ready to be excused from the table. I went into the television room and turned on the BBC, but quickly turned down the volume when I overheard the row coming from the dining room.

Mom and Dad were going at it. Apparently, the box contained an ornately designed sculpture and was to be a gift to my mother as part of their upcoming anniversary. But Mom had opened the package and then tried to reseal the box as if it hadn't been opened at all.

She should have consulted me because I had become an expert at the opening and resealing of things. The previous Christmas, or should I say several weeks before Christmas, I had practiced daily with the Daisy BB Rifle that Dad had purchased for me and would have it resealed every afternoon within its red Christmas wrappings. On Christmas morning, I feigned surprise and delight as I opened the gift for what was probably the twentieth time. Dad was upset because the hundreds of BBs that were supposed to be in the box were somehow missing. But Mom didn't consult with me when she opened Dad's package, and the results were that he immediately recognized her handiwork.

The upshot from all of this was that Mom finally promised to never, ever open anything of his again, as long as he would never smoke another cigarette in his life. She was great at diverting attention away from the main issue at hand or changing the subject matter entirely. Dad didn't believe her and was out to prove his point.

The problem for her was that Dad knew people. He knew lots of people from all walks of life and from all over the world. And he knew the folks working at the mid-Atlantic weather advisories section for Pan American in the Azores. Every morning, rain or shine, those good folks would inflate an enormous weather balloon from their small weather reporting station, and send it aloft carrying a package of instruments designed to measure wind currents, air pressures, and temperatures at various altitudes. All that daily information was vital to the transatlantic flights operated by the airline.

Dad had one of the balloons sent to his office at Heathrow. Deflated, it came in a square cardboard box about three feet by three feet and was quite heavy. The box contained only the balloon and the cylinder of gas to inflate it, but not the extremely expensive atmospheric recording instrument package. As soon as it arrived, Dad had it taken into one of the maintenance hangars, and he and two of the men who worked on the airplanes went to work. They figured out a way to have the initiator cord attached to the lid of the box so that if it were to be opened, the balloon would inflate immediately. He then had the box carefully re-wrapped and sent to a colleague in Johannesburg, South Africa.

He spoke to his friend on the telephone and instructed him not to open the box, but instead to send it to Henry H. Elliott at Longridge, South Road, Weybridge, Surrey, England, and to make sure the words "Private," "Personal" and "Confidential" were emblazoned on all six sides of the box. There was to be no return address affixed to the box, and it was to be wrapped and secured in the heavy brown paper and string. Dad sent along a sum of money to cover the cost of shipping.

Three weeks went by, and things were going along quite well. I remember that Dad received at least one letter from someplace in Asia because Mom held it up to the light to see if she could see what was inside. But seeing me standing there, she cast me a sidewise glance and hurriedly put it on Dad's desk.

A few days later, that box from South Africa was delivered right to the front door. I was in school at the time and didn't see it being delivered, but learned later that the postman carried it inside for Mom and left it in the middle of the television room floor. It was a Friday. The next day, I was off for the weekend, and Dad was scheduled to return from his business trip in Brussels, Belgium, by the afternoon.

Friday night, we were watching television, and that box was sitting in the middle of the floor. South African stamps were all over the top of the package, as well as several customs stamps that I collected. There it sat, untouched by human hands, at least until Saturday morning.

My sister, Mimi, was off riding Matilda, her horse, which was kept in the corral Dad had built at the back of the garage. My brother, Mike, was attending boarding school at a military academy. I think my sister, Sherry, was upstairs playing. I was outside in the hothouse doing some of the important things that needed seeing to — at least, in my mind, they were important.

It was mid-morning, and it was quite warm inside the hothouse. The scream that emanated from the house shook me back to reality, and I thought someone had just been murdered. I ran from the hothouse into the kitchen while yelling for my mother. The commotion was coming from the center of the house. As I approached, I noticed a thin, wispy cloud of a fine white powdery substance floating in the air, quickly spreading throughout the first floor. Slowly, I walked forward into the ever-thickening cloud of smoke.

"Oh, my God!" exclaimed my mother from the television room. "Oh, my God!"

I went from the kitchen into the pantry and heard my mother struggling against the forces of some unknown evil presence. The wispy white cloud of smoke or dust, whatever it was, was becoming thicker, and as I walked from the pantry into the foyer, I could see the entrance to the television room off to my left. There was the unbelievable sight of an opaque white, rubbery sphere quickly and dramatically becoming larger by the second, filling the room. And there was the loud hissing noise as the gas from the cylinder very quickly inflated this enormous balloon. Within seconds, it was bulging from the television-room doorway and protruding into the foyer.

"Mom?" I heard myself yelling.

"Ugghh," came the muffled response from somewhere inside the TV room.

The hissing stopped, and the balloon stopped inflating. It was impossible to walk into the television room because the enormous rubbery shape was applying an airtight seal to the door.

"Mom?" I yelled again.

I could hear some struggling from within the room, and the faintest movement to the stretched skin of the balloon could be seen. I ran to the kitchen and quickly retrieved a steak knife from the top drawer. Running back to the room, I plunged the knife into the side of the shape, but nothing happened. I attacked it again and again, but still nothing. I thought of one of my guns, but they were secured above the closet inside the room I couldn't get into. I ran back to the kitchen, retrieved one of my mother's carving knives from the wooden block near the window, and rammed it into the side of the shape. Again, the rubber just seemed to absorb the shape of the knife, and nothing happened.

Then I remembered that my father's sword from the U.S. Naval Academy at Annapolis was in the closet at the end of the hallway on the second floor, so I ran upstairs. Returning a moment later, I pulled the sword from its scabbard and successfully penetrated the side of the balloon all the way up to the sword's hilt. The sound of the escaping gas was not really a hiss, but more like a loud, long sigh. Within a few seconds, it had deflated to nearly half its original size, and I was able to push my way into the room.

"Your father is going to get it!" she yelled. She sounded just like Donald Duck from the helium-gas mixture she had inhaled deeply into her lungs, and I started to laugh in that cartoon character's voice as well. She had been forced into a sitting position by the power of the balloon and fought the quickly deflating rubbery skin as she struggled to stand. She was covered from head to toe in that fine white powder and looked like some strange figure of a ghost.

I stood in the midst of the carnage, sword in my right hand, as the front door opened and Dad walked in. He dropped his suitcase on the floor and, stepping over the remains of the nearly deflated balloon, walked into the TV room. Through all the years I can remember, that was the loudest and longest I have ever remembered Dad laughing.

"Henry!" yelled Donald Duck. "We have to talk!"

By late that night, most of the mess had been cleaned up, and I had several new South African stamps to add to my collection. And that was the very last time I ever remember my mother even taking a second look at any of Dad's letters or packages.

~John Elliott

23

Hair Today, Gone Tomorrow

*Anyone can be confident with a full head of hair. But a
confident bald man — there's your
diamond in the rough.*
~Larry David

I giggled along with my husband, Gerry, as we looked through the before-and-after pictures in the colourful brochure he had received from the hair club. It was hilariously difficult for us to imagine him having hair again after being pretty much bald for the past twenty-some years. Now in his early fifties, he longed to fulfill his dream of once again having a full head of hair.

After much research, he settled on a provider that was seven hours away and would require crossing the border from Canada into the U.S. He was not discouraged by the fact that he would need to go for "maintenance" appointments every four weeks.

This non-invasive procedure was one whereby a custom hairpiece would be created for him out of human hair, coloured to match the little hair he had left, and then fused to his head via a special taping process. When he shared the details of this with me, we both cracked up, unable to quell the notion that this was nothing more than a glorified toupee!

Gerry, though, was still determined to go through with it, and I wanted to be encouraging. After all, I reminded myself, he wasn't out buying an expensive sports car or strutting around in skinny jeans and cowboy boots! If wanting hair would be the full extent of what I humorously referred to as his mid-life crisis, then I would gladly climb aboard for the ride.

Deciding that we would make these monthly trips a little getaway for both of us, I had Gerry drop me at the mall while he went to have his first hairpiece applied. As I hurried back to where he was to pick me up, I felt the laughter begin to bubble up inside me as I tried to imagine what he would look like. Not wanting to offend him, I struggled for control as I pushed open the door and walked outside. I caught sight of him through the car window as he sat waiting for me. As our tear-filled eyes met, I could tell that he was already laughing hysterically, having anticipated my response. Now I was doubled over in mirth as I awkwardly made my way to the passenger side of the car.

It wasn't that the hairpiece looked bad; it didn't. In fact, they had done a marvelous job. It was more the shock of seeing my husband with hair for the first time in many years that had us both consumed in fits of laughter.

Overcoming this initial transformation, we settled into the four-week routine of traveling to the hair club for washing, maintenance and sometimes a replacement of the hairpiece, while stocking up on the many "needed" hair products.

Joking that Gerry was now more the diva in our relationship than I was found me labouring to reapply the mandatory tape to his head in an effort to keep the hairpiece in place.

Upon entering the fourth year of hair maintenance, we now had the wonderful addition of grandkids, which found us lagging a few weeks behind the compulsory appointment dates. We had also run out of the special tape, which meant that Gerry's hairpiece was becoming extremely loose as well as a little ratty looking. Desperate to keep the hairpiece in place, we experimented with various kinds of adhesive and eventually ended up using Krazy Glue. Although the product immediately bonded to the skin, it would only work for a short time, which had Gerry wearing a ball cap over the hair during the day to keep it in place and removing it at night when he slept. After one such night, our little grandson — who had slept over and was eager to wake Grandpa in the morning — saw Gerry for the first time without hair. He exclaimed, "Grandpa! You have bald hair!" Of course, we laughed our selves silly over this, and had to admit at the same time that this whole procedure was getting ridiculous.

Later that same morning, as we were heading into the city to do some shopping, Gerry was again wearing his baseball cap over the hairpiece, which I laughingly pointed out was enormously counter-productive. Yet still holding onto the dream, he simply grinned and gave the brim of his hat a firm tug.

The mall had been well attended that day, and as we exited through the side door, we were forced to follow behind a large line of people who were also making their way to the parking lot. All of a sudden, a strong wind blew up, causing Gerry's hat to fly off his head. I watched in awe as, with lightning speed, he grabbed the hat, but not before his hairpiece took flight! It soared through the air, eventually hitting the ground and rolling like a tumbleweed through the parking lot. Shocked, we stood there motionless at first, along with a growing crowd, staring in disbelief at this bizarre scene.

"Just leave it," I managed to whisper under my breath while trying not to laugh. "Let it go." Abruptly, I began walking and then running toward our truck. Thinking Gerry had heeded my advice and was following behind me, I was stunned to see that he instead was running after his hair! Uncontrollably laughing now and on the verge of peeing my pants, I stared in disbelief as a very large man viciously stomped down on the runaway hair. Picking it up, he handed it to my embarrassed husband and casually remarked, "@#$% happens." Then he turned and walked away. With the cap back on his head, Gerry quickly shoved the hairpiece in his jacket and sheepishly returned to the truck. Seeing the condition I was in sent us both again into uncontrollable gales of laughter. With tears streaming down our faces and our stomachs aching, we got in the truck and headed for the nearest gas-station restroom.

True to form, the humour of this experience far outweighed the embarrassment, so when Gerry finally regained his composure, he said, "I think it's time to let this hair go."

"Set it free!" I chimed in heartily.

As we turned onto the highway, Gerry reached into his jacket, extracted the matted and dusty hairpiece, and threw it out the window. I watched through the side mirror as it settled on the shoulder, much more resembling a dead animal than something one would actually wear on one's head.

Though my husband did grieve his hair loss for a second time, he eventually came to embrace his baldness, happy to be finally free of his need for hair and equally as happy to have such a great story to tell.

Laughter has always been an essential part of our lives, especially with Gerry at the helm, and this outrageous event continues to be one of the best "ha ha moments" we have ever had!

~Jan Kendall St.Cyr

24

Quacking Up

Keep your eyes wide open before marriage,
and half shut afterwards.
~Benjamin Franklin

 h, no, not again. It was 6:30 a.m. and I heard the psychedelic guitar playing of Jimi Hendrix in the back yard. And my wife screeching.

My wife is stubborn and determined. When she wants something she makes it happen. And that is why we opened our pool in April, even though no one with half a mind opens a pool in April in Connecticut. First of all, it is still sleeting, if not snowing, and secondly, and this is important... April is when the ducks are looking for their new homes. They've flown back up from the south and they're setting up housekeeping again, building nests, laying eggs, and starting their next batches of ducklings.

But my wife was the team mom for the high school's lacrosse team, and they were having their team dinner in April. My wife wanted to crank up the heat and give those boys a treat — a pool party in April, two months before it really gets warm enough to swim.

The first year we opened the pool that early we had an unintended consequence: two ducks — a male and a female — made our pool their home. We chased them away again and again, but they kept coming back, and they made our pool unusable for months, because their droppings are *huge*. We finally got rid of them in July and were able to use our pool for the second half of the summer.

Even though my wife is very analytical, she refused to see the light on this one. So, sure enough, she opened the pool in April again the following spring in anticipation of another lacrosse-team pool party. And the ducks returned.

This time she was a bit chastened. And she confessed that this might have been a big mistake. So she set out to conquer the ducks. The former Wall Street analyst in her emerged and she started mapping out a battle plan. She had learned that the ducks didn't care at all if she yelled at them. But she remembered a historical fact that had tickled her fancy — that when Panamanian strongman General Manuel Noriega was being deposed by U.S. troops he had holed up in the Vatican Embassy in Panama City. He wouldn't come out, even when the embassy was surrounded. So the U.S. Army engaged in psychological warfare — by blasting hard rock at Noriega. Their playlist included songs by The Clash, Guns N' Roses, The Doors, and Van Halen. After one week, Noriega, an opera lover, surrendered.

My wife, a child of the Seventies, rolled out the big guns: Jimi Hendrix. She tried various songs and learned that the ducks really hated "Purple Haze." "Purple Haze" would get them moving, and with two-acre zoning we wouldn't be bothering the neighbors. She also learned that the ducks didn't like it if she looked bigger than she really was.

So that's why our mornings began as follows: she would get up, look out the window, and start yelling, "They're back. The stupid ducks are back." She'd rush downstairs and turn on the Jimi Hendrix CD that was preloaded and ready to rock and roll. As the outdoor speakers filled the back yard with electric-guitar riffs, she would run out in her robe and blue, fuzzy dog-paw slippers, grab a pool noodle to look bigger, and start threatening the ducks with the bouncing noodle, all while screeching at them to "go somewhere else."

I'd be watching the whole thing and laughing. The ducks would flap their wings halfheartedly in response to the loud music and the menacing pool noodle and hop out of the pool and onto the lawn. My wife would wave them off a bit longer, and then come back inside and turn off the music.

And the ducks would hop back into the pool.

Thus, we spent a second spring and early summer sharing our pool with the ducks. That meant *they* got the pool and *we* got the hot tub, which was the body of water they did not sully with their droppings. And then, one day, we watched our tenants fly into the pool as we sat in the hot tub. And my analytical wife realized something: ducks take off and land like airplanes. They don't drop straight in like a helicopter. They need a long gradual flight path, and they don't want to be hemmed in once they are in a body of water.

So my wife took every single piece of outdoor furniture we had and arranged them around the pool. It was a wall of eighteen chairs and chaise lounges, all with their backs to the water, making it impossible for the ducks to glide in for a landing like an airplane.

That was the end of the ducks. But for the rest of that summer and for the next couple of springs, our pool looked rather peculiar. Every time you wanted to go swimming you had to move a chair out of the way and then put it back in place when you got out. We had to make sure that the ducks had fully committed to someone else's pool before we could go back to normal, or whatever passes for "normal" in our house.

~Bill Rouhana

25

March Madness

I love being married. It's so great to find that one
special person you want to annoy
for the rest of your life.
~Rita Rudner

My ten-week-old grandson visited us, along with his parents and my son's in-laws. We propped the baby up in a corner of the den's sofa while I, in hush-hush tones, spoke to him as I squeezed his precious fingers. The little guy opened his mouth as though mimicking my expression — as if he too wanted to babble. My daughter-in-law raised her iPhone behind me and recorded our tête-à-tête. She vowed to send it to me later that evening.

After they had all departed, my husband settled into that same nook of our sofa and became engrossed in the March Madness of the Duke University and South Carolina game. Yes, That Game! I watched and occasionally uttered a lame comment like: "Looked like a foul to me!" or "He shot that from downtown!" I've acquired a bit of the clichéd, broadcaster go-to lingo after four decades of cheering on the Blue Devils.

"Want a Tab?" I asked my husband, a Tab aficionado to rival Austin Powers.

"Huh?"

"Tab?"

"Yeah."

I fetched the familiar pink can. When I returned to my niche on the couch, I noticed my phone had beeped. Snuggling into the other corner of the couch across from my hubby, I shouted, "Yay! Jess has already sent me pictures!"

My spouse squinted at the TV set, absorbed.

"Oh, looky here. You *must* see these with you and the baby!" I held up the phone. He didn't look. His eyes focused on the debacle occurring a few yards away. I glanced at the screen and witnessed yet another turnover. "When Coach K gets mad, he resembles Duke's mascot," I noted. "Don't cha think?"

My husband didn't crack a smile.

I shuffled through the photos, grinning at our big boy of ten weeks. "Amazing! You and he have the same expression in this photo." I extended the phone toward my better half. My husband didn't alter his gaze. I heard another beep. Jess had uploaded the video conversation I'd had with my grandson. I perused it. I marveled at his alertness and my pleasant, engaged baby-whisperer voice. Then, lo and behold, I spied my back, where folds of flesh could be discerned in a rippled effect under my polyester shirt.

"Ugh!" I groaned as I pored over the unflattering angle. "Yikes! I look terrible — even with my back to the camera!"

My partner dutifully followed the sad procession back and forth of his losing team and seemed unaware that another breathing human occupied the room, sharing the same sofa.

Finally, I said, not in sotto voce, "Honey, I am so sorry that you have a fat, unattractive wife. Really, I'm sorry."

"Me, too," he said.

I looked hard at him. He turned to look at me.

"What did you say?" I questioned.

"Me, too. Yeah, I'm sorry, too." He looked sincere in being sorry, too sincere.

"*What?*"

"I'm sorry, too," he stated.

"You're sorry you have a fat, unattractive wife?"

"What?" he asked.

"You agreed with me that you have a fat, unattractive wife!"

"Oh! I'm sorry. Duke is losing."

"Me, too," I said.

Then he gazed at me. With bated breath, I expected him to lie. I expected him to add, "You're not fat," or something to that effect. But he said, "You know, I'm fat, too."

At that point, a whistle blew on TV, and another whistle blew in my mind instantaneously. In that nanosecond, I determined three things about the near future: In the morning, Duke wasn't going to be packing for the Sweet 16; I was going to begin a love affair — with salads; and there was going to be a travel ban on a certain someone who frequently travels to Costco to procure humongous, chocolate-chip cookies that this same trekker consumes in large quantities while sipping a one-calorie soda in a pink can. And his wife eats these basketball-sized cookies, too. In one shining moment, epiphanies occurred!

~Erika Hoffman

The Lost Key

A man may be a fool and not know it,
but not if he is married.
~H. L. Mencken

bout ten years ago, my wife and I took a trip to the Grand Canyon in Arizona. I don't like to carry all my keys in my pocket during a hike so I took off the car key and left the rest in the car. We came back, and I put the key somewhere in the car without reattaching it to the key ring. We made a fire, roasted some weenies and marshmallows, and went to sleep in the back of the SUV.

The next morning, we were cleaning up our campsite when I saw a magpie inside my car. It was the only time I had ever seen a bird of any kind inside the car. I walked over, and it flew away. When we got in the car to go home, I couldn't find the key. We searched and searched, even emptying out the car completely, but it was gone.

Then it dawned on me. The magpie must have taken it. After all, they are notorious for stealing shiny things and decorating their nests with them. Keys are shiny. Ergo, the magpie was the culprit! It made perfect sense to me. So, cursing the magpie, I set out in search of its nest.

The next problem: As everyone knows, the Grand Canyon is a little on the large side — 1,902 square miles large — so I didn't like my chances of actually finding a particular nest belonging to a particular magpie in a particular tree in all that space. But what other choice did I have?

My wife was not encouraging. She said, "Are you crazy? You'll never find it! The Grand Canyon is the biggest hole on Earth!" I resisted the urge to give the obvious sarcastic response and marched purposefully onward until her derisive laughter faded in the distance.

I struggled to maintain hope as I searched dozens of trees and tracked every singing bird. The old "needle in a haystack" metaphor came to mind. But, oh, how glorious my victory would be when I snatched the missing key from the magpie's nest!

After two hours of searching and the onset of hypothermia, I finally gave up and returned to the car to find my wife—the only sensible one in our group of two—relaxing in a lawn chair, sipping a hot cocoa and wondering why she married me.

The next challenge was figuring out how to get a new key made. Luckily, another family came through the campsite. They said they were on their way to town. I asked them to send out a locksmith. They promised they would. Five hours later, he showed up. Because of how far away we were, he charged me nineteen times the normal amount for making a new key.

The next day, back in civilization, we stopped at A&W for lunch. I pulled out the recessed cup holder in my dashboard, and the key was sitting right there. Imagine my chagrin. It was the only place we didn't look. And guess who put it there? My wife! We were actually both to blame because I had pushed the cup holder back in without noticing the key. I got out of the car, looked up at the heavens, fell to my knees, raised my hands and screamed, "Whyyyyyyyy???" It was like what tennis players do when they make a game-winning shot, except without the happiness.

My wife on the other hand, has derived a great deal of happiness from this memory, mainly from enjoying my embarrassment as she has told and retold this story at parties and gatherings in the decades since it happened. It has also become sort of an ace up her sleeve. When we can't find something and neither of us knows who lost it, she simply asks, "Remember the Grand Canyon?"

~Mark Rickerby

Victoria's Worst Kept Secret

*The rate at which a person can mature is directly
proportional to the embarrassment he can tolerate.*
~Douglas Engelbart

As Valentine's Day approached this year, I was at a loss regarding how to surprise my eternally patient and positive wife of twenty-six years. I wanted to find her a gift that would truly show my love and appreciation to her for not smothering me in my sleep or encouraging me to overdose on chips and salsa long ago. My daughters had presented their Valentine's wish lists (yes, wish lists) shortly after Christmas, so I had already financed their gifts. But my wife (who never asks for anything other than that I avoid playing with that app on my phone that makes 500 different bodily noises—in church) was a harder nut to crack.

Then the clouds parted when I checked the mail to find, addressed to me, a special offer from Victoria's Secret. Aha! I had done a little online shopping with this establishment before, and now my creepiness was being rewarded with a coupon for free underwear. When I first heard about Victoria's Secret several years ago, I assumed the business was named after the legendary nineteenth-century English monarch. But once I realized what they sold, I knew I was wrong. Based on the historic images of Queen Victoria I've seen, she would more likely have done her shopping for the royal unmentionables at Sears—in the hardware department. Whoever this Victoria was, I owed her one for keeping her secret between us as I did my online shopping in the semi-privacy of my own bathroom (semi-privacy because I rarely manage to get the door shut and locked without interference from at least one child or pet).

My internal rejoicing over my coupon was suddenly interrupted, however, when I read a horrifying phrase in the fine print: *In-store only.* I didn't think men were even allowed in that place. In fact, whenever I go to the mall, I risk contact with the mall kiosk salespeople selling bespangled phone cases, Turkish beauty cream, and Dippin' Dots as I veer away and avert my eyes from the Victoria's Secret entrance, festooned with mannequins who forgot to put on their pants. This time, though, I was determined I wouldn't let my self-respect keep me from making a romantic gesture — at a discount.

As I entered the store, my mind was racing with "what-ifs." *What if one of my college students sees me? What will they think, and how will it affect my instructor evaluations?* "Well, Mr. Graves teaches a great lesson on Cavalier poetry, even if he is a creepy weirdo who snoops around in the clearance bras." *Worse yet, what if someone from church sees me? Will it endanger my third-grade Sunday school teaching position? Will I be relegated to boys' bathroom monitor or parking-lot duty in the senior-adult area?*

Pushing these thoughts aside, I pressed on to find the items pictured on my coupon. Apparently, underwear at Victoria's Secret is categorized according to how much of it is missing. At any moment, I expected to see a table display with nothing but spools of thread. When I finally found something I could identify as human garments, I then had to find the correct size, which involved rifling through storage bins below the display table and constantly looking over my shoulder like some kind of maniac to see if anyone was watching.

Sure enough, it didn't take long for a sales associate (wearing all black — presumably for my funeral) to show up and ask, "May I help you, sir?" just loud enough for mall security to hear. I had no choice but to be completely honest, so I told her I was looking for house slippers and socks, to which she replied at full volume, "You're in the wrong drawer. Those are the cheekies."

Once I had finally made my selections with the help of the panty police and was making my way to checkout, I did notice a few other men in the store with their wives. One appeared to be examining a hairline seam in the wallpaper while his wife browsed through the hip huggers. Another was counting ceiling tiles while his wife demanded that he smell the glittered body sprays with her. One man who was there with his teenage daughters glanced at me with a defeated look of solidarity in his eyes, and I could have sworn he mouthed the words, "Please, help me!"

Unfortunately, I could offer no help to these fellow sufferers, as my main goal at that point was to escape without further humiliation. Those hopes were dashed, though, when I saw the enormous checkout line. Of course, I was the only male in line, and I was determined to salvage what little masculinity I had left — which isn't easy when you've got a handful of lingerie. I tried to be nonchalant and held them in my fist like a baseball. While I stood there in disgrace, a woman behind me in line actually leaned forward to say, "Your wife certainly is lucky you shop for her here. My husband would never do that." *Of course, he wouldn't,* I thought. *It's called dignity.*

The experience didn't improve when I reached the cashier. I tried to conceal my embarrassment by making jokes. "Do you have a dressing room? Do these match my eyes?" The cashier just raised her eyebrows and avoided making eye contact. She was probably reaching for a panic button under the counter. Her response to my humor was to hand me my merchandise in a ridiculously scorching-pink bag that was specifically designed to humiliate me as I walked through the mall and out to my car. This bag of shame, which was billowing with fuchsia tissue, made me look like I was on my way to a baby shower for Lady Gaga.

As I sat in my car to recover with "We Are the Champions" playing on the radio, I felt a wave of satisfaction come over me. I had swallowed my pride (and a heavily iced slice of Great American Cookies cookie cake), saved some money, and purchased something special for my wife for Valentine's Day. In fact, I'm already planning next year's Valentine's gift. I wonder what she would think of some Turkish beauty cream and a Dippin' Dots gift card?

~Jase Graves

28

Showing Off?

Against the assault of laughter, nothing can stand.
~Mark Twain

The property in rural, southern Ohio where I grew up was straight out of a Norman Rockwell painting. Consisting of nine acres with a gigantic front yard, a wooded ravine, and a small pond, it was the perfect place to raise seven boys.

Situated next to the ravine, our house dominated the landscape. From the sink at the kitchen's corner window, Mom could look over the entire back yard, where nothing escaped her surveillance.

The only reason that we lived in such an awesome house was because of my Dad's Herculean efforts. Dad was a hard-working man of Irish descent, but not averse to the occasional clowning-around-for-a-laugh. And Mom knew that all too well.

One summer, Dad and his older sons decided to build a tree house in an elderly oak just beyond the backyard fence. This led to a beautiful Saturday afternoon in June, with my dad hammering away on the only portion of the tree house that was almost done — the floor. At the time, my brothers and I were working beneath the oak, doing menial tasks that Dad assigned.

Suddenly, we boys heard a branch snap and looked up to see one corner of the floor give way.

My brother screamed "Dad!" while I watched in horror.

Dropping his hammer, Dad grabbed for the nearest branches, but to no avail. He slid on his hands and knees down the sloping floor, and his body was launched headfirst over the side.

Inside the house at that precise moment, Mom happened to step to the sink, where she saw Dad execute a perfect somersault in mid-air and land safely on his feet.

Immediately, she stormed out onto the back deck and yelled, "JACK, QUIT SHOWING OFF IN FRONT OF THE BOYS!"

After Mom traipsed back into the house, Dad looked at his sons, and we all busted up laughing. If Mom only knew…

~John M. Scanlan

29

Hittin' the Sauce

Man does not live by words alone, despite the fact
that sometimes he has to eat them.
~Adlai E. Stevenson II

s a vegetarian, my husband Michael stands firm on his meatless convictions and flaunts his supper snobbery by eating alternative meals each night. He eschews turkey, pork, beef, and on more than one occasion, has referred to chicken as "a fowl thing to eat." Anything that has a face is off-limits, never to touch his pristine lips. Hoping to herd us into his meat-free camp, he glances at our dinner plates and shares sordid tales about the slaughterhouse that once corralled our T-bone steaks. I shoot him the I'm-not-deterred-by-your-hormone-horror-story glance and place my fork to my mouth, enjoying my beef tips — savory and hardy — while he stabs at his bowl of leafy greens, so lifeless and limp, searching for substance.

But I still love the guy and worry if he'll have enough to eat every time I grill a porterhouse. Priding myself on my culinary skills, I'll admit that his refusal of my gourmet meals baffles me as he eats a peanut butter sandwich while the rest of us dine on pork chops stuffed with couscous, currants, and toasted pine nuts. Thanksgiving makes me even more anxious, and I triple the number of side dishes to make up for the absence of turkey in his tummy. In short, his eating habits are a pain in my rump roast.

As if meals at home aren't a big enough problem, his self-imposed food limitations affect our social life. Before being seated at a restaurant, Michael critiques the menu on its vegetarian friendliness. "No, thanks," he says, and hands the menu back to the hostess. "Not much for me here."

And we leave the restaurant.

Once settled at an acceptable establishment, Michael sets to work, creating his culinary masterpiece through rearrangement, deletion, or substitution.

He scrutinizes the breakfast menu. "Can I forgo the bacon in today's special?"

The question throws off the waitress, and she says, "I'll have to ask the cook. I think the quiche is pre-made."

"Never mind," Michael says, recalculating. "What about substituting the side of sausage for one of your whole wheat pancakes?"

The waitress scribbles on her note pad. "I'll have to ask the manager."

Annoyed, Michael points to the picture of the sausage link. "I'm fairly certain this here costs more than a pancake, right?"

"Probably."

"Then it'll be saving you money."

"Yes, and I'm sure it won't be a problem." She smiles. "But I still have to ask."

"That's okay. Forget it." He flips the menu back open.

"I really don't mind asking." Her eyes dart to the left, distracted by the hostess seating a large family in her station. Michael has obviously exceeded the time limit for ordering.

Michael sighs, as if he, too, is exhausted by the effort. "Why don't you go ahead and ask then."

The waitress turns to me, and I'm tempted to ask for whatever is left over in the back to make up for the previous complications. "The Southwest omelet," I blurt, keeping it simple.

She hesitates, thinking I must have similar food hang-ups to be married to the man who reads menus as if they're battle plans. But I remain silent.

"That's it?" she asks, her shoulders relaxing.

I nod, and my food arrives first, which I believe is no accident.

Over the years, the guests at our dinner parties have dwindled as most have voiced their tofu trepidation or, as my father claims, an abhorrence to that "slimy, rubbery, tasteless crap." Whenever we're invited to family get-togethers, the night grows awkward as Michael places his hand over his plate and rejects the hostess's edibles. Out of guilt, she offers him a substitute meal.

"No, no," he says. "I don't want to be a bother."

I silently call malarkey, remembering the thousands of alternative provisions I've prepared for him over the years.

The hostess scurries to the kitchen to whip up something less offensive to his taste buds, not only feeding his appetite but also his ego.

On the way home, I place a to-go bag of cookies behind the driver's seat and catch a glimpse of a few small plastic packets. I reach under the seat and retrieve them. Shocked, I crouch behind the seat as my hostility boils over like a pot of beef-laden chili. I contemplate how I'll confront Michael without punching him in the throat.

I pop up from behind the seat. "What are these doing in your car?"

"What?" he asks, playing innocent.

I dangle the packets in his face. Caught committing a culinary crime, he shifts his gaze to the dashboard, and I stare at the packets of Arby's Sauce and Horsey Sauce, feeling like a jilted chef. "At the very least, you owe me the truth," I say. "How long have you been hittin' the sauce?"

"A few years," he whispers.

"How often?" I ask, bracing myself for the full extent of his cheating.

"A couple times a month."

"So, all this time that you've been requesting special meals each night, you've been a closet carnivore?"

He sighs. "Look, once in a while I need a quick protein hit, okay?"

"Quite the dirty little secret you've got going on here." I picture him ditching his fast food bags in the neighbor's recycling bin before pulling into our driveway, then heading straight to the bathroom to brush and floss the roast beef residue from between his teeth.

I look him in the eye. "I believe you have a problem, Michael."

He stares straight ahead.

"Are you willing to go to AA?"

"AA? What are you talking about?" he asks.

"Arby's Anonymous," I say before buckling over with laughter.

Word eventually got out, and it wasn't long before Michael became the pork butt of family jokes. These days, while the kids and I "ooh" and "ahh" over our rotisserie chicken, he eats a quinoa salad, attempting to re-establish himself as a strict vegetarian. The dinner charade continues, but he doesn't fool us. We smile, knowing he probably scarfed down a smoked brisket not an hour before.

~Cathi LaMarche

And the Award Goes to...

*Silence is golden when you can't think
of a good answer.*
~Muhammad Ali

R are is the time when I am actually all caught up with my
schedule. Such was the case this past week. I was very
much happy with the fact that I was on schedule, and I
had everything in hand. Nothing makes me feel better.

Of course, this is mostly delusional, at least for me. If there ever
was an award for being delusional, I am quite certain I would be at
the top of the list.

As I was wallowing in my delusion and enjoying every moment
of it, the Gracious Mistress of the Parsonage came and said rather
sharply, "Are you ready to go?"

At that moment, I had no idea what she was talking about. And
so I responded, "Huh?" I'm not sure if that is really a word or not, but
it accurately described my delusional moment at that time.

"You haven't forgotten what day it is, have you?" she asked.

I was tempted to say, "Of course not. It's Tuesday." Fortunately, I did
not yield to that temptation and just responded with another "Huh?"

With a disdainful look, she said, "You would forget your head if it
wasn't attached. Today the grandchildren are getting awards at school."

I'm not quite sure if I forgot or if I was not listening when the instructions came my way. At this point, I was not going to let anybody know, particularly my wife.

"Oh, yes," I said, getting up from my chair. "I'm all ready. Let's go."

She gave me one of her classic sarcastic grins, and we headed for the door.

Our one granddaughter was graduating from the third grade and the other from the fifth grade. Unfortunately, one was at 8:30 in the morning and the other was at 1:00 in the afternoon. It would make sense to have them all at once, but what has sense got to do with our world today?

I did not want to complain. After all, it is our grandchildren, but I think the planning could have been just a little bit better. After all, sitting in the school cafeteria listening to the award ceremony is about as exciting as it can get.

The chairs we had to sit on were uncomfortable, which was very fortunate for me because I was not tempted to fall asleep during the ceremony. I believe that was done on purpose.

Imagine getting an award for completing the third grade! I cannot remember any such thing when I was going to grade school. Our great award was leaving school and going home in the afternoon. It just doesn't get any better than that. We live in a different world today where everybody gets an award for something — or sometimes for nothing.

Then I remembered my cell phone in my shirt pocket. It is times like this that God had in mind when he invented this cell phone technology. I pulled out my cell phone and started checking my e-mail.

Then I felt a sharp pain in my right ribs and I heard a voice saying, "Put that away and pay attention."

I returned my cell phone to my shirt pocket and tried to pay attention. The problem is that the grade school, particularly the third grade, had more children than just my grandchild. They were trying to give awards and recognition to all the children, and I was only interested in one: my granddaughter.

I was musing on this for a while, and then my companion said, "Look, there she is."

When she said that, out came her cell phone, and she began

taking pictures of our granddaughter walking up to the stage to get an award. I couldn't use my cell phone, but she was at liberty to use hers?

Taking a hint from my wife, I reached for my cell phone, only to realize that I was too late, and the moment was gone. I glanced over at my wife, and all I could see was the big smile on her face and her saying, "I got her picture." I returned her smile and congratulated her on getting the picture.

After each of the award ceremonies, my wife and I went forward, and she took pictures of the grandchildren and me together, which made her rather happy.

All the way home that afternoon, she was giggling and chattering very excitedly. "Her" grandchildren received some awards. According to her, these were very special awards.

I smiled and was tempted to say, "Aren't they *my* grandchildren, too?" But why spoil the moment. She was excited and happy, and it was worth my silence.

I was reminded of what Solomon said: "A time to rend, and a time to sew; a time to keep silence, and a time to speak" (Ecclesiastes 3:7 KJV).

A wise man knows when "to keep silence."

~James Snyder

Chapter 4

My Crazy Family

We're All Nuts Here

Holy Smoke!

They say that no matter how old you become,
when you are with your siblings, you revert
back to childhood.
~Karen White

Wind pushed at our clothes as we stood next to my grandmother's grave on the hill behind her house. We were waiting for her coffin to be lowered into the ground. We had all been crying for hours, and I watched my four aunts praying together, their heads bowed. Even my mother, with her devil-may-care personality, was sobbing as the crank turned, moving the casket closer to its final resting place.

Everyone stood there uneasily, lowering their eyes and murmuring to others in comforting tones. Suddenly, there was a slight shout. How it began I cannot ascertain, but my mother's sisters began bickering. Their mother's burial hadn't even been completed and the fighting had begun. I couldn't believe it.

My mother wasn't part of the fighting, and she pulled me to the side and handed me something, a hard round object.

"Hurry," she said quietly. "Go down to Mama's house and put this under the hood of your Uncle Chuck's new car. I want you to light it, and then run up here and yell at him that his car's on fire."

"Mom," I protested, pointing to the casket making its slow progression into the ground. "Funeral!"

We're All Nuts Here | 113

"Roni," she replied in kind, pointing to her squabbling sisters. "Fighting."

With a nod, I was down the road without a backward glance. I was almost thirty years old at the time, but had no qualms about doing as my mother bade me. As I lifted the hood to his sedan, my cousin Ray came running over to see what I was up to.

"Is something wrong with Chuck's car?" he asked.

Without comment, I nodded, returning to my task and trying to find the most harmless place to put the smoke bomb my grieving mother had handed me. Ray took one look at it and told me I should be ashamed of myself.

"This is the day of a funeral!" he complained, ramming his fists into his pockets. "You're worse than your mom!"

"Who do you think gave me the smoke bomb?" I asked. "Hey, do you have a lighter?"

He handed it over so I could light the wick, and then I closed the lid. He shook his head, leaving me to my mischief as I handed him back the lighter and ran for the graveyard.

As I arrived, I shouted and waved my arms until I got Uncle Chuck's attention.

"Uncle Chuck!" I shouted. "Your car's on fire!"

At once, the arguing stopped, and everyone began hurrying down the road toward the car. You would think that after all the years my mother had pulled that prank on my uncle (not to mention the others assembled there) that someone might have guessed she was the culprit. But she had never left the gravesite. And no one would suspect sweet little me.

Chuck threw up the hood to his car, the remaining smoke puffing out from underneath, and began checking the entire engine, looking for the source of the problem. After some time, he scratched his head, glanced around for a moment searching the faces of everyone there, and then spoke.

"That smells almost like an electrical fire. Daddy?" He called to my Great-Uncle Duke. "You reckon it could be an electrical problem?"

Uncle Duke was no fool. He and my mother had been in some sort of personal prank war over the years, and that man knew the smell of a smoke bomb like a cat knows its milk. He turned his head away, laughing, and I decided to let my uncle have some relief.

"You think it could be that smoke bomb under your car, Uncle Chuck?" I asked.

He leaned his head over to look, his deep brown eyes narrowing as he caught sight of the naughty object, and immediately turned to glare at my mother.

"Irene!" he shouted.

"I didn't do it!" she responded in mock surprise. "I was with you!"

"That's right," he murmured, taking a deep breath and scanning the faces of those assembled. I suppose he hoped to see someone laughing, or at least smiling, but everyone looked on in awe. He caught my mother's gaze hard, and the standoff began. Her green eyes pierced right through him in denial, and no one moved for long moments. Eventually, Uncle Chuck determined he was no match for my mother and turned around to lean on the car.

"Roni did it!" my mother finally admitted, pointing her finger at me. Uncle Chuck immediately started laughing.

"She made me do it," I answered defensively, pointing back at Mom.

Pretty soon, everyone was pointing fingers, looking at the smoke bomb, laughing and calling up old memories. As I recall, we wound up sitting at my grandmother's table eating KFC, picking over old family photographs and reliving old times. The day of my grandmother's funeral ended exactly as she would have had it end: with her family reliving the joy we'd shared with her in her house.

Several years later, while thinking about it, I asked my mother why in the world she had a smoke bomb in her purse in the first place. She said that she had actually bought it just for the funeral. The puzzled look on my face made her smile.

"No one knows my sisters better than I do, and I came prepared," she answered.

I laughed. "Only you, Mom."

"That's nothing," she replied with a mischievous grin. "If Chuck and Duke had gotten fired up, I had a whole box of firecrackers in my purse for them, too!"

~Veronica I. Coldiron

32

It's a Yoder Thing

People who love to eat are always the best people.
~Julia Child

I t's called Yoder Food. Things that the average American would refuse to touch, the Yoder consumes vigorously, with unrestrained delight.

The reason for this has never been clear. Some say it's because of the generations of Yoders who were raised in poverty, watching their peers eat school lunches consisting of sandwiches with real cheese and mayonnaise, while they ate whatever they were lucky enough to have — often dry bread with a single slab of bologna.

Others credit the habit to a family legend handed down through the generations telling of a Yoder who died a slow, terrible death from starvation. This story is told every year with increasing horror to the youngest wide-eyed Yoders, who suddenly rise from their seats mid-tale and rush to the pantry to stuff their mouths with whatever food they can find in a desperate attempt to stave off their impending starvation.

No one is sure which reason, if any, is the culprit, but there is no denying that the love for food has been firmly imprinted into the Yoder DNA. One Yoder has been known to reprimand an upset stomach by packing it full of food. Another Yoder will forget to pack his socks and toothbrush, but he never fails to bring several large bags full of food on a trip. Every Yoder is born with the ability to take a bite of food and then give a breakdown of its ingredients to anyone around, often suggesting the use of real butter to improve its quality.

Yoders are passionate about their food and therefore they are passionate when they argue about food, too. Quite a famous argument occurred one day over a large pot filled with rich, buttery milk warming on the stove. A few of my aunts were making a dish called stewed crackers, which is said to have been the main staple for Yoders during the Great Depression. One of the aunts innocently picked up the kettle and began pouring the milk over a bowl of crackers next to the stove.

"WHAT ARE YOU DOING?" roared a disgruntled Yoder, grabbing the kettle and setting it back on the stove. "You know you don't put the milk over the crackers! You put the crackers into the milk!"

"No, you don't! I was doing it right!" the aunt said, defensively reaching for the pot.

The argument escalated quickly. One aunt paced, shouting her opinion over the din. Another consulted the Yoder cookbook, in which a blue-blooded Yoder cousin had described in great detail the proper method for making stewed crackers. Sides were taken. Insults were hurled. Opinions were voiced loudly, going completely unheard by the opposing party, which was also loudly voicing opinions.

After a few frenzied minutes, a quiet Yoder uncle stepped into the fray and calmly dumped the milk over the bowl of crackers. The din switched off immediately. A few suppressed whines were heard, and then breakfast proceedings continued as normal. Ten minutes later, the entire Yoder family happily dined on the crackers, all former conflict blocked out by the serotonin released from the comfort food.

As my aunt spooned warm crackers and eggs into her child's mouth, she told me about the fire that had taken her childhood home. There had been an explosion, badly burning the boy who would later become my father, and the flames quickly ate up the curtains until the whole house was engulfed in the flames. My grandma herded her children out into the snow, and my grandpa came home just in time to see his house and everything inside burn into oblivion. The family had escaped with their lives and a pan of sausage that one of the girls had been frying.

I listened to the story solemnly, taking note of the sausage. It was perfectly reasonable to a Yoder that sausage had been swiped off the stove in the mad dash out the door because the life-sustaining food was just too precious to be left behind.

All food is life sustaining and precious. That is why two great-uncles were caught engaging in a heated argument in a Cracker Barrel restaurant over which food the other should order.

It is why certain young Yoder cousins keep snack stashes in their nightstands, just in case they should wake up during the night and find themselves hungry.

It is why anyone who talks with a Yoder will find that no matter what topic they start out on, the conversation will always be artfully maneuvered to the subject of food.

It is why Yoder kids fight over dibs on the leftover bean soup because they all know it's so much better after being refrigerated over-night, when the bread chunks have soaked up all the milk and made the soup into a mealy, comforting mush.

It is why everyone loves traveling to a Yoder family member's home. They know that on arrival they will be rushed to a table decked out with the finest array of good food the family could afford.

It is why an indifferent attitude about food shocks and appalls a Yoder and often results in a rant about the importance of food and how disrespectful such an attitude is toward the very sustenance of humanity.

Each meal is planned and prepared with thoughtfulness and talent. Each bite is lovingly regarded as an experience of its own. Table conversations are more often than not centered on food, often debating the pros and cons of different variations of dishes. "Bone-in chicken has a better flavor," says my grandpa between mouthfuls of mashed potatoes, "but you get much better mileage on boneless chicken."

Most people don't understand this affection toward all things edible and even some things inedible. My advice to those people, when descended upon by a Yoder and lectured on the healing power of oyster soup, is to smile and nod. It's a Yoder thing. You just won't understand.

~Hannah Yoder

33

My Incorrigible Uncle Bud

When hospitality becomes an art, it loses its very soul.
~Max Beerbohm

When our kitchen door flew open, banging against the doorstop, my whole family gasped. Soon, a man's voice yelled, "Hey, Sis! You home?"

Being only six years old, I trembled in fear, unable to understand what was going on. I'd been relaxing with my family in the living room on a hot summer afternoon, but now my peace had turned to panic.

Oddly, my grandmother had a very different reaction. "It's Bud!" she cried with delight, trying unsuccessfully to rise from her rocking chair. "My boy has come to see me."

"Gr-r-reat," my mother growled, throwing down the book she'd been reading. "I suppose that senseless brother of mine dragged poor Mildred and the kids along with him again. Why doesn't he call me first?"

Storming into the kitchen, Mom shouted, "Bud, you're impossible! You do this every time. You could have called. You could have written. But, no! You simply hop in your car, drive across the country, and come storming through my door."

My brother, sister, and I peeked into the kitchen to see Uncle Bud grinning broadly as he said, "Well, Sis, I figure you can handle it.

I've just been longing to come and see more of the sights in Seattle. Plus, a guy has to check on his widowed sister and mom every once in a while."

Hearing Grandma call his name, Uncle Bud headed toward the living room to greet her.

Soon, Bud's wife, Mildred, staggered through the doorway, followed by my three cousins. "Ah-h-h," she sighed, "it feels so cool in here! Could I please have a glass of water?"

"Certainly," my mother answered, still glaring in the direction of her cocky brother. While Mom escorted weary Mildred to a kitchen chair, she asked, "Did Bud drive straight through from Cleveland again?"

"Not quite," Mildred explained. "We stayed overnight at a motel somewhere between Ohio and Seattle. But I'm too exhausted to remember where."

"He's got no common sense!" Mom snarled. "If I'd known you were coming, I'd have taken time off work. As it is, I'm serving a banquet at the hotel this evening, so I'm leaving soon. But I'll do the best I can to prepare the guest room for you."

"Thank you," Mildred sighed. "Thanks so much for your patience."

Uncle Bud pulled this stunt nearly every summer. After my siblings and I would recover from our uncle's dramatic entrances, we were thrilled to see him and our three cousins. He'd take over our family's agenda, driving us all around the Seattle area on exciting day trips to the mountains, beaches, and rainforest. All six of us kids would cram into the back seat of Bud's Studebaker sedan and have a blast together. In my opinion, this guy was awesome!

However, that innocent view of Uncle Bud's antics changed when I became an adult. My husband and I were living in our dream home—a log cabin in the mountains of Montana—when our phone rang on a peaceful summer morning.

As soon as I answered, an impatient man grumbled, "Where the heck are you? I've been driving all around and can't find your place."

"Uh... who is this?" I asked.

"It's your Uncle Bud," he answered, "of course!"

Oh, sure, I thought, *I should have known, even though I haven't even seen this guy in almost a decade.*

Nevertheless, I said politely, "Sorry, I didn't recognize your voice. But... where are you?"

"We're at Fireside Pizza on Highway 93," he answered.

Evidently, Uncle Bud had been so excited to hear we were living in the mountains that he figured he had to come for a visit. Intending to surprise us, he'd noted our address from a card I'd sent him the previous Christmas. But when he arrived in western Montana, he got lost on the winding mountain roads, ruining the fun... for him. Not for me, though.

After giving Bud directions to our home, I was relieved that I'd have a few minutes to prepare while he drove from the pizza shop. First, I wanted to warn my husband, John, and our teenage son that Bud would be setting the agenda for the next few days.

John rolled his eyes. "I remember that about him from our visit to his place years ago. Believe me, I'll try to be patient, but this won't be easy."

While I scurried around cleaning our office, which doubled as a guest room, I saw a car easing its way down our driveway.

"He's here!" our son shouted.

Strolling out the door to greet our guests, I assumed it would be just Bud and Mildred, but I saw three adults getting out of the car. Bud had brought his older sister, my Aunt Betty! I was delighted to see her, but all I could think was, *I only have one spare room... one queen bed! Where will I put Betty?* As I watched my seventy-four-year-old aunt limping toward me, she definitely wasn't a candidate for my couch.

"You have such a pretty place here," she gushed, smiling broadly. "And it's so wonderful to see you."

"Well," I said, "it's wonderful to see you, too. But Bud didn't tell me. I mean, I don't have beds for all of you."

My Uncle Bud stood in the background with his arms folded across his chest. Not surprisingly, he wore the same cocky grin I remembered from decades earlier.

Rubbing his chin pensively, he stated, "I knew your bedroom space would be limited, so I booked rooms for us at the St. Mary's Motel."

"Whew!" I sighed, giving Aunt Betty a huge hug before moving on to embrace Bud and Mildred.

Surprisingly, we ended up having a wonderful visit. Yes, Uncle Bud did set the agenda, but he also paid for everything while we toured the area. Awed by the scenery, he hoped to return very soon. So, the following year, my prankster-uncle surprised us by opening our front door and sauntering in — of course, without knocking first.

"Somehow I've got to get even with this guy," my husband growled.

John felt so disrespected that he dreamed of walking unannounced through Bud's front door, but that could never happen. My husband had multiple sclerosis. At that point, it severely limited our ability to travel. In fact, the following year, we had to sell our home in the mountains so we could move closer to the medical services John needed.

Only weeks after we'd moved, I answered our ringing phone to hear my Uncle Bud once again asking, "Where the heck are you?" But this time, he added, "I walked in the front door of your log cabin and found strangers living there!"

I must admit it took a long time for my little family to stop laughing. However, my dear uncle never pulled that prank on us again.

~Laura L. Bradford

34

Double Jeopardy

I feel like a juggler running out of hands.
~Elvis Costello

It was the ninetieth birthday of one of my uncles, so I drove from Colorado to the plains of western Kansas to see him. I had not seen Uncle Harry or his younger brother, Uncle Carl, for years. Both of them lived in the same town of around 25,000 people. It was Harry who was turning ninety.

Within most families I've known, there is a rift of some kind, usually having to do with dispensation of money and property. The same is true in my family. I will skip the unfortunate details, but suffice it to say that my Uncles Harry and Carl have not spoken in twenty years, even though they lived in the same small town.

The family has long since chosen sides, but my mother and I had somehow managed to stay above the fray, remaining on good terms with both of her brothers. Therefore I would visit eighty-seven-year-old Uncle Carl while I was there for Harry's party.

As fate would have it, both uncles wanted to see me the day following Uncle Harry's birthday. It took some juggling, but I arranged to see Uncle Harry during the afternoon and promised Uncle Carl I would visit him at 6:00 p.m. for dinner.

Uncle Harry insisted on giving me a tour of his metropolis. Yes, he still drives. "I eat early. I want to take you to dinner," he told me around 4:00 p.m. Not taking "no" for an answer, we pulled into the parking lot of a place called Montana Mike's, which boasts the best steaks in town.

I hoped to get by with a salad, knowing I had a dinner date with Uncle Carl in a couple of hours. I even thought about claiming to be a vegetarian, but I knew Uncle Harry would have none of it. He ordered me a steak with all the trimmings. "Can't leave my town without a side of beef sticking to your ribs," he declared, already having forgotten about most of the previous day's activities and the mound of cake we had both eaten.

After dinner, I rebuffed his desire to have me stay longer and made my way to Uncle Carl's place. Following my arrival, Uncle Number Two informed me that I needed to see how the town had grown. In his car, off we went on almost the identical tour I'd taken only hours before.

Then it was time to eat… again. Uncle Carl said he was taking me to the best restaurant in town.

You know what's coming. The beef in my stomach seemed to do a flip-flop when we pulled into a parking spot in front of Montana Mike's. Would we get the same booth, the same waitress? If I was a woman, I could have at least pinned back my hair or removed a sweater, anything to slightly change my appearance.

We were seated one booth away from where I had sat little more than an hour earlier. I spotted the same friendly waitress headed our way. Not having a pair of sunglasses to whip on, I took a handkerchief from my hip pocket and tried to play like I had a runny nose, but probably looked more like a bandit about to execute a hold-up. She eyed me suspiciously. At one point, while Uncle Harry had his head buried in the menu, I put my finger to my lips, employing the international sign to keep quiet.

"Don't I know you?" the confused waitress asked.

"Well… they say everyone has a twin."

With confusion etched on the waitress's face, I tried once again to order a salad and a glass of water, but good ol' Uncle Carl, like his estranged brother, wouldn't have it — not at the best steakhouse in town, not for his favorite nephew. "Can't send you back to Colorado without some good Kansas beef down your gullet."

We parted with promises to see each other again, and I headed back to my hotel room, hoping my tummy wouldn't burst. I knew the trip (and the two meals) had been worth it by the happy expressions on my uncles' faces. Now, if only they could reconcile so we could all eat together. I don't think I can handle two Montana Mike's Steakhouse dinners in two hours again.

~Troy Seate

35

Chicken Soup for the Soul

Mistaken Identity

*The embarrassment of a situation can, once you are
over it, be the funniest time in your life.*
~Miranda Hart

My folks had come to visit a few days before we all left on our family vacation. We were headed to the Bruce Peninsula in Canada. We had moved my parents into our bedroom, and my husband Joe and I were on a blow-up mattress in the living room. All was well — or at least I thought it was — when I went down to the basement to get something. When I came back up, things had definitely changed.

I entered the living room and found Joe already in bed. When he heard me come into the room, he said he had something to tell me. Apparently, he had not been aware that I had headed to the basement a few minutes earlier, and he had walked over to the person at the kitchen sink, thinking it was me. When my blind husband reached the sink, he placed his hand on what he thought was my bottom. Unfortunately for Joe, it was not my butt; it was my mother's! She was standing there taking her evening pills. When Joe touched her behind, she swallowed and said, "I'm taking my pills." She then turned to leave, giggling all the way to the bedroom.

My husband was devastated. He had just goosed his mother-in-law. Joe went immediately to the living room and crawled into bed.

Meanwhile, my mom had stopped laughing long enough to tell

my dad what had just happened in the kitchen. My father came out of the bedroom and walked into the living room. He looked down at Joe and said, "Thanks for warming her up for me." With that, he left the room.

Shortly after that, I came to bed, and that is when Joe told me what had just happened. I could not stop laughing. I headed to the bathroom. When I passed my folks' room, I knew they were still up by the sound of laughter coming from their room. I opened the door, and the three of us laughed together. And while we laughed, my husband lay in the living room, mortified.

The next day, the story spread like wildfire. The usual response was uncontrollable laughter. However, a few of Joe's friends actually asked him why he did it. They wanted to know what would compel Joe to do such a thing. Hearing Joe have to convince some of his friends that it was a mistake, and he didn't know it was my mom, only made us laugh more. Just goes to show that when people get to know Joe, they sometimes forget that he cannot see and hold him to sighted standards. I believe that this is the way it should be.

As a result of Mom and Joe's encounter at the sink, my mother has taken to calling out her location to Joe whenever he enters the room. Hearing my mom announce her coordinates always makes me smile. Poor Joe…

~Laura Dailey-Pelle

36

A Basket Full of Trouble

*Be nice to your siblings, they're your best link to your
past and the most likely to stay with you in the future.*
~Baz Luhrmann

My husband, John, and I needed to sort through the
estate of Louisa, my late sister-in-law, but we found
the task overwhelming. The house was packed to
the limit with everything imaginable. It had originally belonged to my mother-in-law, and the place contained all her
possessions as well as Louisa's things. We had no idea how to deal
with the years of accumulation, and so we decided to put the house
and its contents up for auction.

On the day of the auction, we watched the proceedings with
great curiosity, eager to see what price each item would bring. The
crowd was slim due to bad weather, but we hoped there were enough
interested buyers to have good sales.

A few low bids made us question our decision. We exchanged
worried glances when a grandfather clock sold for only twenty-five
dollars. A pair of expensive French lamps went for a mere dollar.

Our spirits soon rallied, though, after a few other items received
much higher than expected bids. John and I looked at each other in
surprise when a cup of plastic drink stirrers (which we had thought
worthless) sold for twenty dollars. A bag of discarded, old photos also

We're All Nuts Here | 129

brought a good price.

With its high and low bids, the auction was beginning to seem more like an entertaining sport. Feeling like spectators, we sat back in our chairs to enjoy the show.

I relaxed until an unexpected item appeared. I sat up on the edge of my chair, staring in disbelief as an old basket with a flat, wooden bottom and woven sides came up for bid. Its distinctive wooden handle had layers of cloth strips wrapped around it to make carrying easier.

Even though I had never seen this piece before in my life, I recognized it immediately from family descriptions. This had to be the infamous basket that had plagued our family for years.

I first heard of the troublesome thing right after John and I became engaged. We planned to meet his relatives so I could get to know them, but we were cautioned about visiting. Certain family members didn't associate with others as a result of an argument. Apparently, when my mother-in-law inherited her mother's shopping basket, her siblings squabbled over it. The brothers and sisters exchanged sharp words, and feelings became deeply hurt. As a result, they hadn't talked to each other since that time.

During our visit, the relatives brought up the basket story. We sensed that they regretted the silly argument, yet they had remained alienated from one another. Why? Had stubbornness or foolish pride prevented them from being reconciled?

I wondered how an old unattractive basket could cause so much strife in a family. Years later, I learned that John's grandmother had used it to carry groceries back from the local market. Her children would have been familiar with the sight of their mother arriving home with that basket full of food. I suspect that the comforting image provided a memory that each one cherished. Maybe this physical token represented a piece of their mother that they desperately wanted to keep.

I glanced at the controversial piece going up for bid and debated about what to do. Should we bid on this heirloom to keep it in the family, or should we allow strangers to buy it? We valued family history, but we finally decided to let the basket go. Despite the fact that the original contenders were no longer alive, we couldn't chance another generation extending this ridiculous conflict. Certainly, our family would be better off without that continual source of irritation.

As the bidding started, I began to wonder why we hadn't encountered this basket during our search through the house. Neither of us had seen his mother use it during her lifetime. Where had it been stowed all this time?

The auctioneer later informed us that he had found it up in the rafters above the garage. It must have remained there, unused and forgotten, for decades. Why had John's mother hidden it in a place where no one was likely to find it?

I didn't understand why until I thought about my mother-in-law's choices. She had no way to get rid of this inherited piece without causing more trouble. If she gave it to one sibling, the others would be angry. If she sold it, the family would be furious at her, and she would lose a possible source of comfort during her grief. Perhaps she did the best thing. She placed the basket out of sight of visitors, hoping time would heal the festering wound in the family.

Unfortunately, relationships between the siblings never seemed to improve. How sad that John's aunts and uncles had somehow lost each other in their desperate attempt to hang onto the mother they loved. Maybe that explains why John's own mother insisted her children keep a promise: They must not fight over possessions after she was gone.

I looked up as the auctioneer announced, "Sold for one dollar!" I shook my head. Our family had been torn apart for fifty years over a basket worth only one dollar!

When we realized that the basket was now in someone else's possession, we sighed with relief. Hopefully, the rift in our family could finally mend.

The young lady who got the winning bid sauntered past us with a big Cheshire cat grin on her face, probably thinking she'd snatched up the greatest bargain of the day. Little did she know all the misery she was carrying away in that old basket!

~JoAnne Check

37

Flying Fish

We should all have one person who knows how to bless
us despite the evidence. Grandmother was
that person to me.
~Phyllis Theroux

When I grew up in rural Kansas, we took Christmas dinner seriously. My grandmother began losing her mind in earnest about a week before the holiday. She would drag out the good dishes that had been purchased weekly at the local grocery store over what seemed to be years. I can remember when she would come home with a new component for the set and make my grandfather place it in the china hutch after she moved every single piece at least twice to find just the right spot for it. I will never forget the time he dropped the new sugar bowl and broke it into two pieces right before her eyes. We won't even discuss what words came from my five-foot-tall grandmother.

She cooked for days — homemade mincemeat pie, fudge and divinity, and the most mouthwatering cloverleaf yeast rolls. There was rarely anything my family could agree on, but everyone loved the taste of those rolls. If there were just one left in the basket, several people would be eyeing it. More than once, my cousin Brian got a fork in the hand for being too slow to grab the roll.

During the most memorable holiday season of my childhood, we had fried fish as well as ham for Christmas dinner. My grandfather would fish for crappie and filet them with no bones. We had freezers full of it, and I grew up spoiled by the harvest from our gardens and from hunting and fishing. We ate what my grandpa provided and were the better for it. Those crappie were special to us. Gran would dip them in a beer/pancake batter and fry them in an old, iron pot with a basket. It was and still is the most delicious fish I have ever eaten.

We ate well that year, until no one could move or eat one more morsel — and then the fight started. I cannot tell you what it was about, but the grand finale of it found my grandmother wearing a piece of fried crappie on her forehead. There was a moment of shocked silence as the fish began a slow descent down her nose and finally to her lap.

The family held a collective breath, not sure what would happen. My grandparents were the stern, silent type. In fact, I was positive there was no humor in them that I could see. My cousins, my father and I very carefully pushed back from the table. It was one of those moments that lasted a hundred years, and we were all at her mercy.

Gran raised a hand, wiped a smear of homemade tartar sauce from her forehead and looked at it. I could feel the laughter bubbling up inside me, and I fought to control it. My cousin Michelle pinched me on the leg, hoping to stop me from committing the ultimate act of childhood idiocy. I thought for a moment that my young life would be over when I heard my father making a noise like a cat coughing up a hairball. We all turned to see him, red-faced and struggling to maintain his composure, but it was clear he would be the first to snap.

All eyes went back to my grandmother, smeared with tartar sauce and stone-faced. My father continued to fight the laughter, and looks bounced between the eighteen adults and six kids around the table, like a tennis match.

Finally, Gran drew in a breath. We all held ours. She lifted the fish from her lap, where it had ended its slide, looked at it and then looked at my father. Then she said, "Oh, to hell with it," and lobbed the fish across the table at him, where it landed on his shirt with a plop. The moment hung there in stunned silence, and then the food began to fly.

I think it took us most of the afternoon to clean up the mess that followed, but it was, in my memory, the best Christmas ever.

After she passed, with most of us kids being adults and starting families of our own, we talked about it and decided to have one more holiday meal together. We gathered at my grandfather's and did all the old traditions. We got out the china and the table, and my aunty tried her hand at the cloverleaf rolls. As we sat together one last time as a family, my cousin Brian gave the blessing, and in a quiet voice he thanked the Creator for flying fish.

~Cj Cole

The Gift that Keeps on Giving

*Even though you're growing up, you should
never stop having fun.*
~Nina Dobrev

For about thirty years, our family has had a love/hate relationship with a culinary wonder known as Potted Meat Product. One can find it in the Spam and Vienna sausage section of the supermarket. The ingredients appear to be meat by-products and various animal parts.

In my family, Potted Meat Product, known as PMP, became the proverbial fruitcake — the gift that keeps on being re-gifted. In the early years of our PMP days, this little can would be disguised under the Christmas tree, wrapped exquisitely as though it was an item of great desire, a package that made us wonder what treasure lay within. It has been festooned with ribbons and hung on the tree as an ornament until it was noticed. It was also found in Easter baskets, under chocolate bunnies and Cadbury eggs. Birthdays were not complete without a PMP sighting, disguised in socks or underwear.

The (un)lucky recipient of the can of PMP was then charged with passing it on to the next unsuspecting family member. We were always aware that the PMP would rear its ugly head at some point in the festivities. The burning questions were: Who would get stuck with the PMP? Which package would it be hidden in?

PMP could be wrapped in a series of smaller boxes inside a big box. It could be hidden inside a Crock-Pot or a new backpack. But as the teenage years came around, the stakes got higher. My older son, Jeff, and I were determined to outdo each other in the PMP Pass-Off.

Being a rookie at creativity and technology, I settled for inserting a can of Potted Meat Product in the center of Jeff's birthday cake. Angel food cake is especially good for this purpose.

Jeff, much more technically advanced than I was, strung up a very elaborate pulley system in my bathroom. When I opened the door, the pulley system lowered the PMP down over the toilet. We had mirrored walls in the bathroom. As I walked in, it appeared that there was PMP everywhere being lowered on pulleys, a frightening scene indeed. I screamed.

But I was not to be outdone.

I gave the PMP to a friend of Jeff's. Their class was flying to Washington, D.C. for a field trip, and she agreed to have the flight attendant serve it to Jeff as his lunch aboard the plane. Unfortunately, she forgot. She did, however, ask her dad to take the PMP with him on a business trip, and he mailed it back to Jeff from Chicago. Nice touch!

Another of my brilliant plans deserves mention. One of the secretaries from the guidance office at Jeff's school was in my bowling league. I enlisted her help and passed off the PMP to her during bowling one night. The next day, Jeff was called out of chemistry class to report to the office, causing some concern on his part and a bit of teasing from the class.

He hurried to the office at the other end of campus and was handed the PMP. He was pretty annoyed to have to walk all the way back to class and face the curiosity of the other students. Unfortunately, it was a short-lived victory. By the time I left work and got to my car, Jeff had walked from his school to my car and rigged up the PMP to my steering wheel. There it sat taunting and waiting for me.

One day, the three of us went for ice cream. As I got out of the car, I noticed some trash on the ground. Unbelievably, there was an open can of PMP among it. It had a plastic spoon in it, and a bite of the PMP was missing from the can. To this day, my boys think I arranged for it to be there, that perhaps I staged that PMP for them to see.

Over the years, our PMP days have slowed down a bit. Every once in a while, it makes a rare appearance. Not too long ago, my husband and I slipped it in an overnight bag to put it in my son's car as he and his wife left to go home after a visit with us. Unfortunately, they became suspicious and discovered the PMP before they drove out of the driveway. He put the car in reverse, stuffed the PMP in our mailbox, and roared off.

In all these years, we never opened up the can of PMP. I think we were afraid to after all the years of passing it back and forth.

The can of Potted Meat Product is currently residing in my kitchen cabinet. I am waiting for that perfect opportunity to pass it off to an unsuspecting family member. The glory of the deed is short-lived. Once it leaves my hand, I know the PMP will be back to darken my doorstep before long.

~Jeanne Kraus

39

Queen of the Porcelain Throne

Some are born mad, some achieve madness, and some have madness thrust upon 'em.
~Emilie Autumn

I'd finally done it. I'd confessed all to my father. Unfortunately, he suggested that I spill the beans to my mom. "I'll tell her if you don't want to," he said, "but I think it's only fair that she knows what's going on with you."

I took a deep breath and shuddered. Mom was such a goody-two-shoes that she'd never handle this kind of news with ease. "Where is she?" I asked.

"On the toilet," Dad said. "Go on in."

"Great," I grumbled. Unfortunately, Mom's bathroom habits had an unusual twist: she always left the door open and allowed family to visit her while she relieved herself.

And while growing up, almost every serious talk I'd ever had with Mom had taken place while she nestled on her white, porcelain throne, royal scepter (book) in hand. Even during my grand moment of starting my first period, my mother had sat like a queen, gathering me a sanitary belt from the medicine cabinet with one hand and a pad from the box on the floor, while keeping her cheeks planted firmly on her seat.

My parents' tiny half-bathroom had its own sliding door, with the commode almost perfectly centered in the doorway, facing out so that Mom could sit comfortably and hold court. And hold court she did. Our family could come and go and it never bothered her in the least. I've always loved my mom, but is that normal?

As a young mother, I thought that maybe she'd kept the door open so that she could keep an eye and ear out for us kids. Actually, I'd done that when my children were little, until two neighborhood girls walked into our house without knocking and entered the bathroom while I was in there. That ended that experiment.

Although Mom kept herself covered, I couldn't understand how a woman who never let us watch R-rated movies, even in our teens, and who insisted my sister and I dress modestly (no miniskirts), felt comfortable with her potty habits, especially as the years progressed.

My stomach felt queasy as I entered my parents' bedroom and even though I'd seen this sight a million times, I couldn't believe my eyes. The queen of the porcelain throne didn't glance my way, but continued reading her book. The absurdity of it all me made me feel as if I'd jumped headfirst into a Monty Python movie, and I suddenly relaxed as my fears washed away. This was insanity at its finest. Who makes announcements such as mine while her mother is using a toilet?

My husband and I had been separated for a year at that time. While he still used our home as a base of operation, he worked out of state where he had a steady girlfriend, and he was rarely back.

My father already knew the details of my new relationship, but learned of the pregnancy while I was visiting them. While my mother knew that my husband and I had basically separated, she knew nothing about the new man in my life. And now, the unthinkable had accidentally happened.

"Mom," I said quietly. "I've got something to tell you." I'll admit I almost started giggling.

"What is it honey?" she asked, eyes fixed on her book.

"I'm pregnant and it's NOT my husband's baby."

"Oh that's wonderful news!" she said. "I'm so happy. I'll have to start on a baby blanket."

I can still picture my mom's reaction that day. With the coolness of a cucumber, my mother had concentrated on the baby part of my announcement and let the rest slide, and I remembered that while we argued a lot, most of our past toilet talks had ended peacefully. Perhaps there was magic in her throne.

~Vera Frances

40

The Zezimas' Christmas Letter

*There is nothing in the world so irresistibly contagious
as laughter and good humor.*
~Charles Dickens

Since I am in the holiday spirit (and, having just consumed a mug of hot toddy, a glass of eggnog and a nip of cheer, the holiday spirits are in me), I have decided to follow in that great tradition of boring everyone silly by writing a Christmas letter.

That is why I am pleased as punch (which I also drank) to present the following chronicle of the Zezima family, which includes Jerry, the patriarch; Sue, the matriarch; Katie and Lauren, the daughtersiarch; Dave and Guillaume, the sons-in-lawiarch; and Chloe, Lilly and Xavier, the grandchildreniarch.

Dear friends:

It sure has been an exciting year for the Zezimas!

Things got off to a rocky start when Jerry had a kidney stone. He is sorry to have to number them like the Super Bowl, but it was Kidney Stone VI. Mercifully, this, too, did pass.

Also on the medical front, Jerry took a CPR class in which the instructor used him as a dummy. The other class members couldn't tell the difference.

To keep in good physical condition, Jerry won a one-day gym membership. He didn't exercise very strenuously, proving to be the biggest dumbbell there, but afterward he went to an adjacent bar and did 12-ounce curls.

Continuing to show his commitment to a healthy lifestyle, Jerry attended a Wine Stomp Party at a vineyard and, re-creating a famous I Love Lucy episode, climbed into a vat of grapes and stomped them with his bare feet. To ensure the health of the vineyard's customers, the grapes were thrown away.

Jerry may not have made his own wine, but he and Chloe did make their own ice cream. They went to a shop where the owner, impressed by Chloe's natural ability to pour in the ingredients but not by Jerry's pathetic incompetence at measuring them, allowed the dynamic duo to make a batch of honey-cinnamon. It was delicious, prompting the owner to tell Chloe, "Now you can say you taught your grandfather how to make ice cream."

Jerry, Sue and Lauren took Chloe and Lilly on their first visit to the zoo, where humans were the wildest creatures, and Jerry, an acknowledged oldster, was carded by a flirtatious young woman while buying beer for the adults in the group. He roared louder than the lions.

One of the proudest moments of the year occurred when Chloe graduated, magna cum little, from preschool. She had a prominent role in the ceremony, which was attended by Jerry, Sue, Lauren, Guillaume and Lilly, and was tops in her class. Afterward, everyone had milk and cookies. Yale or Harvard couldn't have done better.

A milestone was reached when Lilly celebrated her first birthday. Big sister Chloe, who's 4, helped her blow out the candle on her cupcake and, as their little friends applauded, helped her eat the cupcake, too. Talk about sisterly love!

And there was an addition to the family: Xavier, Katie and Dave's beautiful boy, made his grand entrance into the world. Sue and Jerry, aka Nini and Poppie, went on a road trip to meet him, and Jerry quickly learned that changing diapers on a boy is a lot different from changing them on a girl. That's because boys have an apparatus that is not unlike a water cannon or, considering the oscillation, an in-ground sprinkler system. It was a geyser on a geezer.

But Jerry didn't mind because he got to do some male bonding. On a subsequent visit, Jerry introduced Xavier to the Three Stooges, making him giggle uncontrollably by doing Shemp imitations. The women, naturally, were thrilled.

Xavier met cousins Chloe and Lilly on a visit to Nini and Poppie's house. The three adorable children had a ball, laughing, playing and, not surprisingly, proving to be more mature than Poppie.

We hope your year has been fun-filled, too.

Merry Christmas with love and laughter from the Zezimas.

~Jerry Zezima

Chapter 5

My Crazy Family

Childhood Hijinks

41

A Few More Gray Hairs

Childhood and genius have the same master-organ in
common — inquisitiveness.
~Edward Bulwer-Lytton

ummers were always anticipated with great glee in my family. I started getting excited about those summertime prospects as early as the New Year, wondering what exciting things Dad had in store for us. We lived in Brussels, Belgium, for nearly seven years, and most summers we would be winging back over the Atlantic Ocean for a landing in Boston and the six or eight weeks back home in Newport, Rhode Island.

That was the usual pattern anyway, but once in a while Dad had other things in mind. This was our seventh and last year in Belgium, and instead of flying back to the States for the summer, Dad thought it would be a good idea to do some sort of a mini-tour of the countryside. We actually hadn't seen all that much of Belgium, and the thought of doing some exploring sounded pretty good to me. By the end of the fourth day, however, I was having second thoughts.

Mom and Dad's idea of exploring the countryside was for them to load us into the family car and go to museums and art galleries, have lunch and dinner in different restaurants, or perhaps spend a few hours going from one antique store to another. My idea of exploring, on the other hand, was always "down and dirty." If I couldn't find an appropriate cave to crawl into, or if there wasn't something tall enough for me to jump off of, or if there weren't some neat looking airplanes to see, I was bored out of my mind.

I had enough manners to not let that boredom show through and become a complete pain in the butt, but I think my quiet demeanor while feeling sorry for myself must have drawn some attention. By that fourth afternoon, Dad said, "How would you like to spend the day at the beach tomorrow?" Now that got my attention, and I thought things could finally get interesting during this holiday.

The next morning, we were awakened by our parents bright and early and had a terrific breakfast in the little hotel's restaurant on the first floor. Dad had the car loaded and had ordered a packed lunch from the hotel restaurant the night before. That, along with a supply of drinks, was tucked away in a wicker basket for the morning's drive to the beach. I had my bathing suit on while eating breakfast, for I felt there was no time to waste. An hour later, we crested a hill above the small town of Oostende on the coast of the North Sea.

Oostende was more or less centered an equal distance between the Netherlands to the north and France to the south, and sat about forty miles or so across from the coast of England. That morning's weather was warm and glorious, with a bright blue sky and thousands of seagulls dancing in the air above our heads. Dad parked the car right on the sand off the tiny one-lane roadway and, towel in hand, I sprinted to the edge of the surf with my mother's shouts to be careful quickly fading in the distance. The beach was completely deserted. Save for an old black dog that walked quickly up the beach with his nose intently following some unknown scent, we were alone. The town itself in those years was nothing much more than a picture-postcard-sized collection of stone cottages and the barest minimum of shops and a café.

It was low tide, and without so much as a rational thought in my head, I plunged headlong into the slight surf. Only then did I realize just how cold the water was. This was in late June, but the North Sea waters off the coast of Belgium felt icy even in the grip of summer. It wasn't too long before I was out of the water and slowly walking to where my parents sat with Mike and Mimi, my older siblings, who were eating all our lunch.

I looked down at the two of them in complete disgust. They looked back at me while I was wet and happily shivering, with nothing short of blank stares on their faces. How do two perfectly healthy children, ages ten and twelve, not want to run into the surf? Their complete lack of engagement in any sort of physical activity always mystified me. I would much rather be doing some sort of exploring, no matter where we were. On the other hand, they would rather sit around reading or doing something equally mind-numbing. It's amazing how far off base I was when I was young, as now I can't stop reading!

Anyway, I thought I might as well eat something before Mike and Mimi finished off all the food. As I sat there munching on the only sandwich left in the basket, I noticed the glorious warm sun was fading quickly and the clouds were heading in. The wind was also picking up. Before too long, the sand on the beach began its stinging bite into the flesh on my legs as I started to run in search of something to do. Dad yelled after me to come back for a minute, and I was soon being admonished into not straying too far. "We may have to leave if the wind doesn't die down," he said.

Mike and Mimi sat huddled on the blanket with their perfectly dry towels wrapped tightly around their shoulders. Off I ran again, and I noticed that most of the seagulls were no longer in flight but rather gathered in bunches on the beach, their beaks pointed into the quickly approaching maelstrom. I ran on for another couple of hundred yards or so until my parents and siblings were completely out of sight.

The wind was howling now, and it was such a great feeling to have it pushing me as I effortlessly sprinted down the hard, sandy beach. At one point, the wind actually lifted me up just ever-so-slightly off the sand, and I found myself taking a couple of long strides through mid-air. What a feeling this was! I knew I would soon have to turn around for the run back against that wind, but at that moment it was absolutely fantastic.

I began a long turn to my right and toward the foot of the sand dunes before the run back to my parents, and that's when I saw the strangest shapes poking just slightly out of the sand. There were several of them, perhaps thirteen or fourteen in all, and it looked as if the howling wind had uncovered them from the loose, dry sand near the dunes. Walking up to the first one, I noticed its round, black metal covering was rusted, but the German words were still plainly visible. I picked up the thing and thought it must weigh at least thirty pounds or more, as I found it was quite difficult to lift. I carried it over to where the other objects were and noticed they were all more or less the same. They all had the same German words printed on the tops. Oh well, at least I had one souvenir I could take back with me. If my two siblings wanted one of their own, they could just bloody well walk down here and get them.

Within another five minutes or so, I had trudged back through the howling wind to find Mom and Dad futilely trying to fold the blanket against the raging storm. Mike and Mimi were standing nearby still wrapped in their towels. Dad gave up on the blanket and quickly rolled it into a ball before walking toward the car with the picnic basket in his other hand.

"What did you find, Johnny?" My mother was trying to sound interested in the object I held in front of me.

Dad turned to look, and it was as if he had just witnessed some ghastly ghost of a creature from a horrible nightmare. I don't think I've ever seen that actual look on his face before or since. He seemed to turn several shades of pale white as he dropped the basket and blanket and said, "Son, don't move. Just stay very still."

He was walking slowly toward me with that awful look on his face, and his arms stretched out toward me. I started to back up.

"Henry, what's going on?" It was my mother again.

"Honey, take the kids and run into the town."

"I will do nothing of the kind," Mom answered. "Just what is going on?"

"It's a damn landmine. Now get the kids into the town and call the police. Do it now!"

It was one of the very few times in my life when I ever heard Dad raise his voice, and the first time I ever heard it rise with my mother.

Mom took Mimi by the arm and started running like mad. Mike turned so quickly on his heels that he fell flat on his face before righting himself and sprinting after them, screaming as he ran.

"Son, stop backing up. You're not in any trouble, but I've got to take that from you."

"This one's mine, Dad. There are lots of others you can have."

"Okay, but just let me see that one first."

With that, he slowly took the object from me and let out a sigh before very gently placing it back on the sand.

"We'll just leave it here for a little while, okay?" Dad took me by the hand and slowly walked me back to the car.

The police arrived a few minutes later and asked my father if I would be allowed to show them where the other landmines were located. Several hours later, the Belgian Army arrived on the scene, and the small village of Oostende had to be evacuated. It turned out that the landmines were the anti-tank variety of mines placed there during Germany's occupation, but never found until then. Ever fearful of an Allied invasion coming from the sea, Germany had millions of these things sown from one end of the continent's shoreline to the other.

Around 10:00 p.m., well after we had left the immediate area, and while Dad was talking to one of the police officers at a checkpoint more than two miles from the beach, we heard a huge explosion as the army personnel blew up all the mines that had been left buried and unnoticed for all those years. Dad put his arm around my shoulder and said I had probably saved some lives that day. The incident made the newspapers in Belgium and France, and I thought it was one of the best summer holidays ever.

The drive back to Brussels that night was interrupted by my mother turning to Dad and saying, "Henry, if you ever talk to me like that again, there'll be trouble!"

Dad just couldn't win at times, and I think I gave him many gray hairs over the years. And when I look back at all of the events that seemed to shape my life, especially those great interactions with my father, I sometimes have to scratch my head in disbelief. How was I to know then, as a child of eight, that eleven years later would be the start of a lifelong obsession with bomb disposal and the removal of landmines, as well as a forty-four-year working relationship with police officers from all over the world?

As an aside, many years later, my daughter, Mia, and I were jogging along the two miles of sand at Second Beach in Middletown, Rhode Island, one early morning, when we came across a giant squid that had apparently washed ashore at high tide the night before. The creature was enormous, and we had great fun digging around the animal and measuring one of its tentacles. Just that one was over eighteen feet! It's absolutely amazing what you can find on the beach!

~John Elliott

42

The Day My Kids Broke Out of Jail

*When my kids become wild and unruly, I use a nice
safe playpen. When they're finished, I climb out.*
~Erma Bombeck

Our living room looked like a daycare center in the early days, with swings, bouncy chairs, burp cloths, blankets, and discarded clothing covering nearly every surface. On my short break between feedings, I usually went to the basement to get a Diet Pepsi because caffeine intake was critical to my survival. One day, when I returned, two of my babies were lying on the blanket, toys surrounding them, but the other was missing.

Surely, he couldn't have gone far; rolling was a new skill. I scanned the baby debris for wispy brown hair. I checked under the swing, behind the couch, in the neighboring kitchen, still no baby. I started to look more urgently after the search wasn't as easy as I expected. I even called his name. Standing in front of my remaining babies, I stopped, put my hands on my hips and said, "Where is Max?" Rebecca and Logan just blinked their big eyes at me, like they were in on it, too.

Finally, I heard muffled crying and scanned the room again. He had to be stuck somewhere. Tentatively, I stepped into my bedroom, and the crying became louder. Rushing around the bed, I scanned the floor and still didn't find him. Then I heard a quiet thumping and the sound of someone grunting and struggling. I crouched down to find him wedged underneath the bed. When he spotted me, he struggled and squawked more, his blue eyes wide open.

Prior to that moment, I had no idea that any of the triplets were truly that mobile. Sure, they had rolled over a few times, but rolling a significant distance while I was gone for a few seconds was shocking.

When Rebecca, Logan, and Max were born, I had already been a mom for nearly a decade. Three singletons did nothing to prepare me for the triplet tornado I had given birth to months before. On that day, we made the decision to build "the jail" and to keep them in jail for as long as possible.

I pouted the day our beautiful dining-room furniture and good dishes were moved to the dark basement — where they would end up staying for years. In their place appeared bright colored toys that looked like a layout in a Step 2 catalog. "Formal dining rooms are pointless anyway," I announced to anyone who would listen.

Secretly, I sulked about the fact that everyone who entered our home would be greeted with what looked more like a daycare blocked off by big, tall gates with complicated latches (which often required lessons on how to open them for visiting adults) than an elegant dining space. This would be the state of the entry to our home for years.

In time, I learned to love the baby jail we created. It was nice to have a place to contain all the toys and keep the babies out of trouble. There were even days when I could sneak in a quick shower while they were safely entertained in their prison. I considered it an added bonus that they loved their play space.

As the babies grew into toddlers, we would sometimes let them out of their jail to play in the rest of our home. Some days, they would play for hours roaming free. They chased each other and pushed shopping carts round and round with my three older kids running after them, laughing. They sat and played happily with Matchbox cars or they got all the plasticware out of the cabinets and spread it around the entire house. Those days were fun.

There were other days when they destroyed the house in the first ten minutes they were let free, and I dragged them right back into jail, wondering all the while why I thought letting them out was a good idea.

Like all prisoners, their desire to break out of their cell increased monumentally, and they started to find any opportunity to escape. Typically, the gate would get loose or someone would accidentally leave it open, allowing a quick escape. I had to become diligent about making sure they were safely contained whenever I left the room.

One day, I had to tend to a fairly urgent matter on my computer in our home office. Like my dining room furniture, it had been relegated to the basement as our family grew. I sat down at the computer knowing I had left the triplets upstairs in their jail quietly eating a snack. I became consumed with my task, and a few minutes later I was startled to hear what I thought sounded like footsteps above me. Footsteps that sounded like freedom!

I rushed up the stairs. "Babies!" I called accusingly.

When I reached the top of the stairs, I found them standing frozen like statues, guilty expressions on their faces.

"Did you get out of your room?" I asked them. Calling it a jail to their faces seemed cruel.

Giggles escaped from each sneaky face.

Abandoning my half-finished task downstairs, I said, "I suppose you can play out here with me for a while."

It was like I had given them permission to go wild, and they started to run and chase each other, wispy hair flying behind them. As they ran past, I sniffed the air and detected the need to change one of the guilty party's diapers.

Having now experienced many days of well-behaved children running free from their jail on their best, most obedient behavior, I let down my guard. I took my time changing that diaper, talking to my son and tickling him. We were enjoying a rare moment of one-on-one time. Silly me.

As we walked hand in hand out of their bedroom, I spied my other two and panicked. All hopes of a quiet naptime quickly disappeared as I watched Rebecca pass my forgotten mug of cold coffee into the hands of Logan. He guzzled it hungrily like I never offer liquids to my children. Coffee dripped from both their chins and stained their clothes as they eagerly passed the mug and smiled excitedly at each other. Damn my caffeine addiction!

I crept up slowly, knowing what would happen if I startled them.

"Loooogaaan," I said as sweetly as possible, hoping my voice simply sounded like someone who wanted her turn at a little sip. "Can I have the cup?"

"No!" he yelled and took off running, coffee splashing all over my already stained carpet.

"Logan! Give me the coffee!" I was desperate and stupid to think I would win. It was too late. In a panic, he tossed the cup in the air, and I watched in horror as it landed on my couch. The coffee rolled into the cracks and soaked into the cushions. My shoulders drooped.

I cleaned up the couch and the carpet as they played around me. Logan disappeared into the kitchen and got a cup of water off the counter. I could hear the gulping from my crouched position on the floor as I scrubbed.

"Why in the world are you so thirsty?" I asked. No one answered.

Heaving my body up off the floor, I tried my friendly little creep-up act again, which ended the same way. He threw the cup of water, and this time it splattered all over my clothes. After wiping up the second spill, which was mercifully easier to clean, I went to my bedroom to change my wet clothes.

I returned to an empty room. I contemplated crawling into bed and letting them have free range of the entire house, but on further introspection I decided to search out the distant noises I could hear coming from behind the closed door of their bedroom.

"Out!" I screamed as I threw open the door to find they had emptied the entire dresser and had started working on the closet. They all laughed as they ran past me. "Mama!" Max growled like he was taunting me as he passed.

I shoved unfolded clothes back into drawers as I mentally reprimanded myself for not learning my lesson. *They can't be left alone! That's when I froze. *What are they doing now?*

I ran to the kitchen as I heard a crash. The trashcan had been tipped over, and they were into everything. Logan had a beer bottle to his lips and was tipping back like a lush. *Why the hell is he so thirsty?* I mused. Rebecca held an empty yogurt container and was licking yogurt from one finger. Pink goo was in her hair and on the tip of her nose. Max had pulled open drawers and thrown dishtowels and utensils across the floor. He was on tiptoes trying to reach into the knife drawer.

Like an angry superhuman, I flew into action. I did not creep up on Logan this time but instead grabbed that beer bottle out of his hand before he could see me coming—a much more effective method. I slammed the knife drawer shut, scooped both boys under my arms and deposited them right back in their jail cell. They wailed as I secured the gates and went to get my girl. She looked at me and flashed her cutest smile as yogurt dripped from the container and onto the floor. As I whisked her back to jail, the yogurt cup fell to the ground and splattered tiny globules of gunk to the far reaches of the room.

That afternoon, no one napped. Instead, they happily talked and played in their beds, high on caffeine and the thrill of the chase. They remained in their cribs while I cleaned the house. In addition to dealing with the tornado of a mess they had created in less than an hour, I secured the baby gates and opened a beer for myself at 2:00 p.m. on a Tuesday. Like Logan, I just happened to be quite thirsty that afternoon.

When my husband got home, he asked, "How was your day?"

"Oh, it was fine. The babies broke out of jail today."

"Don't you think it's time we take down that gate?" he asked.

"I don't think we are quite ready. Today got a little wild."

He shrugged as he sat down on the couch. "Do you smell coffee?"

~Sarah Lyons

43

Out of the Mouths
of Babes

Children are a great comfort in your old age —
and they help you reach it faster, too.
~Lionel Kauffman

ur family didn't live like most other young families because we didn't hold down normal jobs. As members of the American Guild of Variety Artists (AGVA), we earned our income by doing live western shows. My husband Monty was a gun and bullwhip expert, doing fast draw, gun spinning, and a bullwhip act. He also had a team of men who put on stunt shows. We played all types of venues, from private parties to state fairs, and all types of local community festivals up and down the coast of California. I wore a spangled little outfit, black mesh stockings and high heels, and I held targets in my hands, teeth or on my head for him to cut off of me with his Australian bullwhips. The pay was good sometimes, bad at others, and sometimes we got stiffed. But I can honestly say that it was never dull.

Our older daughter, Michelle, was always a handful. She had a will of her own and a mind to match. I had to keep an eye on her all the time or she'd be into something, whether turning the kitchen into a mess trying to cook a "surprise" or cutting the dog's hair with her daddy's electric razor to make the pooch look like a lion. The stories are endless.

In 1965, the job of a lifetime came along for Monty. He got a contract to work in the *Hello America* show at the Desert Inn in Las Vegas. The show was a family affair that took the audience through all the stages of the movie business, from *The Wizard of Oz* to the big band era and more, including two great stunt spots: a showdown at the OK Corral with a gunfight, bullwhip act and stunt falls, as well as a swashbuckling pirate Errol Flynn-type spot with sword fighting and swinging around the stage on ropes from balconies. Monty was a shoo-in.

We packed up the kids, dogs and cat and headed for Vegas in our ten-year-old Ford. The girls were three and two. Las Vegas was nothing like it is today. Yes, all the well-known casinos were there, but Caesars Palace was just breaking ground, and all the spectacular casinos that rule the strip today were not even ideas yet.

There were no lawns, housing tracts, or shopping centers, other than a few gas stations and bodegas along the highways that circled the town. The apartment building we lived in was near the casinos, but backed up to the strip, separated by a highway and desert that stretched from our front door as far as anyone could see in all directions. The dogs loved it. I had to get used to it, particularly the scorpions. Also, since there were no yards or fences, I had to keep a close eye on the girls all the time. But until our second year there, I didn't work. When I did, the babysitting service from the casino was superb. They came armed (but that is another story).

Anyway, Monty worked two shows a night and three shows a day/night on weekends, so he was home most afternoons to help with the girls and take us shopping or to visit friends. We soon had many friends from the clubs. One single mom who worked at one of the clubs lived a few doors down from us in the same apartment building. She had a seven-year-old daughter, Mary, who became very fond of Michelle. Soon, they were together all the time, coloring, playing with dolls or watching television at either our apartment or Mary's. Anita was still too young to care about not being included and was happy just to have me to herself.

One day, Mary came over and asked if Michelle could go to her house to play. I gave permission, but said I wanted her home for lunch because we were supposed to go shopping that day. When noon came around, she was not home. I went to Mary's apartment, and her mother said that Mary had told her they were going to be at *our* apartment.

Now, it was panic time. I rushed home and told Monty, who looked across the vast desert, only to see nothing but a few cars far on the horizon.

We checked every apartment in the two buildings, but no little girls, so we called the police. Now, Las Vegas in 1965 was like a small town. Call the police for a missing child, and the sheriff and mounted deputies, the police in black-and-white squad cars, the Highway Patrol and the local news were on our doorstep all at once.

Mary and Michelle were found miles across the desert trying to cross the highway to get to the bodega to buy ice cream. The walk had to have taken at least two hours. They were almost hit by a car when trying to cross the highway, but were saved in the nick of time by a highway patrolman.

Mary was released to her mother unscathed. Michelle had a slight scrape on her leg, so they took her to the local emergency room. Monty, Anita, and I rushed there immediately. When we arrived, the doctor assured us that Michelle was fine. She wasn't even scared. In fact, she seemed to be enjoying all the attention immensely. She'd been given an ice cream and was being interviewed for the evening news.

We stood behind the camera as the newscaster recited a highly embellished tale of the brave highway patrolman who rescued the little blond, curly-haired angel from certain death on the highway. Then he reported that her father worked at one of the clubs on the strip. "What does your daddy do, honey?" he asked, holding his mic near her. Michelle smiled broadly and stated on network news, "My daddy turns tricks at the Desert Inn. He does it every night and three times on Sunday."

Monty almost fainted. The news crew and medical staff were cracking up. Michelle just looked around, smiling from ear to ear, and continued licking her ice cream.

~Joyce Laird

44

Be Careful What You Dream

*Dreams are often most profound when
they seem the most crazy.*
~Sigmund Freud

Growing up on our family dairy farm in upstate New York, I accepted that my oldest brother, John, wasn't ordinary. For one thing, he didn't like sugar. This peculiarity wasn't a bad thing because John gave his Halloween candy to my brother Steve and me, while he enjoyed a cavity-free childhood. I also found it odd that John had little interest in sports, music, or movies. In fact, he seemed interested in only one thing: farming. John was the only person I knew, with the exception of my father, who enjoyed doing chores, including milking cows.

John knew each of our thirty cows at a glance and had names for many. But his favorite cow was Polly, a pretty Brown Swiss. John showed Polly many times at the county fair, where he enjoyed talking to people who stopped by the stalls to see her. As he groomed Polly, he explained that he preferred Brown Swiss cows because they gave chocolate milk. He was pleased when people believed him.

One morning when John was seventeen, he came to breakfast limping. He grabbed onto furniture along the way and winced when he tried to put down his foot.

"Why are you limping?" asked Mom.

"Polly stepped on my foot," he said. "I think it's broken."

"You weren't limping last night when you came in from milking," she said. Her eyes narrowed. "When did this happen?"

"In the middle of the night," he said. He grabbed the table and eased himself into his chair. "Oww! I just bumped my foot on the table leg."

"You were milking in the middle of the night?" she said.

"I dreamed I was milking, and when I took the milking machine off Polly, she stepped on my foot hard."

"Are you kidding?" I said. "A cow hurt your foot in a dream?" Steve and I both laughed. What a far-fetched excuse to get out of going to school.

"That's right," he said.

After breakfast, Mom examined John's foot, but could not see any sign of injury — no redness, no swelling — but John continued to cry out in pain whenever she touched his foot. Mom told him he could stay home from school that morning on the condition that he saw the doctor. John agreed. I was beginning to believe he wasn't faking his injury because John hated going to the doctor. The last time he had gone for a shot, he passed out in the waiting room just from thinking about the needle. I had to test his veracity.

"Don't worry," I said. "Maybe the doctor will give you a shot for the pain."

"I don't care," he said, "as long as it helps."

That did it. John was not faking this injury. Whether it made sense or not, his pain was real.

Later that morning, Mom took John to the doctor. The X-rays were negative and there was no sign of an injury. The doctor prescribed aspirin and told John to stay off his foot until it felt better. He gave him a pair of crutches.

When I saw John at school that afternoon, he was hobbling from class to class on his new wooden crutches. He had a heavy sock covering his injured foot. Whenever a classmate asked him what happened, he said, "A cow stepped on my foot." This drew instant sympathy because everyone in a farming community knows that getting stepped on by a cow is a painful experience. When a horse steps on your foot, it picks its foot back up and continues on its way. But when a cow steps on your foot, the cow pushes off and slides its hoof across your foot, inflicting maximum pain. Apparently, cows do this even in dreams.

My brother Steve and I were not happy to have John laid up. Of course, we didn't want him to suffer. After all, he was our brother. But the longer he was incapacitated, the longer we had to do his chores in addition to our own. We wished him a speedy recovery.

After three or four days of walking on crutches, John began to put weight on his injured foot. Within a week, he was well enough to resume his chores. We welcomed him back with a new appreciation for the work he did. But we also gave him the following admonition: "From now on, be careful what you dream."

~D.E. Brigham

45

Busted

Life is either a daring adventure or nothing.
~Helen Keller

My mother was a vivacious, attractive young woman. She was also strong-willed. She craved adventure and the spotlight — a characteristic not shared by her strait-laced folks. Her wealthy parents indulged their only child's desire for piano, dance, and voice lessons, but the only venues available to display her talents were recitals — prim and proper affairs where the only recognition was polite applause.

My mother had ambitions, ones that extended way beyond recitals. Her adolescent imagination was fueled by the films of the time showing glitzy nightclubs where glamorous women in evening dress sipped martinis, their elegant red-nailed hands holding cigarettes, the smoke spiraling from their dark red lips. The men who accompanied these women were sophisticated and debonair, exuding just a hint of danger and intrigue. She imagined bright lights, dangling chandeliers, and white-clothed tables surrounding a tiny stage. The banter was witty, and laughter spilled over in the room like champagne.

When the lights dimmed, all eyes moved to the figure stepping onto the stage. Smoke from the many cigarettes swirling around her shrouded the woman in sensual mystique. The nightclub singer — that's what my mother wanted to be.

After she read an ad in the local newspaper for auditions at a supper club, my nineteen-year-old mother took matters into her own hands.

Feigning a headache, she excused herself and went up to her room. Then as soon as she saw the light go off under her parents' door, she made her escape. Dressed in her prom dress — which she had altered to create a higher hem and lower neckline — and holding her high heels in her hands, she tiptoed quietly down the stairs.

When she got to the club, she was surprised and secretly pleased to see it filled with customers. She greeted the manager and, lying about her age, signed up to perform. If she was experiencing any apprehension, it soon vanished when she was led onto the stage by the chubby emcee with greasy, slicked-back hair and a pencil-thin mustache. He introduced her as Beautiful Beverly.

The lights dimmed, the audience quieted, and my mother nodded to the piano player that she was ready.

"The night is bitter; the stars have lost their glitter." My mother belted out the lyrics to "The Man That Got Away." Whatever she lacked in musical ability was more than offset by her movements. She cradled the microphone, pouting her lips. She swayed her hips and tossed her dark curls. Then, in a move that brought down the house, she sashayed down from the stage and, with the spotlight following, glided over to a man sitting near the front. Rubbing his bald head, she sang into his ear, and then kissed his cheek before coquettishly blowing kisses to the audience amid thunderous applause.

When she got home late that night, the house was quiet, her absence undetected. And her plan would have succeeded but for the call my grandmother received the following day from the owner of Le Club, raving about the audition and offering a certain Beverly Wilterding a year's contract to perform at his establishment on weekends.

If there is such a thing as an escape gene, then my brother inherited it from my mother. Years later, my grounded teenage brother escaped from his second-floor bedroom by tying sheets together, only to be featured the next day in the local newspaper for scoring the most points during the previous night's high school basketball game. Busted! Just like his mom.

~Martha Roggli

46

A Nose for Trouble

*You can learn many things from children. How much
patience you have, for instance.*
~Franklin P. Adams

It was the time of day that every parent cherishes — naptime.
I had just put down both kids. My son, Wesley, was really
"down." He had gotten it into his little head that sleeping on
the floor was a great thing, and he was determined to nap
there. Personally, I didn't care — he was sleeping.

I had just dozed off after watching a rerun of Martha Stewart
showing me how to maintain my massive orchard of apple trees when
a scream pierced the silence. Wesley was in the living room, and blood
was gushing out of his nose. At first, I didn't panic because he gets
nosebleeds from time to time due to his allergies. He was crying, and
in between the snot and the blood, I could not make out why he was
crying. Finally, he said, "A nail crawled up my nose."

What? Surely he didn't say "nail." Maybe he said "snail." After
all, I am not the best housekeeper, and a snail can crawl, albeit very
slowly. I looked up his nostril, half expecting to see the shell of a French
entrée. Sure enough, there was a metal tip more than halfway up his
nose. So much for pulling out a snail.

For those who are not parents, I must digress. I was the first one
to tell anyone when I was childless that I would:

A. Never catch vomit in my hand

B. Only touch my own bodily fluids (i.e., blood, mucus, etc.)

C. Tell a baby he can change his own diaper

D. Never, ever look up someone's body parts when blood was gushing out

Obviously, being a parent changes us. We become impervious to snot, blood, or both coming out of our child's nose.

Anyway, I made the mistake of asking how long the nail was, and Wesley stretched his fingers as far as they could go. Where did this monstrosity come from? As far as I knew, my husband Dave and I were not in the construction or blacksmithing business. Also, how did this nail get into his nose? Wesley kept insisting that it did indeed rudely crawl up his nose. Despite the fact that I had taught him certain things were inanimate, he insisted. I stuffed a kitchen towel in his hand and told him to hold it against his nose to stop the blood. He was concerned about hurting the nail.

I dropped my infant daughter, Regan, off at her grandmother's house and headed to the hospital. The doctor and nurse did a double take when I told them what happened—I guess they were expecting something normal like an ear infection. Wesley was still adamant that he did not push the nail up his nose.

After the nurse stopped laughing, they told me Wesley was going to be fine. They tried to get it out with tweezers even though I told them that Wesley would not stand for it. This kid thinks he's dying when he gets a paper cut. He could win an award for best actor with his tantrums. The nurse medicated Wesley. They declined to medicate me although I believed I needed it more than Wesley. In the space of ten minutes, my three-year-old son was stoned.

"Mommy, Oprah's dress is soooo green." He laughed as he rolled around the hospital bed.

"Mommy, hold my hand," he said as he threw his foot into my hand.

"Mommy, why is Regan a girl and me a boy?"

"Mommy, why do you throw your veggies to the dogs but make me eat them?" *Oops.*

This was getting serious. I knew a nail up the nose was not

considered an emergency, but we had to get out of there before the kid told everyone I color my hair and secretly eat at Sonic for breakfast.

After I explained to Wesley why Oprah was giving away cars, the nurse came in and strapped my son to a cushioned thing that looked like a papoose. Any other time, Wesley would have screamed like he was being forced to eat squash. This time, he giggled. The doctor opened the door and came in carrying a sinister-looking tool designed to pull out railroad spikes. I felt lightheaded just looking at it; Wesley laughed uproariously. This had to be the plot of a Mel Brooks movie written by Stephen King.

In the space of two seconds, the doctor had pulled out a quarter-inch screw. He asked if I wanted to keep it as a souvenir. I thanked him and asked if I could have the T-shirt instead.

That night, Wesley finally admitted that the screw did not deliberately climb up his nose, but he put it up there to see if it would fit. He thought it would not. I suggested he not try that again, but I didn't make a big deal of it, as I don't want my children ever to stop exploring or asking questions.

To be on the safe side, I ran a metal detector through the house.

~Christy Breedlove

Crazy about Her Brother

Brothers and sisters are as close as hands and feet.
~Vietnamese Proverb

The good Lord blessed us with four children, all born in fairly rapid succession in the 1980s. Two, separated by a mere sixteen months, are particularly close.

Sarah, the older, and Brian, the younger, were constant play companions as toddlers. That bond continued throughout their childhood, and became even stronger when sports became a big part of their lives. No matter the sport, the two would be in the yard or the driveway — one the quarterback, the other a receiver; one a pitcher, the other a catcher; one a shooting guard, the other a defender.

But among the variety of sports that our children tried, hockey seemed to bring the clan closest together. As Brian progressed through the youth-hockey ranks beginning at age six, Sarah became his biggest fan. She wouldn't miss a game. Whether it was at our community rink on the other side of town or a three-day tournament across the border in Canada, she would be cheering wildly from the bleachers.

As he entered his preteens, Brian became a pretty good defenseman and was selected to play travel hockey. As the competitiveness increased on the ice, the intensity also increased in the stands.

Sarah's dedication to her brother never waned. But, as kids often do, Sarah would occasionally break a household rule and face some discipline from Mom and Dad.

On one occasion, she did something worthy of a punishment. Sending her to her room seemed a little childish, and taking away TV privileges was no big deal to her, but she needed to face some consequences for the infraction.

So, as parents, we told her (and I quote), "We're not taking you to Brian's hockey game on Saturday."

Well, you would've thought she had been sentenced to life in prison. She begged, pleaded, ranted, raved and negotiated for a different punishment. But we stuck to our guns and reaffirmed, "We're not taking you to Brian's game Saturday."

It was a local game, and at age twelve, Sarah was old enough to be left home alone for a couple hours, no matter how mad she was. As the rest of the family headed to the rink, I felt like we had achieved a parental victory, assured that she had accepted her punishment.

The winters in our hometown of Oswego, New York, are harsh, but this was an especially bitter February day. Not only did we have our usual several feet of snow on the ground, but we were also dealing with sub-freezing temperatures.

During a stoppage of play about midway through the first period of the game, I happened to look across the rink and was shocked to see Sarah walk in. I immediately went over to my wife and asked, "Did you go home and get Sarah?"

My wife and I were usually on the same page when it came to disciplining the kids, so she looked surprised and asked, "No, why?"

I could only point across the rink and mumble, "I think that's her."

I wasn't certain looking that far across the expanse of ice, but her blue-and-gold winter coat was unmistakable. Some of my uncertainty came from looking at her face, which was as red as a tomato. I was also stunned because she had been grounded from the game, and neither my wife nor I had backtracked on the punishment.

The first period ended moments later, so we approached her. Her face was indeed bright red, and she had ice in her eyebrows.

"I thought we told you that you couldn't come to the game today," I barked.

"No," she replied as if she had rehearsed this line. "You said you weren't 'taking' me to the game."

Though I was an English teacher and have studied linguistics, I was speechless.

Darn, I thought. *She's right. I did say "taking."* But how did she get to the rink? When I asked her who brought her, she replied, "Nobody."

Considering the wind-chill factor, and taking into account the two miles from our home to the rink, I knew she couldn't have walked, but I had to ask anyway. "Did you walk?"

With a look of stubbornness and sheer determination, she looked me in the eyes and stated, "Nope. I rode my bike."

No way! I was dumbfounded. In a climate where sometimes SUVs with snow tires and four-wheel drive get stuck, she rode her bicycle two miles to watch her brother play a hockey game?

I actually thought she was joking. I figured she had cajoled an unsuspecting grandparent into giving her a ride. I was sure that I had hung the kids' bikes on hooks from the garage ceiling for winter storage.

Again, I said, "No way!"

"Yep," she boasted as only a defiant twelve-year-old can. "I got my bike down with a ladder, pumped up the tires, and here I am."

Still not believing, I said "no way" for a third time and added, "Where's the bike?"

"I parked it out in the snow bank," she replied.

I had to confirm. With the Zamboni still doing its intermission resurfacing of the ice, I went outside to investigate. Sure enough, her purple ten-speed bicycle was propped up in the snow that had been plowed from the parking lot.

As a parent, I always hated to be outsmarted by my kids, but I chalked this one up in the loss column. Technically, Sarah didn't disobey us. We didn't say she couldn't go to the game; we said we weren't taking her! In addition, she demonstrated independence and resourcefulness in getting to the game, while continuing her loyalty to her brother as his number-one fan.

As bizarre as it seems for a twelve-year-old to ride a bicycle two miles on a February day in the snowbelt of Upstate New York, Sarah wasn't just crazy; she was crazy about her brother.

~Mike McCrobie

What Goes Around...

*Karma has a surprising way of taking care of
situations. All you have to do is to sit back and watch.*
~Author Unknown

"**P**eter! Get back in here." I grabbed my brother's shirt and tugged him toward me as he raised his little leg over the windowsill. "You can't climb out your bedroom window and sneak off just because Mom and Dad aren't home. Where do you think you're going?"

"To the store," he said with a pout, now back in the bedroom on both feet. "I want an ice-cream bar."

He was five. And I was fifteen. When our parents were out, I was in charge. But Peter didn't care. Headstrong, stubborn, and oh so cute, he had the whole family on high alert.

Mom hated taking him to the mall. The round racks of ladies' shirts and skirts spun in a circle, first clockwise then counter-clockwise as Peter pulled and pushed to amuse himself. "We're going to the next store," Mom would announce. "Where are you, Peter?"

No answer. The clothes racks were motionless.

"Come on, let's go."

Still no answer. After five minutes, Mom would be frazzled. "Where are you?" she'd shout. And that's when we'd hear muffled giggles, and then a grinning, dark-haired, brown-eyed imp would jump out of the clothes, springing up in front of Mom and yelling, "Here I am! Couldn't you find me?"

I swear, if Mom could have had some kind of tether on him, she would have. Instead, he did it over and over, at least whenever he could pull his tiny hand out of Mom's and play that maddening game.

His shenanigans fizzled out as he grew up, but he always had a wicked sense of humor and a deep, bellowing laugh, followed by a grin that went from ear to ear. His handsome looks and debonair charm went a long way. Later on, he married and had kids.

Then, one day, he called.

"Hey, Sis, have I had chicken pox?"

"Chicken pox? I don't know. I can't remember. Why?"

"Because Amanda came out of her bedroom with spots all over her. I think they might be chicken pox."

Amanda was eight, with the same fiery stubborn streak and self-assured grin as her father. Her behavior blew Peter away most of the time. I had to stifle my own giggles many times when he recounted her capers. Not this time. This could be serious.

"Peter," I said, "you'd better call Mom. She'd know. Call me back and let me know."

The phone rang an hour later. "Mom said no, I didn't have them as a kid."

"Then it could be bad if you get them when you're an adult. What do you see now?"

"The spots are pink, mostly on her belly, with a few on her face. I ran out and got calamine lotion and some kind of oatmeal bath. That's what it said to do on the Internet."

"Okay, good luck." I felt sorry for him and asked him to call again over the next few days.

Later in the week, after I hadn't heard from him, I gave my brother a call.

"Hey, what's up with Amanda? And did anyone else catch it?" I asked.

"The next day, after I talked to you, Amanda had even more spots.

They were spreading all over her arms and legs."

"Oh, boy. What about the other kids? Have they had it?"

"No, no one else has had it, which is why we were so concerned. We quarantined Amanda in her room and kept applying the lotions. But nothing worked. Finally, my mother-in-law came over to help out, and that's when the you-know-what hit the fan."

I started to smile on my end of the phone. There was something coming; I could feel it.

"It seems her grandma took one look at those chicken pox and knew right away they weren't real," Peter said. "We looked real close. It was magic marker. Hot pink, non-washable marker."

"What?" Now I almost doubled over. "You've got to be kidding."

"Nope. Amanda had been putting the spots on herself. And when we confronted her, she denied it. Said it was *real* chicken pox. But by this time, we could tell they weren't real. So I said to her, 'Where's the marker?' She kept saying it wasn't a marker. But I could tell by the look on her face she was caught, and she knew it."

I stifled a laugh, but managed to squeak out, "That's funny, Peter."

"Not really. It cost me forty bucks and a ton of worry. Finally, by the time she did 'fess up to lying, I wanted to laugh, but only because she was so darned smart."

"Hmmm, seems like I remember someone else who used to cause his mom and dad a lot of undue worry."

"Yeah, I know. You've all told me that. I just never thought my eight-year-old daughter would get the best of me."

"Well, get used to it. What goes around comes around. And you are way overdue."

"Thanks a lot, Sis."

"No problem," I replied.

~B.J. Taylor

Drama in the Negev

The cure for boredom is curiosity.
There is no cure for curiosity.
~Dorothy Parker

e lived in Beirut, Lebanon, for more than a year, and I found lots of ways to get in trouble, including getting hit by a car when I tried to chase a boy across the highway. My dad worked for Pan Am, so we lived in a variety of places, and I was an inveterate explorer and adventurer in every one.

One time, Dad singled me out for a three-day trip to Israel for a series of meetings he was attending in the Tel Aviv area. He knew I would enjoy being around some pretty exotic airplanes and seeing the huge airport.

At the end of it all, Dad had been invited by some of his colleagues to a semi-abandoned airfield in the heart of the Negev desert, near the southern tip of Israel. The thought was that the airfield could once again be utilized by commercial airline carriers, as the Israelis wanted to transform the southern tip of the Negev into a possible tourist mecca. Many years into the future, that is exactly what did happen, as the small town of Elat, on the Gulf of Aqaba, has sprung up as one of the favorite tourist destinations in the region. The pristine and clear waters of the northern gulf, combined with the white sandy beaches and tropical breezes, is a huge attraction for scuba divers and beachgoers from all over the world. Back when Dad and I were in the region, however, Elat was a grimy little town with little or no activity whatsoever. Aside from the Israeli military presence in the town, the area seemed to be devoid of any life at all.

We had driven for what seemed like hours through the hot desert until we finally came to a series of low hills in the distance. The driver took a left-hand turn onto a small paved roadway and drove on for another twenty minutes or so until coming to a stop directly in front of a series of airplane hangars that looked to have been abandoned many years before. While stepping from the back seat of the car with Dad, my heart sank as there wasn't one airplane to be seen anywhere.

Dad was accompanied by several men, and I lagged behind as we walked from the cars to the expansive parking apron on the flight side of those old hangars.

And then I saw it! The hangar directly behind us had its enormous doors wide open, and within its shadows sat the most beautiful sight — a World War II-era North American P-51 Mustang fighter airplane. In my mind, this was the most treasured of airplanes in the world and definitely my favorite aircraft type. I had read stories of the fantastic P-51, heard accounts of its maneuverability and its mastery of the skies over Germany and Japan during the war, and there it stood. This one had the blue Star of David emblem painted on its sides and wings. As I walked slowly toward it, the afternoon sun shone through the open hangar door and glinted off the polished aluminum fuselage. This was great!

Dad yelled at me to not get into any trouble, and I sort of acknowledged him with a grunt and the wave of my hand. He and the group of men began walking in the general direction of a row of buildings that seemed to border the airfield a few hundred meters away. They were soon out of sight.

I walked around the P-51 in absolute awe and gently touched its polished aluminum structure. The canopy sat wide open, and I thought the airplane was actually beckoning me to climb up on its wing and sit in the pilot's seat. That little inner voice we sometimes hear so very clearly can either save us from some unforeseen danger — or get us into so much bloody trouble. It was a lesson I was to learn pretty well that day.

I was quickly up on the left (port) wing and had one leg already halfway inside the cockpit when that little voice in my head spoke. "Climb down off the wing and remove the wooden chalks from in front of the wheels."

So I backed off the wing, ducked down near the left main wheel and kicked at the wooden block. That one was removed and thrown off to the side, and I quickly went to work on the other one. Within another minute, I was back up on the wing and strapping myself into the harness of the seat-mounted parachute inside the cockpit.

I actually believed that I was going to get the airplane up in the air — for what purpose, I still do not have a clue. I knew the layout of the cockpit pretty well, having studied photographs of it back home in my books, and I knew the exact sequence of switches to throw in order to get that enormous Rolls-Royce Merlin engine cranking over. The only troubling part was that I was barely able to reach the two rudder pedals with my feet. Hey, I wasn't quite nine years old yet and still had a long way to grow!

If push actually came to shove, I figured I could stretch my legs out just a little further once airborne, so that controlling the rudder pedals wouldn't be such a problem. I forgot that the rudder pedals also controlled the direction the airplane traveled while on the ground. To use the brakes on the ground, one had to push the rudder pedals all the way forward.

My right hand easily found the power toggle, and, to my amazement, lights flashed on in the cockpit, needles within gauges started swinging into place, and a satisfying hum could be heard from somewhere behind the instrument panel that stared back at me. The fuel selector switch was right where it was supposed to be, and I easily turned it to the center gas tank I knew was somewhere behind where I was sitting in the cockpit. All that was needed to get that huge Hamilton Standard propeller spinning invisibly in the air at the business end of this fighter plane was for me to push up on the engine start switch.

My left hand found the throttle, and I pushed it forward just slightly.

I was so engrossed in what I was doing that I never even noticed the gaggle of uniformed men racing for the entrance to the hangar. By the time I looked up, smoke was belching from the twelve exhaust stacks on the sides of the Rolls Royce engine, a split second before the whole thing caught and the engine roared to life. At that same instant, several sets of very rough hands were grabbing at me through the still-open cockpit, and other hands were reaching in and shutting off everything.

My arms were held in vice-like grips, and I was soon unstrapped from the parachute and dragged out of the cockpit. Several of the men were yelling in Hebrew, and two of them had me by the back of my shirt while they dragged me out of the hangar. About a hundred yards away, I saw Dad and his colleagues running at a sprint in my direction, with Dad in the lead. I didn't know whether I should be happy or really worried just then because that's when I realized I definitely should not have paid any attention to that little inner voice. Either way, I figured I was well and truly in an enormous amount of trouble.

Within another ten minutes or so, however, everything seemed to have been pretty much sorted out. A couple of the Israeli military guys were even smiling at me. One brushed his hand roughly through my unruly mop of hair at the top of my head in what I presumed to be a gesture of friendship. Dad held onto the back of my shirt collar as he and his colleagues walked back to the waiting cars.

The long drive back to Tel Aviv that afternoon was punctuated by some laughter and jokes, at my expense I'm sure, and I received several glances and smiles from the other two men in the car.

That night, Dad and I had one of our heart-to-heart discussions. To this day, I'm not quite sure if Dad was actually angry with me or in an odd sort of way, somewhat proud. I could have been punished severely for what I did, yet I was not. Dad actually wanted to know if I wanted to be a pilot. I told him I would like nothing better, and he replied, "Alright, Johnny. We won't mention any of this to your mother, as she wouldn't be too happy. And I'll see what we can do about those flying lessons."

Hindsight again being 20/20, my take on that incident so many years after the fact was that Dad knew if my mother ever got wind of what happened in the Negev desert, there would be so much more trouble for him than for me. It was such a closely held secret that she only found out about the Negev desert drama when she was in her early eighties, and the look she shot my father from the other side of the kitchen table in Newport, Rhode Island some forty-five years later could have frozen the Dead Sea solid!

By the way, Dad did arrange those flying lessons, both the official ones and the unofficial ones. The official ones started when I was twelve, the minimum age when it was allowed, and the unofficial ones happened every time Dad took me up in one of Pan Am's airplanes, where he made sure I sat up in the cockpit with the pilots.

Sometime after this incident, Dad and I were having a quiet talk, well out of earshot of Mom. He mentioned that the P-51 had been part of the Israeli Air Force's reserves and had been assigned to the Negev airfield for routine training. Apparently, nothing much was said about the incident by the Israeli military guys either, as they would have been in some pretty hot water for not guarding their airplanes better.

As an aside, two years after that incident, we had moved to England where Dad was the Station Manager for Pan American's operations out of Heathrow Airport. As was his routine, he left for work every weekday morning at precisely 6:30.

We kids had the week off from school, and I was bored out of my mind. Instead of doing anything sensible, God forbid, I decided I would stow away in Dad's brand-new Morris Minor for the morning's ride into the airport. The thought of getting into any trouble never really entered my mind, so I climbed into the car and quickly hid on the carpeted floor right behind the back seats.

Within a few minutes, Dad climbed in, started the motor, and off we drove. About ten minutes into the hour-and-a-half drive to the airport, Dad lit up his first cigarette of the day. The moment I smelled that forbidden smoke, I knew there was no way I would be getting into any trouble. As he pulled to a stop in his parking space, I popped up like some sort of Jack in the Box from behind the seat and said, "Hi, Dad!"

"What the...!" I heard Dad exclaim. He almost had a coronary, but I knew that I would be getting my way as long as I promised not to tell Mom. At any rate, I was taken into Pan Am's VIP lounge and pretty much treated like royalty for the entire ten hours that Dad was at work.

~John Elliott

50

Halloween in May

You're never too old to do goofy stuff.
~*Ward Cleaver*, Leave It to Beaver

"**I**f I tell you this story, you're gonna think we're all crazy." My mother-in-law sat across the table from me, laughing. My husband, Greg, knew where she was headed. He was laughing, too.

One of the reasons I fell in love with my husband was because of his Cleaver-like family. Growing up, my dad was married five times, my mom four. The first two marriages were to each other, though, so I'd lived through some fairly dysfunctional times. I had one full-blooded brother from that first marriage, a half-sister from my mom's third marriage (second husband), a half-sister from my dad's fourth marriage (third wife), and a slew of stepbrothers, most of whom had been left behind in the wake of multiple divorces. I doubted there was a thing this woman could tell me that I'd find crazy.

"Lay it on me, Mom," I said.

And so she did.

***

It was a warm, May evening in 1985. Greg had a few friends over to ring in his thirteenth birthday. Once all the usual birthday festivities had taken place — cake, ice cream, and games — the boys were bored. And it was only 9:30.

Now the thing one must understand about my mother-in-law, Pat, is that she is the kind of mother who would take her boys and their friends to an empty soccer field at midnight, leave the car headlights on to provide light, and read a book while they kicked around a ball until 3:00 am.

She is the kind of mother who, despite her own fears, allowed her sons to catch and research every kind of snake native to Kentucky... even after one escaped in the house.

And another in the car.

She is the kind of mother who, when the boys were watching a scary movie in the basement, reached over the deck to tap gently on the window with a broomstick.

Repeatedly.

So when the boys were bored that May 18th, it was no surprise that she suggested they go trick-or-treating. A neighbor who had a great sense of humor was having a Bunco party. Wouldn't it be funny to show up in full costume, asking for candy, in springtime? Of course the boys jumped at the chance. Quickly, they all donned ripped clothing, monster masks, and face paint. Not to be left out, Greg's mom sported a black hooded monk's robe and painted her face white. They knocked on the door and everyone got a good laugh. And they scored some candy in the process.

Now running on adrenaline, the boys weren't ready to call it a night. A favorite teacher lived in the neighborhood, only a few blocks away. A math teacher, she was a mentor who treated them like young adults instead of children and affectionately called everyone, "Babe."

Pat gave the boys the green light. So off they ran — even Greg's friend, Tony, who was on crutches.

Little did they know that teacher had been receiving threatening crank calls over the prior couple of days.

Little did they know that the teacher had been to the police station that very day.

Little did they know that the teacher's neighbor hadn't slept in days, because he had newborn twins in the ICU.

But the boys were in full Halloween mode now. Wouldn't it be funny if, instead of knocking on the door, they scratched on her window screens and the sides of her house? Wouldn't it be funny if they grabbed sticks and tapped the windows upstairs? Wouldn't it be funny if they circled her house for ten minutes and screamed in the back yard while hoisting a table into the air?

Since the boys had run ahead, Pat wasn't in on the prank's evolution. So, as she approached the house, she was shocked to see Tony rapidly hobbling toward her on his crutches. The teacher's neighbor, wearing nothing but boxer shorts, had just hurdled the fence and tackled two of the other boys. Now carrying one under each arm, he was quickly gaining on Tony.

"MRS. STOCKER! MRS. STOOOOOCCCKEEEEERRRR! HELLLLLLP!"

Pat sprinted to the man in boxers. Sheepishly, she lowered her monk's hood.

"It's Pat Stocker. I.... I go to church with you."

The neighbor froze. They knew each other well.

"I'm sorry. The boys are with me," she said.

He dropped the boys. Without a word to Pat, he turned and knocked on the teacher's door.

"Karen, it's me. It's okay. It's the Stockers."

Karen creaked open the door, a whiskey in one hand, and a cigarette in the other. Wide-eyed, she looked from one guilty face to the next.

"Babe, I was petrified."

Even when terrified, she still called everyone "Babe." The boys stifled their laughter as sirens became audible in the background.

"Oh, yeah. I called the cops. You guys better get out of here."

When they got back to the house, the boys begged to trick-or-treat at a few more houses. For once, though, Greg's mom said no.

"The neighbors are going to think I've lost my mind."

By the time the shock wore off, the embarrassment began to sink in. Pat wondered how she could ever show her face in church again. She sent the boys downstairs and padded to her bedroom. Although she tried not to wake her husband, he rolled over when she slipped into bed.

"So… How'd it go?"

* * *

I looked around the table as my mother-in-law and my husband howled at the memories. My father-in-law, in his usual fashion, sat shaking his head, silently amused. I thought about the memories that Greg and I were making for *our* children. I thought about the birthday parties to come, the midnight soccer trips, the snakes, the pranks… that was the kind of mother I wanted to be, too. I wanted to be the kind of mom who took her kids trick-or-treating in May. I caught Mom's eye.

"I don't think you're crazy," I said.

"No?" she asked, still giggling.

"No," I answered. "I think you're amazing."

~Shannon Stocker

Chapter 6

My Crazy Family

Grand and Great

51

Granny's on the News

Have the fearless attitude of a hero
and the loving heart of a child.
~Soyen Shaku

I received an urgent call from my aunt. "Turn on the TV. Granny's on the Channel 10 news."

I clicked on the TV just in time for the teaser: "And stay tuned for a daring story that happened just this afternoon, and a criminal who didn't realize what he was getting into."

What on earth?

I stayed on the phone with my aunt through the commercials. Finally, the newscasters were back, ready to tell this heroic story.

It turned out that Granny had made a sandwich run for her office and was stopped at a red light downtown. She had the window rolled down to enjoy the breeze when a man rushed up to the driver's side window, intending to carjack her.

Now, what the would-be carjacker couldn't have known was that this woman simply wasn't "a granny." This was Nancy Johnson — the same woman who owned and lived on a Texas cattle ranch, drove her own tractors, and dug her own post holes to lay fence. The week before, she had shot a rattlesnake and chopped off its head with a shovel. She was the proud owner of the new minivan she was driving, as one of her Brahma bulls had head-butted her former car into oblivion after seeing its own reflection gleaming in the door.

In other words, she was not your normal kind of granny.

The carjacker leaned into the open window, one hand stuffed in his pocket, and said, "Get out of this car. I have a gun, and I will shoot you."

A statement like that would have terrified anyone else. Instead, Granny saw it as a challenge.

"If you really had a gun in your pocket, you would've pulled it out and led with that first," she snapped at him, completely unfazed.

She was right. The criminal didn't have a gun. She had called his bluff, so he instead lurched into the window, grabbed her, and tried to pull her out of the van. He yanked open the door, wildly clutching at Granny's arms.

Granny leaned her shoulder into the steering wheel to blast the horn and started yelling to make a scene. With the door now open, she looped one arm through the steering wheel and started kicking the man anywhere her foot could make contact. At 5'9", the woman has quite a reach.

After a well-placed kick to the crotch, the man was done, and attempted to release her and run. But Granny wouldn't stand for that.

It was now her turn to grab onto him, her hands made strong from hours and hours of ranch work. That poor fool didn't have a chance.

She yelled for help to bystanders, and they rushed to her aid. With Granny leading the charge, a group of strangers came together and pinned the man to the sidewalk, holding him there until the police came.

A silver-haired woman — who loved being out on her tractor as much as she loved making brownies and crocheting — had just made a citizen's arrest.

When asked by the starry-eyed young reporter covering the story why she fought back and wasn't scared, Granny's answer was surprisingly simple: "No, I wasn't scared of that little twit. I'd had my brand-new van for less than two days and a pack of good sandwiches for my office. And there was no way he was going to get either of those!"

And this was quintessential Granny. The local newspaper ran it as their lead story the next day. She proudly clipped it to her kitchen fridge, wedged between pictures of her grandkids.

At first, we were furious with her. "Granny, don't you realize you could've gotten yourself killed?" we said.

But we all learned an important lesson from her that day — the same lesson that had been building through the years, all centered around one theme.

It was there when she would kick us grandkids out of the house at 8:00 a.m., telling us to be back at sunset. It was there when she taught us how to climb into the tractor, which at the time seemed scary yet simultaneously thrilling, surrounded by unknown machinery and perched well above the fields. It was there when she very carefully showed us how to load and shoot a shotgun.

She encouraged us to push boundaries and expectations. But even more so, she taught us fearlessness.

~Kristi Adams

Bubby Gets Her Way

*One should be able to control and manipulate
experiences with an informed and intelligent mind.*
~Sylvia Plath

My grandmother is a hilarious mixture of morbidity and humor. She has a line prepared for nearly every situation. Upon hearing that someone she knows is going to Israel, she responds, "Oh, really? I'm also going to Israel soon. I'm going in a box. I have an apartment waiting for me there on Har Hazeisim (a large cemetery in Israel). I heard the scenery is beautiful there."

During the summer, Bubby is always sure to tell us that it's so hot because God is reminding her of what's waiting for her after she dies.

And when her freezer is very full, she says, "You couldn't fit a cockroach in my freezer."

Some of my fondest childhood memories took place in Bubby and Zaidy's house. Sitting on the old green carpet telling jokes with my cousins. Playing with her bristle blocks and her toy gas station. Making sure not to touch her fragile glass coffee table. Watching her bake kugels and cakes. Trying to count how many plants she had in her living room.

I was always fascinated as I watched the chickens turning round and round in her rotisserie, or the vegetables sliding out of her grinding machine as she made gefilte fish from scratch. I can still smell her delicious chicken soup and hear the clang of our spoons against the old glasses she used to serve her homemade ice cream.

A couple of decades have passed since I was a kid. Nowadays, Bubby is one of the most active eighty-seven-year-olds I know. She still bakes and shops for her grandchildren every week. Every Friday night, Bubby and Zaidy are all smiles as their children, grandchildren, and great-grandchildren gather in their little apartment. They have somehow managed to live together with minimal help. Bubby's sense of humor helps her get through the hardest times.

Some things have changed since my childhood, but many of my favorite things can still be found in Bubby and Zaidy's house. My children know not to touch Bubby's glass coffee table. They still play with the gas station that I loved when I was their age. The bristle blocks are gone, along with the rotisserie, the vegetable grinder and the ice cream glasses, but the feeling of home is still there.

My grandparents recently faced a difficult time when Zaidy needed a hip replacement. He was admitted into the hospital, leaving Bubby to spend her nights alone at home.

The day after the surgery, my aunt Rachel took Bubby to visit Zaidy in the hospital. Knowing that the hospital security guards require all visitors to present a photo ID, Bubby had prepared hers in her pocketbook. Then, when it was time to go, she accidentally took a different pocketbook.

When the guard asked to see her ID, Bubby smiled nervously. "I don't have it," she said, "but my husband is a patient here. He just had a hip replacement. And this is my daughter, Rachel. She has ID, and she can vouch for me."

"I'm sorry, ma'am." The guard waved her away. "I can't let you in without a photo ID. Hospital rules."

My grandmother stood as tall as she could while holding onto her walker. "Excuse me," she said in a pleasant voice. "Do I look like a murderer to you? Are you afraid that I will murder the patients if you let me go see my husband?"

The thought was ridiculous, but the guard was not easily persuaded.

He refused to allow her to enter the hospital.

Finally, Bubby turned to her daughter and said, "Okay, Rachel. You go up and see Daddy all by yourself. Take your time. You can stay for a few hours if you want. I'll stay here and keep this nice security guard company. I will make sure he won't be bored, and this way he can make sure that I'm not murdering anyone. Send Daddy my regards, and remember — don't rush back. Feel free to stay for a few hours. The guard and I will have a good time together."

"Okay, lady, you can go up this time," the guard said with a huff. "But next time, we really won't let you in without ID."

Another victory for Bubby!

~Chana R. Rubinstein

53

Dragging the Gut

The winner ain't the one with the fastest car,
it's the one who refuses to lose.
~Dale Earnhardt

When I visited my grandparents in Pawhuska, Oklahoma, Grandma and I always "dragged the gut," which meant riding up and down the main street to see what was going on. We did this as often as possible after any excursion. The main street in Pawhuska is called Kihekha (as Pawhuska is the seat of the Osage Nation), and runs from east to west. It is about ten short blocks. Even though it runs right by the police station, most people go faster than the standard twenty miles an hour.

One Sunday, Grandma and I were coming back from picking chokecherries and had four full baskets in the back seat of the car, along with our red hands and mouths. As it happened, we were stopped at the light by the triangle building (the middle of the block), and a young man pulled up in what would now be called a "muscle car" — a 1976 Mustang — revving the engine and shouting out the window. Grandma looked calmly over at the young man and asked what he wanted. He said that he could "clobber an old woman driving a big car," and did she want to drag? Now, this was before seat belts, and her car was a new Cadillac with a V-8 engine with overdrive.

If there was one thing that my grandmother could not pass up, it was a challenge. I had a really bad feeling about this as she put her left foot on the brake and commenced revving her car to match the noise level of his car. I told her that the police station was just down the block, and we could go to jail for racing down the main street. But she just smiled sweetly at me and said, "Don't worry. I have enough money to get us out."

Our light was about to turn green, and both cars were growling and making little jumps forward. Now is a good time to point out that my grandmother was only 4'2", and she sat on the Tulsa Yellow Pages so she could see out the windshield.

Well, the inevitable happened. The light turned green, both cars popped forward, and I looked briefly over at Grandma. She was leaning as far forward as she could get on the wheel and still reach the accelerator pedal. She had that car floored.

Both cars raced for about six blocks before anything happened, and then it happened with such quickness that it was hard to follow. The Mustang, seeing that he was not going to win this race quickly, cut in front of Grandma, and in her reflex to miss the Mustang, she hit the brake. Several things were set in motion like a ripple effect as she swerved the car and hit the brakes: The chokecherries started flying over the seat and hitting the front windshield, making it a sloppy red; I had a grip on the door handle for dear life; Grandma's butt slid off her phone book as the car stopped, and she landed on the floorboard; and the car kept going forward as her foot slipped off the brake. I knew then that the Lord was coming to take us home.

The next thing I knew, the car was stopped, Grandma was out of the car, and she was chasing that Mustang down the street on foot. When she hit the floor, she must have clamped her hands down on the brake to stop the car because, Lord have mercy, we were stopped. That poor youngster did not have a chance. The next light turned red, and instead of jumping it, he stopped, and my tiny grandmother caught up with him.

She reached in the window, grabbed his ear, and started telling him the positive attitude he should have toward his elders, since she now recognized him as one of the leading citizens' sons. She finally let him go and calmly got back into the car, and then we drove home.

The next day, not only did she get a written apology from his dad, but also four baskets of chokecherries were delivered at the front door.

I asked her how she had gotten this done, as she had also been dragging the kid. She looked at me with those dark Cherokee eyes, cocked her head to the side and said, "I simply reminded his father by phone last night that I taught him how to treat his horses for the bloating when he had allowed them to overeat on his dad's farm. I thought it was about time that his dad knew how he had learned the cure."

She decided she had won the race by "default," and we canned the chokecherries that day.

~Pamela Dawes-Tambornino

54

The Jacket

A grandma is warm hugs and sweet memories.
She remembers all of your accomplishments and
forgets all of your mistakes.
~Barbara Cage

When I was a child, our family would go to my grandparents' every Sunday night for dinner. We'd walk in the door, and the first thing to greet us would be the wonderful aroma of roast beef cooking in the oven.

But what always made the visits extra special was dessert. My grandmother would always scoop ice cream for my sister and me, smother it with chocolate sauce, and top it with a maraschino cherry. Then she'd look around slyly as if someone might be lurking. If the coast was clear, she'd always put an extra cherry on mine. (I don't remember if she did the same for my sister, but I'm guessing she did.)

She was the stereotypical grandmother — caring and doting, spoiling her grandchildren, always willing to help out my mom. But there was her other side. She took no sass from two daughters, nor from her sons-in-law, and definitely not from her grandchildren. She had no qualms about doing "the right thing," no matter the consequences or embarrassment she might inflict. That leads me to another kind of grandmother memories.

It was a beautiful fall day in 1968, a Saturday. I was eleven years old and on my way out the door to see a movie with some friends.

"Take your jacket. It's chilly outside," my mom called from the kitchen.

"Okay!" I yelled back and raced out the door. I could see my friends already at the corner waiting for the bus to take us downtown.

Yeah, it was a little chilly outside, but certainly not enough to warrant a jacket. Cool eleven-year-old boys did not wear jackets unless the temperature dipped into the low forties. Really cool boys didn't wear jackets until the temp hit freezing. It didn't matter if our skin turned blue and goose bumps covered our arms. It just showed how tough we really were. Besides, it had to be about fifty degrees that day, and the sun was out. Not even close to jacket weather. So, out the door I went, sans jacket.

As I trotted down the driveway, my grandmother pulled up in a white car. I stopped to give her a quick peck on the cheek and a "hello."

"What do you think of my new car?" Her voice was full of pride.

"Looks great." I barely noticed, more concerned about being with my friends.

"Shouldn't you be wearing a jacket?"

I shouldn't have said what I did, but my friends were waving frantically, signaling the bus was in sight.

"Mom said it was okay." I took off running toward the bus stop.

Best-case scenario: Mom and Grandma would never mention it to each other, and I'd get away with it. Worst-case scenario: My mom would find out I didn't take my jacket, and I'd get grounded. But what could I do? The bus was on the way.

The bus picked us up, and we took our seats in the back, like we always did, as far away from the adults as we could.

Not six blocks away from where we boarded, the driver stopped to pick up another passenger. As the bus started to roll, it came to a sudden stop, blaring the horn as the passengers lurched forward. The horn stopped, and the door opened. Up the steps climbed my grandmother. The bus went silent as this small, elderly lady tromped to the back of the bus, locking me in a death glare. When the passengers saw whom she was scowling at, all eyes turned toward me. How could anyone not notice my face turn a bright shade of red?

She never said a word as she stood in front of me, her arm extended, my jacket dangling from her fist. Sheepishly, I took the jacket. Still without a word, my grandmother turned around and exited the bus.

As soon as the doors closed, everyone on the bus, friends and strangers alike, erupted in laughter. I felt about two inches tall, and wished I was so I could hide. Still beet red, I looked out the window to see a shiny white car back away from where it had blocked the bus. The bus continued on its route, my friends teasing me relentlessly, and smiles flashed on all the passengers' faces. I'm sure they all had a great story to tell when they got home.

I came home that afternoon, and my mother never said a word about sending Grandma after me. For my part, I thought it best to keep my mouth shut, too. For the rest of the day, we pretended that nothing happened. I was able to put the incident behind me. But the following evening was dinner at the grandparents'. How should I act? She had made me a laughingstock — something my friends would never let me forget.

It turns out nothing happened. My grandmother never said a word. And when it was time for dessert, there was an extra maraschino cherry on top of my ice cream. All was forgiven.

~David Fingerman

55

Toaster Perfection

*A grandfather is someone with silver in
his hair and gold in his heart.*
~Author Unknown

"**H**ow much longer 'til Grandpa and Grandma get here?" my little sister Kris asked.

"Probably only an hour or so," Mom assured her.

Ten minutes less than the last time you asked, I thought.

"Aww, really?"

"Yes," Mom told her, "and there's still a lot to do to get ready."

I looked around the living room we'd been cleaning. This was the cleanest our house had been since last year's spring-cleaning. I couldn't imagine what else we needed to do.

"Joy, go fix the couch cushions. Kris, go dust the stereo."

"But we already dusted it," Kris complained.

"Look at all that dust in the corner."

I turned toward the couch and rolled my eyes, sympathetic to Kris's situation, but not willing to get involved. This was just the way it always was when Grandpa and Grandma came to visit. No matter how hard we tried, there'd still be a problem of some sort, especially...

"Oh, no! What about the toaster?" I called to Mom.

This was a real crisis. I couldn't believe we hadn't thought of it sooner.

How would we tell Grandpa the toaster was broken again?

My grandpa was a bit of a fix-it guy. He had a shop in the corner of his basement where he loved to fix things. This shop was where all items with flaws of any kind went to be repaired — cracked croquet balls were repainted, tilting knick-knack shelves were realigned, and used toasters were rewired.

And that was the problem. Years before, on one of their visits, Grandpa had discovered that we didn't have a toaster. Our old one had quit working, and with our family's tight budget, we hadn't replaced it. Grandpa found this completely unacceptable and vowed to get us a new one.

In the weeks to follow, I'd thought about that new toaster, imagining what it would be like to be the first to push the lever on the shiny new machine and to smell the toast browning inside. We didn't have new things in our house at that time so this was really exciting.

What I had forgotten, unfortunately, was that Grandpa didn't do "new" like some people did. In addition to working in his shop, Grandpa loved to go to auctions. He'd always find something banged up or broken and take it home to his shop for repairs. This time it was a toaster, which he proudly presented to us on our next visit to his house.

"Now, you have to jiggle the handle a bit sometimes, and you have to watch it so it doesn't burn," he told us. "Don't run off and forget it, girls, or you'll have black toast. But, look! See, it works great!"

Grandpa looked around at us all, his eyes shining with pride, and we readily agreed that it was perfect.

For weeks after we took that toaster home, we wiggled the handle and watched our toast. Sometimes it would get burnt, but many times we had perfectly browned toast for breakfast — until the morning it quit working all together.

"Well, that was good while it lasted," Mom said. "It was nice of Grandpa to try."

That Thanksgiving when Grandpa asked me how our toaster was working out, I wasn't sure what to say. I hated to disappoint him, but

I couldn't lie.

"It stopped working," I told him reluctantly.

"Really? I wonder why." Grandpa seemed truly perplexed. "Did you forget and leave it on too long?"

On their next visit, Grandpa brought us another toaster.

"Now, this one pops up great," he told us, "but sometimes the toast is not quite done, so you just have to push the bread down again. Two or three times should work," he told us with confidence.

Two or three times was in fact about right — every day for several months before it quit on us.

This pattern continued for several years. There was the toaster that only worked on one side so we had to toast one slice at a time, and the toaster that only toasted one side of the bread so we had to flip it around. One of the toasters only toasted the bottom two-thirds of the bread. We just had to turn it upside-down about halfway through.

Now, as we frantically prepared for our grandparents' arrival, Kris asked Mom, "Why don't we just buy a new toaster and tell Grandpa we don't need one anymore?"

It seemed logical to me. Mom had a new job, and we could afford a few things now. We'd just gotten a new microwave. A toaster couldn't be that expensive.

"We can't," Mom explained. "It would hurt your grandpa's feelings."

"Really?" Kris asked. I agreed. Grandpa didn't seem to have a lot of feelings. He never hugged anyone, never cried and rarely even laughed. He was a very straight-up kind of guy.

"Grandpa doesn't always know how to show his feelings," she explained. "The toasters are his way of showing he loves us."

The idea quickly grew on me. Fixing things for people was the only way Grandpa could let people know he cared. So, having agreed to once again explain things to Grandpa and await a new toaster, I turned to my couch duties, determined to make sure Grandpa knew how much we loved our toasters.

Grandpa's gone now, and I have a home and family of my own. We don't own a toaster. I've tried several times to buy one at the store, but it never seems quite right. Maybe someday I'll find a good one at a yard sale — one that only toasts on one side or doesn't always pop up right. I'm not sure any other kind will do.

~Joy Cook

56

She Did It Herself

*A woman is like a tea bag — you never know how
strong she is until she gets in hot water.*
~Eleanor Roosevelt

y grandmother was only in her sixties when Grandpa died. She continued to run their junkyard in the small Kansas town of Sabetha, sculpting her biceps with her newly acquired welding and cutting-torch skills, and sorting metals into neat piles. During the Depression and World War II, the A.M. Henry Salvage business had been a major employer that helped the town weather those troubled times. Grams, who had previously handled the bookkeeping, saw no reason to close the business and embraced some of the outdoor work that Grandpa had hired others to do.

She was much older when she ceased doing business, but she never quit working. I well remember the summer day that my husband Ray and I, along with our two young sons, drove the ninety miles to Grams' home and found her up on the roof nailing on shingles. She was then in her early eighties, measured five feet tall, and weighed her age. Ignoring her protests, Ray quickly took over the job for her. When she led the boys and me into the house, I noticed her shiny hardwood floors and realized they were newly refinished. "I did it myself," she said matter-of-factly. "Just stripped off the old varnish and brushed on the new. It wasn't that hard."

She had also painted her kitchen a soft mint-green. Hoping to be of belated assistance, I asked, "Grams, would you like Ray and me to move out your refrigerator and range and paint behind them?"

"Why, honey," she replied, "I already did that."

"How on earth did you move those heavy objects?"

"I just went out to the iron pile, got a steel pipe, hoisted up the appliances and rolled them out. When the paint was dry, I rolled them back."

Back in the living room, I noticed a baseball bat by the door. Grams explained, "Our neighborhood has been having trouble with burglars lately. If one comes here, I'll hit him with the bat." Any burglar who encountered Grams would wish he had taken up a different line of work.

Grams was brave, but never foolhardy. At eighty-six, when she climbed a tall pear tree, she asked my great-aunt, aged ninety-something, to act as spotter. Suddenly, Grams plummeted about fifteen feet, landing with a thump at Aunt May's feet. When Aunt May could not revive her, she presumed the worst and went into Grams' house to call the mortuary. She was talking to the funeral director when Grams — shaken but otherwise unhurt — walked in the back door.

When we were alerted to the accident, we drove to Sabetha and insisted on taking Grams to the doctor. He lectured her sternly, "I don't want you climbing any more trees."

"I won't climb any more *pear* trees," Grams promised. And until her productive life ended at almost ninety-one years of age, Ruth Moriarty Henry was true to her word.

~Marsha Henry Goff

57

Grandma Was a Nun

If you're going to have a story,
have a big story, or none at all.
~Joseph Campbell

Our seven-year-old daughter walked through the door and dropped a bombshell on my wife and me. She could hardly contain her excitement as she exclaimed, "Grandma was a nun!"

This was news to me, and I looked at my wife for answers. Why had my wife not told me her mother was a nun? This was highly unusual. Nuns seldom get married, yet my mother-in-law was. Nuns devote their lives to God and so did she. Nuns don't swear, and neither did she — a miracle since I was her son-in-law. Maybe she *was* a nun!

When had she been a nun? How did she escape the convent? Could she help me get some bonus points with the big guy upstairs? All of these questions popped into my head.

I analyzed this and thought perhaps my daughter was going through a phase. Maybe she was starting to make up stories. A lot of children get creative around age seven, so maybe my daughter wanted to get some extra attention with an interesting tale.

I was about to quiz her on the nun thing when she chimed in again.

"Papa even showed me a picture of Grandma when she was a nun." Now I was even more puzzled.

There was photographic proof, and it was never shared with me.

Was this a dark family secret? I wondered if I needed to ask for time off from work for an appearance on the "Dr. Phil" show.

How could my mother-in-law have been a nun and I didn't know?

My wife is the most honest, trustworthy and forthright person I know. She would have certainly told me that her mom had been a nun. If she had withheld this information from me, there had to be a reason. Maybe my mother-in-law had been in the Witness Protection Program. Maybe she had to seek refuge in a convent.

My wife finally spoke and said to my daughter, "You must be wrong. Grandma was never a nun."

My daughter was not convinced. She repeated, "I saw the picture of her." My little girl was certain that her grandma had been a nun.

My wife asked, "Who showed you this picture and when?"

Marissa replied, "Papa showed me the picture when we had lunch after we wrapped gifts and decorated his Christmas tree."

My wife was on the telephone within seconds. I heard her ask her father, "What is this nonsense about Mom being a nun?"

I could hear the roar of his laughter through the phone receiver. Apparently, my father-in-law thought it would be fun to do some storytelling. He had found an old Halloween picture of my mother-in-law. She had been dressed up as a nun for an adult Halloween party. He knew that he could convince our daughter that Grandma was a nun.

My wife also learned that Grandma was gone during the time he told his story, so no one was around to refute it. It was the perfect plan, and it was pulled off brilliantly by a man who loves to tell stories.

When the phone call ended, my wife breathed a sigh of relief and laughed. She didn't know what to make of it, but she smirked and marveled at her father's creativity.

I laughed and thought, *Wow, I should go to this man for some pointers on future stories.*

My daughter was confused at first but then laughed loudly. She knew Papa loved to tell stories and realized he was just having fun with her. She loves him deeply and was not going to let this fabrication stop him from sharing more tales with her.

This "Grandma Was a Nun" story from my father-in-law got me thinking. Had his past really been as exciting as he told us it was? He had told us stories of having Elvis's pillow and then giving it back. He had us convinced that he rode a horse bareback to school each day. He had amazing tales of being lost in the wilderness and almost drowning in a canoe. His military experience included crazy characters and creepy night watches. He had lived through a car hitting him, a dresser falling on him, and more. He had carried a baby alligator home from Florida to Ohio.

My wife confirmed his stories and another thought came to me. Did I really care which of his stories were true and which were not?

My father-in-law has a gift: He's a great storyteller. His stories are interesting. They have humor, suspense, action and even a dramatic twist on occasion. He tells them with a baritone voice that any deejay would envy. He tells them with a twinkle in his eye and enthusiastic joy. He tells them to anyone who will listen, and he tells them well.

In a world of texting, tweeting and "reality" TV, my father-in-law has managed to entertain the old-fashioned way. He sits down and tells great stories that make people laugh. His stories make us want to come back for more.

My mother-in-law isn't a nun and never was. We won't get a chance to be blessed by her, but we did get a surprise gift from my father-in-law at Christmas time. He shared his gift of storytelling, and now we have a memory that will last forever!

~David Warren

58

The College Fund

*That which seems the height of absurdity in one
generation often becomes the height
of wisdom in another.*
~Adlai Stevenson

appy Birthday, sweetie," Grandma Marlene said as she hugged me tight and then handed me an envelope. "Here's your gift, but don't pay a bill with it," she said sternly.

I smiled. Grandma Marlene's birthday cards always contained exactly four dollars. And every year, she admonished me that I had to spend the money on something fun, rather than paying a bill. And every year, I thought the same thing: *I wish I had a bill that was only four dollars.*

Grandma Marlene had never had much, but she gave as much as she could to her family. Her one regret was that she wouldn't be able to leave an inheritance to her grandchildren and great-grandchildren. It really bothered her — until she hatched a wonderful plan to raise a ton of money.

Grandma Marlene invested in the booming Beanie Baby business.

It started out rather small. Instead of her usual birthday card that contained four dollars, Grandma Marlene started giving each family member a Beanie Baby. We got them for Christmas as well.

She kept a detailed log of which family member she'd given which Beanie Baby. We were cautioned not to remove the tag because "these were going to be worth some serious money someday."

And that's when Grandma Marlene started hanging out at the flea market.

All. The. Time.

She made friends with Bob, the man who sold Beanie Babies at the flea market. She began following the trends in the Beanie Baby market like a floor trader at the New York Stock Exchange.

One day, she called me all excited. "Sweetie, the price of the purple bear I gave you two Christmases ago just spiked," she said. "Can you come down to the flea market so Bob can see if it's still in mint condition?"

I gulped. Did I still have the purple Beanie Baby from two years ago? Where exactly would I find it now? "Of course, Grandma," I said confidently.

I found the Beanie Baby under my toddler's bed. I piled him and his little brother into the car, and drove an hour to the flea market. Bob was thrilled to see me and did indeed declare my purple bear to be in mint condition. He grinned broadly and announced, "I can offer you eleven bucks for this baby."

"But my grandma said the price had really spiked," I said.

"Oh, it has," Bob answered. "That's almost double what she paid for him."

I didn't bother explaining that I'd piled my two young children in the car and driven an hour to sell a purple bear for eleven dollars that my dear Grandma Marlene had bought for six bucks.

The five-dollar profit didn't even cover my gas.

The next time Grandma Marlene called to tell me that the price had spiked on one of the Beanie Babies she'd given me, I asked a few more questions. "Bob offered us twelve dollars this time," she said, beyond thrilled.

I did a terrible thing. I promised Grandma Marlene that I would take the Beanie Baby to Bob so he could evaluate its condition and see if it was indeed worth the twelve-dollar price tag.

And then I didn't go.

I didn't think Grandma Marlene would find out, but she called me a week later, very disappointed because Bob claimed that he hadn't seen her beautiful granddaughter or the twelve-dollar Beanie Baby.

"I'm sorry, Grandma," I said. "I meant to go to the flea market, but this week has been very busy."

"But the price could go back down any minute," she said. "If we're going to make serious money at this, we've got to take it seriously."

"I know, Grandma, but it's hard for me to go to the flea market all the time because it's a long drive," I tried to explain. "I have to take the boys with me, and they don't like to ride in the car for that long."

"But we're doing this for them," she said. "We're doing this to pay for their college."

My heart melted. As usual, Grandma Marlene was thinking of her family. She wanted so badly to leave an inheritance for her great-grandchildren. But that didn't change the fact that driving an hour to sell a Beanie Baby for twelve dollars just didn't make any sense.

I offered to sell them online, but she was convinced that Bob was the only one we could trust to give us a fair price. I told her that if Bob offered us twenty dollars for one of the Beanie Babies that maybe I could make the drive then. I tried to explain things as gently as I could, but I know I hurt her feelings, and we both wound up in tears.

"I'm sorry I bothered you," she said. "I'm old, and my kids are all grown up. I guess I forgot how busy you must be with your little ones." She sighed. "I think I'm the only one who has time to care about all of these silly Beanie Babies I bought."

"Grandma, it's not that we don't care," I said. "It's a nice thing that you did for all of us."

"No, it was a nice thing I *tried* to do," she said sadly.

Grandma Marlene continued to collect and give out Beanie Babies until her death a few years later. By the time she died, she'd given dozens of assorted Beanies to my husband, my children, and me.

After her funeral, our family began the arduous task of cleaning out Grandma Marlene's house. She'd collected many things with the same passion she'd collected the Beanie Babies. Her house was full of dolls, toys, stuffed animals, and every kind of collectible you can imagine.

"What are we going to do with all of her stuff?" a family member asked.

But I knew exactly who to call: Beanie Baby Bob from the flea market. I'd seen him at the funeral, and he'd been beside himself at the loss of his friend.

Bob came to Grandma Marlene's house, and he brought friends with him: Donna, who collected and sold dolls at the flea market; Mary, the Precious Moments lady; and Sarah, whose stall at the flea market contained a little bit of everything.

"Has your family been able to choose a few things to remember her by?" Bob asked me quietly.

I nodded. "Yes, but we won't need them. No one who met my Grandma Marlene ever forgot her."

Bob smiled sadly. "You're right about that, honey."

Bob and his friends spent hours going through Grandma Marlene's things. When they'd taken what they wanted, Bob called more flea-market friends, and they did the same thing.

For a whole week, our family took turns manning the giant sale at Grandma Marlene's house. And when it was over, we'd raised enough money that each of her great-grandchildren had $1,000 with which to start a college fund.

None of us ever sold a Beanie Baby for any serious money, but Grandma Marlene's greatest wish had come true after all.

~Jenny Wilson

59

Gangsta Billy

*Smart phones… making the world look drunk and
literate one auto-correct at a time.*
~Author Unknown

It started when we got my grandmother an iPhone. Technology
had never been her forte; we had laminated lists and handwritten directions on sticky notes all throughout her house
to help guide her through things like changing the input on
her television so she could watch a movie, and then how to change
it back again to watch cable. Despite these notes and directions, I
would often get a phone call when she wanted to do something tech-
nological that I had helped her with on a previous day. It was endear-
ing, and any reason to talk with my grandmother was fine by me.
But I could sense her hesitation with the smart phone, and I would
be lying if I didn't admit I had my own misgivings when the family
wanted to get her set up with one.

She had had an iPad for a few months and seemed to be managing
well with Facebook, e-mail, and copying recipes and pictures. There
were a few extra features that made the iPhone more complicated, plus
the screen and keyboard were smaller. Nonetheless, we all took a deep
breath as a family and embarked on this new adventure of teaching
our grandmother to use an iPhone.

It took a little time, but she caught on quite quickly. Before I
knew it, I was receiving text messages… from my grandmother! It was
incredible, since I knew quite a few people in my parents' generation

who were still resisting the move toward smart phones. I loved being able to communicate with my grandmother more frequently throughout the day, and thought she was the coolest grandma ever.

We set up a group text for her so she could text all of us at once when she had a message of common interest, for example the next morning, when she was making biscuits and gravy for everyone. She texted us all to come for dinner when she wanted to use her new spaghetti serving-bowl. My grandmother loved nothing more than to cook, entertain, and have her family together in one room.

So texting proved to be convenient for everyone, and my grandma liked how connected it allowed her to be with the family throughout the day, despite everyone's complicated work schedules.

I have found the most difficult thing about texting with people of a certain age is the use of acronyms or abbreviations, such as LOL (laughing out loud) or SMH (shaking my head). These are standard abbreviations for younger people, but more difficult to figure out for people who did not grow up with smart phones.

We were texting as a family one evening — all of us spread out across the state of Colorado — and my grandmother created her own shorthand. We were getting ready to sign off, and she sent a text that said "gnstgbyaily." She was answered with many question marks, but then my aunt replied, "Think about it."

Hmmm, the more I thought about it, the more confused I became. Another text from my aunt came through: "Think about what Nanny always says before we go to bed." That did it. It was the magic light bulb that triggered all of our sleepover and childhood memories with our grandmother. Before we went to bed, she would always say, "Good night, sleep tight, God bless you, and I love you" before gently kissing us on the forehead and tucking us in to sleep.

"Gnstgbyaily" became a ritual. It was how everyone in the family started signing off at night.

Then, one night, I had gotten a new phone. When I signed off and typed in my "gnstgbyaily" to signal to my family I was heading off to bed, my phone auto-corrected before I realized it, and I sent the words "Gangsta Billy." Oh, man! I quickly began typing to correct this silliness of auto-correct when I got an uproarious response of laughing emojis and LOLs flooded my screen. "How did your phone even auto-correct to that?" my aunt inquired. I had to admit, it was quite hysterical, and became our new family favorite. My phone lovingly contributed and learned this new habit of mine when I texted within my family. The first time my husband saw "Gangsta Billy" written across my phone from a text my grandmother had sent to the family, his face scrunched up, and he inquired, "Who is this Gangsta Billy your grandmother is talking about?"

I couldn't stop laughing, but I eventually settled down and told him the origin of our newest family member.

~Gwen Cooper

60

All by Himself

Small cheer and great welcome makes a merry feast.
~William Shakespeare

My second year in college had started. I hadn't decided whether to fly home for Thanksgiving yet. Although I had missed the holiday the year before, and I didn't want to miss it two years in a row, I didn't have the money for the ticket, plus I wasn't sure I could get enough time off from my job.

All that wondering changed when my mom called. She got right to the point: "Your grandmother isn't doing well. Your dad and I decided I should fly out there for Thanksgiving." Mom was an only child, so that made sense to me. But I was not ready for what I heard next. "We decided you would want to come along so I covered your ticket."

My mom was a whiz at logistics. "I will fly from Alabama, and you can fly from Minnesota. We will meet in Northern California the afternoon before Thanksgiving. Your dad and the younger kids will stay home for Thanksgiving at our house. I will have all the holiday preparations done so they can just pop the turkey in the oven on Thanksgiving morning."

As always, Mom's plan went off without a hitch. I met her at the Oakland airport, and we took a taxi to our hotel.

When we got in the door, Mom promptly called my grandpa. "Would you like us to come over and get the holiday meal ready for tomorrow, Dad?" She was disappointed when she hung up the phone.

"Your grandfather doesn't drive at night anymore, and your grandmother is already resting for the night. He will pick us up sometime tomorrow morning."

Mom was anxious to see her parents, especially her mother, who was really fragile. But Grandpa didn't show up until well after nine in the morning.

When we finally got to their house, we got to say hello and then Grandpa helped Grandma lie down again and banished us to the living room, telling us we would eat Thanksgiving dinner at noon. He went into the kitchen.

Mom paced the floor. Finally, I asked her what the matter was. She didn't appreciate the question. "He can't cook," she hissed. "How's he supposed to fix a Thanksgiving meal for us?"

I tried to reason with her. "Can't you smell dinner? It smells divine to me. Grandma is upstairs resting. Grandpa is the only one who could be cooking." But we couldn't see through the kitchen door.

She had an idea. "Let's sneak out the front door and see what's going on. Then we will know who is really cooking." Grandpa was very hard of hearing, so he didn't hear us leave. It was a crazy plan, but I followed her around the house to the kitchen windows. There we watched Grandpa fill water glasses and make coffee, undetected. "When did he learn to make coffee?" Mom asked out loud. We ran back around the side of the house and into the living room.

We should not have done that because it made Mom worse. "I tell you, he can't cook." She continued to pace in the tiny living room. Finally, Grandpa came through the kitchen door. It was almost noon by then.

Speaking directly to my mom, he said, "I am going to get your mother up and bring her down to eat with us. You two — go sit down at the dining room table. Stay out of the kitchen!" So we did.

When Grandma got situated at the table, Grandpa sat down and said grace. Then he got up and started making trips back and forth through the kitchen door: first he brought the water, then the coffee, then a couple of relish trays, rolls and individual lettuce salads he had poured out of one of those premixed plastic bags. You get the idea.

It took forever because he moved slowly, and he only brought out a couple of things at a time.

Then we heard the oven door squeak open. Mom's eyes got big. She stopped answering Grandma's questions because she was listening so hard. The kitchen door opened again, and Grandpa came through with a potholder in each hand. He served Grandma first, with a flourish, and then Mom. The smell of the food was so good I didn't think I could wait any longer. Grandpa came through the door one last time and set hot food in front of me, and then himself. The food was still too hot to eat, so we sat in silence.

Finally, Mom spoke. "Wow, I can't believe it, this smells so good." I started shoveling food into my mouth, careful not to make eye contact with Mom. If I had, surely I would have choked to death from laughter. But I could tell by Grandma's eyes that she had been in on planning this Thanksgiving dinner.

You see, Grandpa had truly made the Thanksgiving dinner all by himself. He had heated and served each of us one of those TV turkey dinners on little metal trays. You know the kind: a little mound of stuffing with a slab or two of pressed turkey on top, a blob of whipped potatoes with not enough margarine and a pile of really bright green peas, but no dessert. It tasted as good as it smelled, and I really don't even like peas.

I guess it shows that it's who's around the table, not what's on it, that makes the food taste so good.

~Pamela Gilsenan

Chapter 7

My Crazy Family

Sometimes You Just Have to Laugh

61

Never Tell Anyone

A secret remains a secret until you make someone
promise never to reveal it.
~Fausto Cercignani

onday night! I've had a pretty awful day at work and a worse forty-five-minute-turned-seventy-minute commute home. After eating something cold out of the fridge, showering and getting in my jammies, I'm just in time to watch *Everybody Loves Raymond*. Feet up on my couch, I'm in for the night. The phone rings.

"Yes?" I answer, barely taking interest.

"You need to come over." It's my dad.

"I'll be right there."

"It's nothing bad," he adds.

"Then I'm not coming; my show's on." Raymond and Robert argue in the background. Yes, I'm recording it, but I intend to stay planted.

"You've got to come. It's good news. And don't tell anyone that you're coming."

"Dad, I'm not going anywhere. I'm already showered and in my pajamas."

"You have to come."

My very cute, very Italian parents, who reside six minutes from the first condo of their only daughter, frequently have insignificant emergencies. Today they have caught me on strike from the world. "You're going to have to tell me what's up or I'm not budging."

A sigh… "Your mom won the lottery."

"A lot of money?"

"A lot! But don't tell anyone!"

"Okay," I say, "I'll get dressed. And who am I going to tell?"

Driving the six minutes to my parents' house, I contemplate getting rich before my soul mate materializes. How will I know if he's interested in my money or me?

Getting to the house, I find my grandmother on the stairs with her walker, my uncle and aunt flanking her. "I'm so happy!" she says when she gets to the top, grabbing my hand and hugging me. This was the grandmother who never hugged.

A party is starting before my eyes. Everyone greets each other warmly like it's been so long since Sunday dinner at Grandma's house yesterday. All the liquor in the house is now on the kitchen counter. Most of the bottles, some still in boxes, have a layer of dust on them. My brother Jim grabs my hands and tries to lead me in a weird jig.

At the kitchen table, Mom writes a list. She has been allocating her lottery winnings. First on the list are the retired nuns. *Retired Nuns? Where did that come from?* Second, she intends to pay off Jim's car and my own; that's fair, I think sarcastically. Jim's car is a new sports car that he rolled off the lot last week; I've made about 180 of 350 payments on my far more practical used car, but whatever.

Suddenly, I remember a friend who said a prayer for my mom in Rome. Prior to his trip, he had collected everyone's intentions and was praying throughout his sabbatical. He'd told my mom that when he'd actually seen the pope waving from a distance, all he could think of was "Marie Farella's special intention." She'd beamed when he'd told her that.

"Mom," I ask, "was this the special intention you'd asked Ron to pray for you in Rome?"

She looks down, blushing and smiling. Guilty as charged.

"Well, I'm happy for you!"

I hear my father announce that he has called the state lottery number, but they don't know that there's a winner yet. That doesn't sound right. I walk over to look at the ticket on the counter. Next to it is the newspaper, open to yesterday's winning numbers.

Uncle John is leaning over it, matching the numbers. I hear his brain wheels turning. Looking over his shoulder, I stare at the newspaper and the ticket in turn. Stupidly, I hear myself ask, "Wait, could she have won more than one lottery? These *all* seem to match yesterday's. All the winning numbers match for *each* type of lottery."

He snaps out of it. Grabbing the ticket, he looks to my mom. "Wait! This is the slip from the gas station! The one they print out when you ask for yesterday's winning numbers. Where's your lottery ticket from yesterday, Marie?"

Mom looks like she's been slapped. Reality hits the entire room. Mom looks for her purse. When she returns with the actual lottery ticket that she'd purchased, it has only three matching numbers. Everyone has been reveling in the winning numbers on the print-out given to her *today* by the cashier at the gas station, which displays the winning numbers from yesterday and looks very much like a lottery ticket. We all look at her dumbfounded. Ours for only minutes, the treasure is gone.

"You ruin everything!" my brother yells at me. All of this is suddenly my fault. New dust gathers on the champagne and the other bottles. The celebration ends. No nuns, no car payments, no special intention prayer to the pope answered. We are middle-class-broke once again.

We all look to my mother. She sits at the kitchen table, completely deflated. "Promise me," she calls to us all, "you will never, ever tell anyone about this."

~Gina Farella Howley

62

Saturday Morning Wrestling

[Television is] an invention that permits you to be
entertained in your living room by people you
wouldn't have in your home.
~David Frost

My great-grandmother was a hefty woman less than five feet tall, with hands that were gnarled from years of arthritis. Her swollen legs were encased in stretchy elastic bandages. The floors in her modest home were uneven, so she steadied herself by pressing her hands against the wall as she moved about.

Though her short body was bent and disabled, her mind was as sharp as a tack and she was always at her best. I never saw her wearing anything but a black dress with a dainty, crocheted lace collar. Her peppered white hair was always braided into a bun.

I rarely saw her smile, and when she did it was ever so slight. She didn't have much to say about anything either, unless it was in a very meek and quiet voice. She only spoke when she felt she really had something important to say, which wasn't often.

Her six-foot-tall husband towered over her. He was definitely the voice of the family. He was tall, strong, and vigorous; she was short and quiet, but kind.

They spent their early mornings at the kitchen table with freshly brewed coffee and some fabulous baked treat just recently pulled from the oven. There was always room for something sweet, and Grandma made sure it was on the table each day.

She wasn't one to show her emotions, so her children had a hard time buying her gifts that would seem to make her happy. When they bought her one of the first televisions in their small town she said it was an extravagant gift and a total waste of money.

There wasn't much on the tube in those early years except local news shows, some children's programming — and wrestling. The satin-clad wrestlers would enter the ring, each sporting some kind of flashy outfit to set him apart. Muscles bulged, and strength exuded from every pore. Grandma was transfixed.

With each slam to the floor, she would scream at whoever was winning and say how mean he was. If the tables turned, and the former victim now had his opponent in a hammerlock, she rose to the defense of the new underdog. It was comical how she shifted from favoring one to the other. Everyone tried to tell her that it was staged, but she was convinced that it was absolutely true.

She'd wring her lace handkerchief tightly around her twisted fingers. Her wrinkles seemed to deepen as she became involved in the "contest." When it was over, she ranted on and on about the savage behavior of the two wrestlers. She didn't miss an opportunity to tell anyone about what she had witnessed and how vulgar it was. For the rest of the week, she'd be talking to the mailman, milkman, neighbors, pastor and everyone else in town about the barbaric behavior going on in her living room each Saturday morning.

Who knew a tiny screen in a huge console could hold someone captive for one hour a week and give her enough to talk about for seven days? The following Saturday, she'd plant herself in front of the TV and watch the mayhem all over again.

Simple pleasures.

~Kathy Boecher

63

The Spurs Don't Suck

*But I learned that there's a certain character that
can be built from embarrassing yourself endlessly.
If you can sit happy with embarrassment,
there's not much else that can really get to ya.*
~Christian Bale

It wasn't Aunt Susie's ample bosom, colorful wardrobe, or ever-changing hairstyle that cemented her status as the "crazy aunt" of our family. One would be hard-pressed to find anyone who wouldn't agree that it was because Aunt Susie always said whatever she wanted, whenever she wanted. No matter who was around.

As a young woman in my twenties, I found Aunt Susie's blunt style to be incredibly embarrassing. Despite this, there was something about the way she told a story. Call it morbid curiosity on our part, but when Aunt Susie spoke, the family gathered around to listen.

It was 1999 when I arrived at my parents' home for a family dinner to find Aunt Susie sitting on the loveseat with a Poodle in her lap and a Miniature Dachshund standing guard at her feet. The entire family was there, all seated around the odd trio. My sister motioned for me to pull up a chair, and then leaned over and whispered in my ear, "Aunt Susie is telling us about her day. She said something crazy happened. Don't worry, she just started."

Great, I thought. *I hope this doesn't take all day.* I could smell the pot roast from the other room, and my stomach growled.

Aunt Susie looked in my direction and nodded at me before addressing our tribe. "I'll start again so Melissa doesn't miss anything."

I groaned internally as my aunt began her story for a second time.

"Now y'all know that I recently took a job with the newspaper," Aunt Susie said proudly.

Yes, we all knew. Aunt Susie had started selling newspaper subscriptions for the *San Antonio Express-News*. We agreed it was the perfect job for her. It got her out of the house and allowed her to do one of her favorite things — talk to people.

"Well, in celebration of the San Antonio Spurs' recent NBA championship victory, the newspaper put together a commemorative package they are offering to new subscribers. The Sunday paper even contains a large fold-out poster of the team!" Aunt Susie added.

I wonder if Mom made mashed potatoes and gravy, I thought to myself. I wasn't a huge basketball fan, and I wasn't sure where my aunt was going with this story. Hopefully, she'd make it quick.

"I'd just arrived at the drugstore to set up my subscription table," Aunt Susie continued. "I pulled a large Spurs promotional poster out of the car and set it on the ground. That's when I heard a car honking and some crazy woman yelling at me for no good reason."

"Oh, no. What did she say?" my cousin asked.

"She said, 'The Spurs suck!'" Aunt Susie answered with a solemn look on her face.

Oh, my. I may not have been their number-one fan, but the Spurs definitely didn't suck. The people of San Antonio were incredibly proud of their team. Everyone loved the Spurs, or so I thought.

"And she just kept screaming it over and over… 'The Spurs suck, the Spurs suck.' When I wouldn't respond to her, the woman started making frantic hand motions… pointing her finger at me."

"What did you do?" I wanted to know, now fully invested in Aunt Susie's story.

"I just ignored her. She finally threw her hands up in the air and drove off. At the time, I figured she saw my Spurs poster and was trying to stir up some trouble. Anyway, I gathered my papers and my poster, and I went inside the store. I began to set up my subscription table when a woman came over, put her hand on my shoulder, and began to whisper in my ear." Aunt Susie paused for dramatic effect.

It worked. The family all leaned in closer.

"The woman whispered, 'Excuse me, ma'am, but your skirt's stuck.'"

Aunt Susie looked out over our puzzled faces before clearing things up.

"The back of my skirt was tucked, very deeply I'm afraid, into my pantyhose. As soon as she told me, I twisted around to get a look for myself, and let me tell you, she wasn't lying. That's when I realized that the woman honking at me in the parking lot wasn't saying, 'The Spurs suck.' She was yelling, 'Your skirt's stuck.'"

My mouth fell open. I was embarrassed—no, make that horrified—for poor Aunt Susie. She sat on the loveseat looking from person to person. I met her gaze just as her lips started to curl up and that "Aunt Susie twinkle" came alive in her eyes. She started to chuckle, and then she began to laugh. Hard. One by one, my entire family joined in until we were grabbing our sides with one hand and wiping away tears with the other.

That was the day I decided I was no longer embarrassed by Aunt Susie. As a matter of fact, I hoped to be just like her one day... a woman who speaks her mind, doesn't take herself too seriously, and is able to laugh in the face of life's most embarrassing moments.

I'm in my mid-forties now, and I proudly wear the "crazy aunt crown" passed down to me from good ol' Aunt Susie. I still haven't mastered the bright clothes and crazy hair, but I've got a pretty good grasp on all the rest. I did, after all, learn from the best.

~Melissa Wootan

64

My Forward Thinking In-Laws

Be kind to your mother-in-law but pay for
her board at some good hotel.
~Josh Billings

My mother-in-law didn't know me well yet when I stayed at her home while my new husband was at his twelve weeks of boot camp. She became over-protective of me, and automatically assumed I'd require her constant guidance and help with everything.

But in reality, since both my parents held full-time jobs, I'd done all my family's cooking, housework, chores, and after-school errands since age nine. I had developed organizational skills, including the habit of resetting our family clocks on the Saturday evening before every switch between standard time and daylight savings.

On that particular Saturday evening, I set the bedside clock and my wristwatch one hour ahead before going to sleep. Sunday morning, while I was at church, Mom-in-law took for granted I'd need her assistance. Convinced I couldn't possibly know or remember on my own, she didn't even bother to check the time. (It hadn't dawned on her that I'd somehow managed to get up, bathe, dress, and leave for church on time.)

She entered my bedroom and set the alarm clock an additional hour ahead. Earlier, she had murmured to her husband that if left to my own devices, I'd certainly arrive an hour late for work Monday morning. Later, unaware that she'd already remedied that possibility, he too entered the bedroom and added yet another hour.

Before retiring on that Sunday evening, I double-checked the alarm-clock setting. How strange! It was two hours fast. So I fixed it.

At breakfast, Mom-in-law sat gloating at the kitchen table. "See — you'd still be in bed fast asleep if it wasn't for me."

"What do you mean?" Dad-in-law chimed in. "She's got me to thank. I'm the one who set the alarm clock ahead for her."

I grinned, bid them good morning, then followed my usual preparatory ritual, and headed out to my office. Still deeply entangled in their intense debate over who deserved the credit, they both lost track of time and arrived late to their jobs, where their co-workers teased them about forgetting to set their clocks ahead for daylight savings time.

~Florence C. Blake

65

Can You Hear Me Now?

Give up all hope of peace so long as
your mother-in-law is alive.
~Juvenal

My mother-in-law was from the "old country." Her knowledge of modern technology was, to be polite, limited. Very limited. Just about nonexistent. She was perfectly capable of understanding how to use these newfangled devices, but she had no interest in learning. She was content with the old ways. They had worked for her for years, so please don't try to show her any new contraptions, even if they would make her life easier. Her mind was made up, and she knew she was right.

She did love watching television and didn't ever want to miss her special shows, so she mastered the on-and-off switch and channel-selector dial very quickly. But forget about teaching her to use the remote control. We tried so that she wouldn't have to get up each time she wanted to change the channel. It was a lost cause.

My family and I were into technology. We had computers, cell phones, fancy TVs — all the latest things. And, oh my goodness, we even had a machine that answered our phone and recorded messages for us when we were out. What a novel idea! We told my mother-in-law about the answering machine, showed it to her and explained how it worked. Over and over. We played the greeting for her that I had recorded. It was such a pleasant greeting. Good luck with that! She just looked confused. The concept didn't register. She couldn't figure it out.

My mother-in-law would call our house and, if we were out, my voice would greet her and ask her to leave a message. That was the first problem. She wasn't absolutely delighted with me in the first place because I had married her son. Truth be told, she wouldn't have thought anyone was good enough for him, so I tried not to take her attitude too personally. But now she liked me even less. She felt that I was being very rude and insulting to her when I answered the phone but wouldn't talk. And why did I tell her to leave a message? Why didn't I just talk to her?

Here's something else about my mother-in-law that is important to understand: When she would call at night and we were not home — and if we had forgotten to tell her we wouldn't be home — that meant something was terribly wrong. She knew we were all dead. In a ditch. Or we were in the hospital having major surgery and were not expected to live. Or we were lost in the mountains without food or water, and we were going to freeze to death. Couldn't we just be out to dinner, or at a party with friends, or at a movie? No way.

So when she would call and get our answering machine, she would freak out. And how did we know this? We would listen to her messages when we got home.

"Hello, Barbara. I want to tell you that Aunt Rose called." (Long pause.)

"Barbara? Hello? Can you hear me?" (Longer pause.)

"Barbara! Don't you care? Talk to me. Well!"

And then she'd hang up and call right back.

"Hello? HELLO?? HELLO! Barbara? BAR-BAR-A!! I know you are there. I can hear your voice. Why don't you talk to me? Well!"

When my name turned into three syllables, I knew I was in trouble.

The best part is when she would decide that our number was not working correctly and have the operator try to call. Wow, would she get mad. Poor operator. When we would come home and listen to our messages, we could hear the entire conversation.

"Madam, there is nothing wrong with this number."

"Then why can't I talk to them?"

"I'm sorry, Madam. I don't think they are at home."

"Then why does my daughter-in-law answer the phone? She's there."

"Ma'am, that's their answering machine. It's a tape. It's just her voice."

"What do you mean? A tape? Why is her voice on a tape? I know she's there."

"Ma'am, they have a machine that answers the phone when they're not home."

"How is that possible? I know they are there, and they're just not talking."

"LISTEN, LADY. Leave them a message. There is nothing I can do."

"Well, you have some nerve talking to an old lady like that!"

You get the picture. There was just no way for her to grasp the concept and understand this type of technology. When we would get home, listen to our messages and call her back, she would tell us there was something wrong with our phone, and that she had to call the operator to help her. Then she would berate the operator for not doing her job and not being able to get her call through to us because she knew we were there. Of course, she knew I was there because I had answered the phone!

My mother-in-law is no longer with us. She never, ever did understand the concept of an answering machine, and we stopped trying to explain it to her. She never, ever completely forgave me for marrying her son either, but she and I did eventually make our own kind of peace. And now every time I hear my own voice on my answering-machine tape, I remember those messages she would leave, and it makes me smile.

~Barbara LoMonaco

66

Papa's Biggest Mistake

*So many tangles in life are ultimately hopeless that we
have no appropriate sword other than laughter.*
~Gordon W. Allport

It was Papa who flushed the toilet. Mama said that was his biggest mistake ever.

Papa had a doctor's appointment that morning, and he was in the house getting ready. Mama knew we had a friend coming over to knock down our old brick well house, which was too small. He had told Papa if we ever needed to have work done on the well or the pump, there would be a problem because there was just no room to work in there. Papa wanted to make sure we never had that problem and decided to have the small brick well house torn down and a bigger well house built around the equipment.

Mama decided to check and make sure nothing needed to be moved out of the old well house. She told us she removed the top, looked in and saw about a gazillion spiders, which she knew had to be black widow spiders because they were… well, black. Not wanting to bother Papa or make our friend mess with the spiders, she decided to get rid of them herself. She had the perfect solution… or so she thought. Mama took a bug bomb, opened the top of the well house, clicked on the bug bomb, dropped it in the small brick structure and slammed the top back down.

Mama had just reentered our house when... *ka-boom!* When the windows stopped rattling, she heard Papa yell, "What the...!" and the phone was ringing. Mama went for the phone because, as she said, it sounded like Papa was, well, busy.

"Did you hear that explosion?" an excited neighbor hollered in her ear.

"Uhh... well, yeah," Mama said as she glanced out the window. The pump was wobbling back and forth, but thankfully it was still in place. "I... uhh... I have to check on... I'll call you back."

About thirty minutes later, our friend arrived. "I thought you needed me to tear down the well house. It's gone, and there are bricks all over your yard. Have the grandkids been playing with the old bricks?"

Papa turned around, raised an eyebrow, looked at Mama and then back at him. "Yep, it's gone alright. Seems my wife decided to give you a little bit of help this morning." Then he proceeded to explain what happened. I listened because I was curious, too.

He explained calmly, "I was in the bathroom, sitting down, minding my own business. I reached behind me and flushed the toilet. That flicked the switch in the well house. The switch sparked and ignited the fumes from the bug bomb. There was an explosion so powerful that it blew up the well house, sending bricks all over the yard. It also sent the water pressure from the water pump back through the pipes and up through the toilet, nearly knocking me off the throne."

After hearing the explanation, I can honestly say I have to side with Mama. Papa was the one who flushed the toilet and blew up the well house. All Mama did was kill the spiders.

~Debbie Sistare

67

My Brother's Haircut

*Laughter gives us distance. It allows us to step back
from an event, deal with it and then move on.*
~Bob Newhart

My father was an eye surgeon and a very practical man who would never waste money. One Saturday morning, he was sitting in our dining room when I returned from Volpe's, the local Italian barber. As I handed him the change from the ten-dollar bill he had given me, he frowned, and I could tell he had something to say.

"We're spending far too much on haircuts in this family." His voice echoed through the first floor of the house. My father was a large man at six feet, four inches tall, and he intimidated my brothers and me. "We need to cut back on what we spend." I took a couple of steps back as he began to talk.

"Those barbers charge far too much. All they do is cut your hair!" He took a deep breath. "*Anyone* can cut hair. *I* could cut hair. There's nothing to it. I could cut hair for everyone in the family — and it wouldn't cost a cent." I could see my father was worked up because his face was turning red in a way I'd never seen before.

"But you've never cut anyone's hair. Don't you think you should let the professionals do it?" My mom spoke softly and frowned as she looked directly at my father.

"How hard is it to cut hair?" He paused. "I know I can do it as well as anyone."

"Are you sure?" My mom's voice wavered a little.

"No problem." My father smiled as he ran his hand through his own hair. He was thoroughly convinced he could cut our hair — and cut it well. He was used to facing medical challenges like corneal implants and detached retinas. When he was determined to do something, there was no stopping him.

"So what are you going to do?" my mom said anxiously.

"I'll do Jimmy's hair. It's long and needs a good cut." Jimmy was my younger brother and was five at the time.

I had this sinking feeling in the pit of my stomach. My father had no idea how to cut anyone's hair, and I was afraid of what he'd do to my poor little brother.

"Jimmy, come down here right now." My brother was upstairs in his bedroom playing with his toys.

Dutifully, my brother came downstairs and into the dining room. "I'm here." His voice was full of trepidation, not knowing the fate that awaited him.

"Jimmy, I'm going to cut your hair so it'll look really nice for church tomorrow."

"Okay," Jimmy said slowly, his eyes watching my father carefully.

"Just sit up here on these phone books I've put on my chair." He then looked at my mom. "Could you get one of those big bath towels for Jimmy?"

Obediently, my mom went off down the hall to the linen cupboard and grabbed a large mauve bath towel. Within a minute, my younger brother was ensconced on two thick phone books stacked on my father's armchair at the end of our dining-room table. The towel was wrapped around his neck and flowed over most of the chair.

The first thing my father did was run his comb through Jimmy's hair, an unruly blond mop. After three minutes of my dad working, I couldn't see any difference. It was still a mess. Then he reached into his "doctor's bag" — a black faux leather bag he brought home with him every evening. Out came a pair of surgical scissors, the kind used to cut sutures, and my father began to cut my brother's hair.

Snip, snip, snip. From where I stood, it looked like he was cutting hair at random — a chunk here and a chunk there. Lots of blond hair was falling on the mauve towel, and some tumbled onto the floor. I could also see two cuts on my brother's scalp.

I knew I couldn't stand to watch my father hack away at my brother's hair, so I retreated to the den at the back of the house. I don't remember what was on television, but it was better than watching the drama unfolding in the dining room. Every couple of minutes, I could hear my brother say "Ouch." And then there was one loud shriek of pain followed by a long period of silence from the dining room.

About twenty minutes later, I heard the grand announcement: "We're all done." My father's voice echoed through the whole house. I didn't want to see what had happened to Jimmy's hair, so I just stayed in the den watching TV. Five minutes later, Jimmy made his way through the door of our den, his blue eyes glazed over.

After thirty seconds, I looked up. "Wow!" was all I could say. Some parts of his scalp were bare, while other places had hair that stuck out in short spikes. I could also see half a dozen places where he'd been nicked by the scissors, but fortunately the cuts had stopped bleeding.

I was at a complete loss for words. I just turned back to the television, which proved to be a good distraction.

The next day, we missed church for some reason, but we ended up going out for dinner Sunday evening. As it happened, we were seated at a table near the main door of the restaurant where all the customers had to pass. Without exception, those who walked by turned to look at my brother and either gasped or looked at him with an expression that said, "We feel your pain."

Throughout the meal, my father, who was always the most talkative one of the family, remained silent. I'm sure he soon knew what all the other diners were thinking. None of us, of course, had the courage to mention Jimmy's haircut, although we were all thinking about it. It was a very awkward dinner.

An older lady with perfectly coiffed gray hair turned to look at Jimmy as she was leaving the restaurant and let out a loud gasp we all heard. The look on her face was a mixture of shock and amazement. She stood on the spot for a long time and then turned slowly and left.

Within a minute, my father announced, "Time to go. We're leaving now." None of us had finished our dinner, but that made no difference. We were all hustled out the door and into the car in under a minute. From that moment on, my father never once mentioned cutting our hair, and his surgical scissors disappeared, never to be seen again.

The next day, my mom took my brother to Volpe's and had his hair shaved completely. A week later, his scalp was fully healed from the injuries, and all was forgiven.

~Rob Harshman

68

Teaching an Old Dog New Tricks

A moment's insight is sometimes
worth a life's experience.
~Oliver Wendell Holmes

My father-in-law is a loud-spoken, gruff man. He is known for yelling and talking harshly. He came into my life when, at seventeen, I started dating his youngest son. The funny thing, though, is that while his own children were intimidated by his tone, I found his loud demeanor funny and bonded with him immediately.

For some reason, I just "get" him and generally love spending time with him. But there is one exception… technical help. I was the one he called when he decided to enter the world of computers, when he bought an iPad, or whenever he gets a new phone. I receive calls when these items "don't work," and I have spent hours on the phone trying to explain why these devices aren't working. And, yes… it is always user error. We live hours away from each other, and trying to picture what he is doing or looking at is often a challenge, to say the least.

Thus, I swore I would never introduce him to another device. Then Christmas rolled around. I must have temporarily lost my mind when I decided we should get him an Amazon Echo, which is the machine you talk to by saying, "Alexa." I hadn't yet seen the very funny *Saturday Night Live* skit about trying to teach an elderly relative to use the device! You can watch it if you search for "SNL Alexa seniors" in your web browser.

We arrived with the Amazon Echo, and I really thought it would be easy since my college-age son was with us to help set it up. Nothing was easy! My father-in-law's gruff behavior was in full force.

The first problem was that he couldn't get her name right — he kept yelling "Alexia" over and over. Once we got that straightened out, I told him to ask her to play his favorite music.

"Alexa... fifty!" he yelled.

"Fifty?" I asked. "What does that mean? Do you want her to play fifties music?"

He got angry. "Yes, that is what I said."

Complete sentences were a foreign concept. We went over it again and again.

"Alexa... Fox."

"Fox?" Again, I explained, "You need to give her more. What is it you are asking?"

We spent all afternoon teaching him the skills needed to use the device. And as we pulled away, my entire family agreed it was the worst gift we could have given him because we were sure he would never understand it.

The next day, my son received three phone messages from my father-in-law asking why he received notifications in his e-mail that he has a Pandora password. My son explained what Pandora was. Once again, we said, "This was the worst gift idea ever!"

How wrong we were. The other day, I received the following e-mail from my mother-in-law.

I am really enjoying Alexa. I don't have a radio downstairs, so now I can play music or listen to the news while I am working in the kitchen and cleaning. Thank you so much for such a thoughtful gift.

I also love the fact that she is training Tom well. He is realizing that it's not how loud you talk; it's HOW you ask when you want something. I could have used her sixty years ago.

So, I guess maybe you *can* teach an old dog new tricks.

~Susan Sanchez

69

Never Let a Genius Plan Your Funeral

*In all affairs it's a healthy thing now and then to hang
a question mark on the things you have long
taken for granted.*
~Bertrand Russell

My dad is a genius, former math and science teacher, perfectionist, procrastinator, always late, and refuses to spend money. One can never win an argument with him. Not a good mix when planning a funeral. My grandfather passed and was cremated. Dad was responsible for the funeral. He did not believe in spending a ridiculous amount of money on an urn, especially when he could make a seal-tight plastic PVC pipe container and encase it in concrete. Not only was this cheaper, but he felt it would withstand years of inclement weather, deterioration, and possible rising from its buried depth if the soil became too saturated.

The family drove from their individual locations to Grandfather's graveside service. It was time for the service, but no Dad and no ashes. We waited... and waited... and waited. Approximately an hour later, Dad showed up with Grandfather's ashes. He was running late because he had waited too long to make his masterpiece, and the concrete hadn't set up enough in time. My deceased grandfather, a preacher and gentle soul, would be rolling in his grave. However, he couldn't

Sometimes You Just Have to Laugh |

because he was firmly encased in PVC and concrete.

Then my grandmother passed. Time for her burial in the same cemetery. Dad had realized how expensive it was to bury Grandfather, so he decided it wasn't necessary to pay all those fees, and he didn't set up anything with the cemetery. However, we didn't find out about this until an hour before the service, when it was raining and he had me, in my dress, and my brother, in his suit, dig a hole with the shovels he had brought. He also brought a tamper to ensure solid compaction. My cousin, who is a preacher, and aunt and family (all very proper) drove in from out of town for the service. They arrived shortly before the service, after we had dug the hole on our own and put away the tools. My preacher cousin was going to perform the service. He began the service as we placed Grandmother, also in her sturdy PVC and concrete, into the ground.

In the middle of the service, we began to hear sirens. My side of the family was aware we had dug our own hole without permission. We watched as the police car headed in our direction, turning onto the outer road of the cemetery. I accidentally let out a variation on "oh shoot" during the middle of my cousin's traditional religious service, and that whole side of the family was appalled, having no idea what was happening. Just as quickly as the police came toward us, they continued to drive past and on to their emergency, which luckily was not ours.

After the service, I apologized for my outburst and said that police make me nervous for some reason. We couldn't tell them what we had done. My aunt did ask how I got mud all over my shoes and dress, but the pouring rain had helped wash away a big part of it.

So, my grandparents were buried and hopefully at peace. But then my mom passed. She was cremated as well. Of course, by now my dad feels that cemetery fees are totally outlandish. Therefore, he wants to wait until he passes so we can bury them at the same time and only incur one digging fee and cheaper overall cemetery fees. Mother, bless her heart, sits on the kitchen counter now, spending another three years to date in the place where she was stuck the majority of her life. Dad has not yet made her PVC urn.

Maybe it's a good thing he wants to be cheap and wait until he passes to bury Mom. That way, we'll be in charge. We'll let Dad have his PVC pipe and concrete urn combo, but Mom will have the sweetest, most beautiful urn we can find.

~Becky G.

70

Am I Dead Yet?

*Painful though parting be, I bow to you as
I see you off to distant clouds.*
~Emperor Saga

My father-in-law, Bill Senior, decided he was ready to die. He had suffered a paralyzing stroke a few years earlier and every part of his body was starting to fail. He was in pain and he felt useless. He was always saying that he had no purpose anymore. Little did he know how important he actually was, how much the family still revolved around him and depended on him.

My husband Bill and I were in New York City for a theater weekend when we got a phone call from my sister-in-law Debbie, with whom Senior was living, informing us that we needed to visit him right away. He wanted to have one last talk with each of us before he passed away. We rushed out to Long Island to say our goodbyes.

We solemnly entered the house and joined our other family members as we waited our turns for an audience with Senior. It was really hard to keep it together, knowing this would be the last time we talked. I loved my father-in-law — he was smart and funny, and we spent a lot of time teasing each other. I admired him, too. He had been the youngest son of a couple who had emigrated to the U.S. from Lebanon. When his father abandoned his wife and four children, his mother ran a restaurant — the first Lebanese restaurant in Manhattan — serving a Wall Street clientele. Bill Senior grew up helping out at the restaurant and learning about finance from the customers. There was no college for him, but his World War II Army service in India provided an excellent further education. When he came home from the war he got into the wine business and ended up owning quite a large wine distributor, one that allowed him to raise four children of his own in much better circumstances than he had experienced as a child.

Now I was going to say goodbye to this amazing man, one whose mind was still sharp at age ninety. Bill Junior talked to him first, and Senior took the opportunity to tell my husband how proud he was of him, something he had found it hard to say over the years. When it was my turn, Senior asked if he had been a good father-in-law. He had, I assured him, and he had done a wonderful job welcoming me — and my children — into the family when I married his son thirteen years earlier. Then he apologized that he would miss my son's wedding the next year.

He ended our talk by telling us that it was a difficult decision but it was time for him to go. It was very sad, and we left in tears, deeply missing him already. We were sure this was really happening — because Senior had decided. And we'd heard stories about elderly people who announced they were going to die, put on their Sunday best, lay down, and did just that.

The next morning, Monday, Bill Senior woke up and said, "Debbie, am I dead yet?" She assured him that he was still alive.

Tuesday morning was a repeat: "Debbie, am I dead yet?"

"No, Dad, you are still alive."

By Tuesday night, my husband was wondering what to do. He had called his father every night for twenty years, except for the last two nights when he didn't want to bother him while he was dying. I'm not sure why we are all convinced that Bill would die when he wanted to, but we really believed that he had it within his power to do so that Sunday.

By Wednesday night, my husband had resumed calling his dad. He just skirted around the issue of the impending death.

Thursday morning, Senior announced that God had spoken to him during the night. In what sounded a bit like Borscht Belt comedy,

God had said, "So what's your hurry?" So Senior decided that he might as well get out of bed and have some breakfast.

Two weeks later, Bill Senior presided over the party for his 91st birthday. He was in good spirits — telling stories and cracking jokes as he sat at the head of a long table in the dining room, one that was packed with his children and grandchildren. We all pretended that our heartfelt goodbyes hadn't happened.

When Senior died five months later, it was in accordance with his wishes. He was in his own bed and there were no doctors, no needles, and no interference. He couldn't speak or open his eyes by then, but he had already said his goodbyes months before. He did such a wonderful thing for the family, giving us the chance to have our "final" talks while he was still lucid and unhurried and capable of conversation.

Harriet Beecher Stowe said, "The bitterest tears shed over graves are for words left unsaid." My father-in-law was a wise man. He made sure that no words were left unspoken.

~Amy Newmark

71

A Diamond in the Rough

The trick to being smart is knowing
when to play dumb.
~V. Alexander

My son has always been a great student. He was always in advanced placement classes in high school. My husband and I have always said he is "book smart" and we are very proud of him but, on the other hand, he doesn't have much in the way of "street smarts." And we all know that you need "street smarts" to get along in the world.

When you have a responsible son, you can trust him with things like credit cards, even in high school. So we gave him a Chevron gas card. But our son couldn't get it to work, no matter how hard he tried. Finally, my husband went to see what the problem was — was our book smart son putting the card in the gas pump upside down or backwards?

My son had a sheepish grin on his face when he came back home. My husband just smirked. Of course the Chevron gas card hadn't worked… my son tried to use it at a Shell station.

I tried to do everything I could to prepare our son for life away at college. I taught him about banking, cooking, which gas card went with which gas station, and even sent him off with a first-aid kit.

I must have done a good job. The first quarter of college went off without a hitch. He did very well in his classes and seemed to settle into college life without too many questions or problems. My husband and I felt great about how mature our son had become and were so proud of his ability to live independently.

Thanksgiving came along, and our son was coming home, flying alone for the first time. Still not ready to completely give up my "mother" responsibilities, I checked him in for his flight from my computer, texted his boarding pass to him, and arranged for the shuttle service to pick him up at his dorm and take him to the airport. All went well. I met him at the airport when his flight landed and he proceeded to share his flight experience with me on our drive home.

"I really lucked out, Mom," he said. "I was seated between two hot girls."

This surprised me because he is on the shy side, so my question was, "Did you talk with them?"

"Yes, I did."

He then told me the three of them talked about a bunch of different things until one of them started feeling sick. The plane was almost empty, and with so many rows of vacant seats, she decided to lie down in her own row. He and the other girl kept talking.

We got home and as our conversation continued, we heard lots of stories about school and college life. Then we all went to bed. While lying in bed, I reflected on the many stories he had shared, including the one about the "hot girls" on his flight… and then it hit me. Why did he sit between the two girls with all the empty seats that were available on the plane? That would be very out of character for my shy son.

In the morning I met him in the kitchen and asked, "Why did you sit between those girls if there were so many empty seats?"

His response was: "I had to sit there. That was my seat number."

Seat number? Your seat number? I began to laugh so hard.

You see Southwest Airlines does not have assigned seats. Between giggles, I explained that Southwest has what they call "festival" seating. Another foreign word to him. He didn't have a clue. I explained that is what it's called when you go to a concert but do not have an assigned seat. You sit anywhere.

He looked at me with a confused look on his face. "But Mom, I checked and the boarding pass you gave me had my seat assignment… B12."

"Oh no! That was not your seat number; that was your boarding group number."

The reality of the situation hit him. We laughed until tears were running down our faces. Those girls must have thought this 6'2" cute guy was so self-assured and bold… or crazy… that he wedged himself between them in a middle seat on an almost empty plane. When we finished laughing my son said that he had actually never felt so confident and he had even asked one of the girls for her phone number. I guess in this case it was good that he wasn't so street smart.

And I guess no matter how hard we try to prepare our kids for life's adventures there are always things a mother forgets to teach her kids. Again, in this case… maybe that's not such a bad thing!

~Michelle Campbell

Chapter 8

My Crazy Family

Blending In

When a Salad
Is Not a Salad

*There is no better way to bring people
together than with desserts.*
~Gail Simmons

erging two families into one through a marriage
is a time full of learning, loving, compromise,
adjustment, and sometimes flat-out humor. The
first time I brought my soon-to-be husband to
meet my extended family was one of those situations.

To set the scene: My wonderful fiancé grew up in a family that
not only knew the names of lots of weird veggies, but knew how to
cook them. When they say they're having salad for dinner, they mean
that salad *is* dinner. It will be both healthy and filling, with sprouts
and nuts and three kinds of dressings made with vinegar. Some sort
of lean protein will be involved about half of the time.

Growing up, my family was more of a meat-and-potatoes group.
We had veggies with every meal, but they were a side dish. Corn
with the chicken. Broccoli or green beans alongside the ham. Strange
vegetables that require lots of preparation need not apply. And as for
sprouts, forget about it.

My fiancé didn't know this.

All unaware, I led my trusting future husband to that minefield known as the "meet-the-family dinner." My young son, my parents and sister, my aunt, uncle and cousins, my ninety-year-old grandmother all gathered around a table with us. The wine was flowing, accompanied by prime rib, baked potatoes, green bean casserole, salad, rolls and our traditional Jell-O salad.

If you've never had a Jell-O salad, it may take some explaining. There are many tasty ways to make this dish, but in this case my grandma (who raised two daughters in the 1950s) makes it with those cinnamon red hot candies, melted down and added to applesauce and lemon Jell-O. This is sandwiched around a middle layer of cream cheese, mayonnaise, walnuts and chopped celery. All of this amazing mixture of things that should not go together, but somehow do, was about to be presented to my fiancé — the one who grew up eating real salads made with actual vegetables.

"Some salad?" my mother asks him, holding out the glass Pyrex pan full of delicious, wobbly, spicy redness.

"Yes, please," he replies. He takes the pan and looks down.

Uncertainty flits across his face, leaving a trace of skepticism behind. He considers the tray in his hands. His future mother-in-law definitely said "salad." He took the "salad." She didn't switch pans on him as she handed it to him, so this must be it. Leaves do not seem to be involved. Lettuce is not making an appearance.

His brow wrinkles in confusion. He actually lifts the pan, since it's see-through, and checks the bottom just in case. Nope. No vegetation on the bottom, either. Sprouts are not waving their little, feathery green heads from inside the red wobbly mystery. Not even a lonely crouton bobs on top of the thing in his hands.

Because he is such a wonderful man, and this is the official meet-the-family dinner, he takes a spoonful and plops it on his plate. This stuff really plops, with some extra splatter and little dribbles of red cinnamon juice. It's a joy to behold. He tries a bite.

By now, everyone at the table is watching him chew.

"It's good," he says to the crowd of fascinated faces. "But this is not salad."

And this is why my husband tells people to this day that he married into a family who calls "dessert" a "salad."

~S.E. White

73

Graduation with My Three Husbands

*Our family is just one tent away from
a full-blown circus.*
~Author Unknown

ollege graduation challenges the multi-wedded. I've
been married three times, and my daughter Star has
a loving relationship with each father figure. So naturally, when David and I celebrated her graduation, my
two ex-husbands were invited.

It was a June evening at Seattle's Pike Place Market. I was talking
to Tom, Ex-Husband No. 1 and Star's biological father, who came to
the restaurant with his mother, Joanne. Twenty-three years divorced,
Tom was considering another go.

Sharing a picture of his girlfriend, he said, "We're talking about
getting married."

"Wow. Congratulations!" I said.

His mom added, "Tom's seeking an annulment from you so they
can remarry in the Catholic Church."

My raised eyebrow signaled, *You don't say!*

But what I was thinking was, *He wants to invalidate the union that
brought your only grandchild into the world? Is that a polite comment to
make to your dinner hostess?*

No time to gnaw on that bone because along came Ken, Ex-Husband

No. 2, with girlfriend Deirdre. I noted his red flannel shirt and jeans, which contrasted with our dressy evening wear — always the rebellious criminal lawyer. Miffed, I pretended not to see him.

Ken tapped my shoulder, and I turned, startled. "Hey, you made it!"

"Of course. You remember Deirdre?"

Deirdre radiated a classy friendliness, and we embraced like old friends. *What is she doing with him?* I thought.

Walking in, our daughter Star's eyes widened in joy, and she grabbed us in a group hug. "I'm so happy you're all here!"

Chic in a black cocktail dress, Star's open back artfully centered her Capricorn tattoo. Red rhinestone pins clipped back her dark, wavy hair. Vampy.

Patrick, her boyfriend, looked brave. Consider the poor twenty-one-year-old consort meeting three dads and Star's mother for the first time. Could one blame him for saying, "Gin and tonic, please?"

My three marriages were flying discreetly under the radar until Grandma Joanne insisted on snapping photos in front of the restaurant. How many combinations can one come up with?

Tom, Star and Joanne

Ken and Star

Deirdre, Ken and Star

Tom and Star

David and Star

David, Star and me

Then Joanne said, "Now I want a picture of the *original* family."

Clenching my grin, I posed with Tom and Star. This led to Ken's request for one of himself, Star and me.

Honestly, how did Elizabeth Taylor do it? It's exhausting. Can we eat now?

At the table, Deirdre shared with me snippets from her life with Ken and waxed devoted. He sat distracted, rubbing his temples while observing others in (no doubt) negative character studies.

Ordering food is good for fifteen minutes of animation.

"I hear the swordfish is great!"

"Ooh, they have lamb."

"I can't eat prawns."

While discussing likes and dislikes, Deirdre said, "You know how Ken can be. You know him better than I do on that subject."

Ain't going there. I laughed, "Oh, no. That's not true. He's very different with you."

Elsewhere, my husband David talked about science. Bio-dad Tom probed Patrick's ambitions while Star nodded encouragement to her champion. A bit tipsy, Joanne peppered the air with non-sequiturs.

Once dinner orders were taken, we went quiet.

Ken zoomed in on Star's boyfriend. "So, Patrick, where did you say you're from?"

"Flint, Michigan."

Ken said, "Well, a lot of people don't know where that is, but I do."

"Yeah, it's way out there," admitted Patrick.

"I'll say! It's where the men are men and the sheep are nervous!"

We could only stare. Patrick looked confused, obviously unfamiliar with animal sodomy.

Ken the merrymaker continued, "What's your state bird anyway — the mosquito?"

I grabbed his arm, rolled my eyes and whispered loudly to Patrick, "Pay no attention. I never did."

Ken shrugged me off, pleased at his ability to loosen everyone up. Deirdre stepped in (gingerly, over the doo-doo) and once again engaged Patrick.

"So Star says you like music."

"Yeah."

"What kind of instrument do you play?"

"All kinds. I can play anything."

"Really? What's your favorite instrument?"

"No favorite, I like them all. I can play them all."

"The piano?"

"Well, no. Not the piano."

"Oh. Most musicians who can play more than one instrument usually play the piano...."

Silence.

Deirdre continued awkwardly, "But I guess not..."

"Toasts! Toasts!" screamed Joanne.

Regrouping, stepfather Ken said, "I propose a toast to Star. Congratulations on your graduation. We are proud of you. A job well-done."

Cheers and clinks.

Bio-dad Tom raised his glass. "Star, I love you with all my heart, and we are so proud of your achievement."

Star looked radiant with the fanfare.

Then Grandma gushed, "Mamma! Now it's Mamma's turn!"

Heck, I memorized my toast a year ago. Dramatic pause.

"Your degree does not define you. What we all want for you will not define you. How you handle the challenges that will come to you will tell us who you are. And if history is any indicator, you will never disappoint."

Approving murmurs. I looked over and knew Ken was reworking another toast in his head — competitive bastard.

The food arrived amid lively camaraderie. We heard about the latest in the law from Ken and what was new in the world of viruses from David. Asia was a hotbed of new architecture, according to Deirdre, and Star fended off all attempts to share memories of her childhood with Patrick.

During dessert, David offered his toast. "Star, we see you now, and you are beautiful. You've always made us proud. And a special toast to Patrick because it took a lot of guts for him to come here tonight and deal with all of us."

We laughed at our bond. Weathered warriors, we knew what lay beyond the door for our little girl — the Real World. School had been her cocoon, and soon she would fly free.

Suddenly, our butterfly took us by surprise. Star's red fingernails held her merlot up high.

"Now I want to make a toast. Thank you to my mom and David for hosting this dinner. And thank you all for coming. This evening is very, very special to me. My entire family is here, and it means so much to have you all together at one table." Star's voice cracked. "I love you all, and I know what it took for all of you to be here today. I will always remember this night."

David's eyes went shiny. Tears rolled down my face. Deirdre sniffled. Tom smiled, and Joanne blurted out, "Honest to God, you're just like me!"

Ken brought an official end to the evening when he announced, "My leg is cramping up. I gotta go."

We sighed collectively. Never before had this group assembled in the same room. Chances were against a repeat performance, but for Star we would lay aside our pride, fears and versions of what happened when. This night was our own milestone in moving forward.

Yes, it was our graduation, too.

~Suzette Martinez Standring

74

A Bountiful and Blessed Meal

*Within our family there was no such thing
as a person who did not matter. Second
cousins thrice removed mattered.*
~Shirley Abbott

I grew up thinking I was related to the entire county. Seriously! My mother was the fourteenth child in a family of fifteen. You know your family is overly large when every possible crush you have is heralded off-limits because "he's your cousin." Needless to say, years later, all those cousins have married and our family has expanded. Every year, we celebrate with a reunion and Thanksgiving meal together, thankful for each other and the past year's blessings. Last year's head count was 641 souls — all from Gerrit and Rolena and their fifteen children.

Technically, we are a small village, and there are always new faces and missed faces. When we walk into the reunion on Thanksgiving evening, we are met with a loud hum of voices and laughter, the squeals of children playing games, and the mixed smells of apple pie, pumpkin pie, turkey and stuffing. We always serve buffet-style, with a notebook at the beginning of the line in which the direct descendants are required to sign our names, which of the original fifteen we belong to and how many people we brought to the reunion.

So it happened that about a month after another epic Thanksgiving reunion, just a few days before Christmas, my cousin, Teresa, was stopped by a gentleman with two little pig-tailed girls in tow at a local store.

"Hello, I'm sorry, but I recognize you from the meal held on Thanksgiving," he said to her.

He went on to explain that the day before Thanksgiving, his wife had left him and his two daughters. Devastated but determined to uphold Thanksgiving for his children's sake, he had dressed and bundled up his daughters, intent on finding a restaurant for a Thanksgiving meal.

There were no restaurants open due to the holiday, but he noticed a large number of cars at the community center and deduced that there must be a community Thanksgiving meal. He took his daughters inside and was met with the crazy chaos of my very large family. They were greeted like they belonged and encouraged to take off their coats. The father pulled up a chair and watched as his daughters quickly took off with new friends to play tag in the gym. He knew a few of the others in the room, but most were strangers.

When the children were summoned from the gym to gather for the prayer and meal, he began to realize this might not be a community meal after all. He noticed families grouping together to get in the buffet line. But his giggling girls were hungry, and the food smelled amazing, so with two little hands in his, he joined the line. However, when he reached the notebook, his suspicions were confirmed.

It wasn't a community event at all. He and his daughters had just crashed a family event. So, he humbly wrote his name in the notebook and noted they were a party of three. He was certain someone was going to call him out on it, but no one said a word. His family enjoyed the meal, and then sat a while longer to have dessert and play a few more games. Then, he bid everyone "goodnight," to the dismay of his daughters, who begged to stay just a little longer.

At this point, Teresa smiled and hugged the newest unofficial member of our family. She told the man he was most welcome, and invited him to come again next year as our family blossoms in all sorts of ways. And, by our deduction, since he does live in our county, he most likely is a cousin anyway!

~C. Joy

75

Who's Who?

What's in a name? That which we call a rose by any
other name would smell as sweet.
~William Shakespeare

My father married his brother's widow
Which quite confused me when I was little.
My aunt, they said, was now my mother
And her son, my cousin, became my brother.

Was I to call him Cuz or Bro?
He looked the same. How could I know?
And saying Mom instead of Aunt
Seemed all wrong. I couldn't. I can't.

Then Father had a son with her.
What was he to me? I wasn't sure.
But now my guesswork had improved.
Maybe "second something once removed?"

But who was I in all this mess?
Just a nobody is what I'd guess.
I wondered, "What is *my* name now?"
"What will they call *me*, anyhow?"

On top of this there came another.
A cuz? A bro? Something or other.
I finally learned, from this crazy litter,
My family name was "Babysitter."

~Kay Conner Pliszka

76

R You Listening?

For years, I'd go to the movies and see guys
doing Boston accents and think, "Oh please,
God, I hope I never have to do that."
~Michael Keaton

I am the product of a mixed marriage — my mother was a Red Sox fan from Boston and my father was born and bred in New York City. I live in Greenwich, Connecticut, in staunch Yankees territory, but only twenty miles south of the Red Sox Nation border. The American League East is at war in my blood. My cousin on my mother's side has worked at Fenway Park his whole life and he gave me a Red Sox hoodie that I love wearing when I am safely outside my local area.

But where I live? Forget it. I dared to wear my Red Sox hat *once* while walking in our neighborhood. And sure enough, I took it off for one second when I got hot, and a bird pooped right on my head — a big pile right where the emblem with the two red socks had been. Even the local birds had noted my treachery.

Boston is on my mind a lot because my son and daughter-in-law live there now, surrounded by people who sound just like my mother. Why do I bring this up? Because I remember fondly the day more than twenty years ago when I was talking to the kids about "foreign countries" and they insisted they had already been to one. They explained that every time we visited my parents we went to a foreign country.

In reality, my parents lived twenty minutes away. Where had they gotten the idea that Grandma and Grandpa lived in a foreign country? Well, they explained, Grandma had a foreign accent and she lived in a place with a foreign name — Chappaqua — in New York State. So "New York" must be a foreign country. I had no idea that for years I was getting credit for taking my children on exciting weekend trips out of the country!

My mother's "foreign" accent was always a source of amusement in our family. When she drove me to my freshman year of college, she actually said the very cliched "oh look, they opened the gates so we can pahk the cah in Hahvahd Yahd" as we pulled up to the front of my dorm. I always teased my mother and dared her to pronounce words with an "r." She would struggle and slowly enunciate the words, with only the faintest trace of an "r" no matter how hard she tried. But give her a word like "idea" and up popped an "r" right where it didn't belong. What's an "idear" anyway?

One of my favorite stories about my mother's accent was when she tried to buy some dark chocolate bark a few years ago in a candy store in touristy Annapolis, Maryland. Mom told the salesclerk that she wanted some of the "dahk bahk" in the glass case. Considering all the foreign tourists who visit Annapolis, the home of the Naval Academy, the clerk assumed that English was not my mother's first language. She explained that she couldn't understand my mother's accent, so would she please spell what she wanted? My mother proceeded: "D-A-AH-K B-A-AH-K." No luck. She left the store empty-handed, foiled by her Boston accent.

After my mother had a stroke, which resulted in her losing some language skills, I had to pull the speech therapists aside and explain to them that her Boston accent was not the result of aphasia. I didn't want them to try to reinstate an "r" sound that had never been there anyway. They had actually been trying to teach her how to say words with R's in them, so they appreciated the heads-up.

At my mother's memorial service I told some stories about her various unique characteristics, including her Boston accent and how she was often misunderstood. My cousin who works at Fenway "Pahk" came up to me after and said it was the best funeral speech he ever heard but he didn't really understand my comments about my mother's accent because he "had never noticed that she had one."

And that's why I love going to Boston, where the pahking is difficult and the snowy, cold winters are hahd. In the meantime, I still get to talk to the other side of the family, the New York side, which can't pronounce R's either. It wasn't until my Park Avenue aunt died that I learned that her best friend's last name wasn't "Shera," but was "Sherer." And we love to tease my Brooklyn-born husband about his R's. And his L's too. He can't for the life of him pronounce one of his favorite beverages, the "Arnold Palmer," so he always has to order a half-iced-tea-half-lemonade.

~Amy Newmark

77

Stepping Up to the Plate

It takes a strong man to accept somebody else's
children and step up to the plate another
man left on the table.
~Ray Johnson

"**A**re you out of your mind, Imogene? He has three kids! He's in the Army Reserve and could be called up. He has a lousy civil-service job! His mother is part of the package. And he has no money! Are you crazy?" As my red-faced aunt stormed out of the house, she turned to me with one last parting shot.

"Your mother," she snarled, "is out of her mind! It's as easy to fall in love with a rich man as with a poor one."

Aunt Dorothy was Daddy's older sister, and the only relative of his we had. I knew she missed Daddy as much as we did. Daddy died when he was forty-five, after a lifelong battle with juvenile-onset diabetes. When he died, I was eight, and my little brother was four. Because Daddy had been sick for so long and couldn't always work, we had very little money. We did have a large, three-story ramshackle house and a car, but that was about it. Mommy was working full-time, but not earning very much.

On the afternoon Aunt Dorothy marched out of the house, I had more things to worry about than whether or not my mother was crazy.

Mommy had told me that Bob Mitchell was going to be my stepfather.

"I know it's only a little over a year since your father died. I'll always love him, and no one can take his place," she explained. "I hope you will learn to love Bob, too."

I already liked him, his three sons, and his mother, who had been taking care of his boys since his wife died. She would be living with us, too.

My problem? What could I possibly call Bob Mitchell now that he was going to be my stepfather? I couldn't call him Mr. Mitchell after he and Mommy got married. Mommy suggested that I call him Uncle Bob during their engagement, but I knew that he wasn't my uncle so that would be a lie. I couldn't call him "Daddy," the term I always used for my own father. "Dad" was too close to Daddy.

While I was trying to come up with a name, I didn't call Bob Mitchell anything, which was awkward. I made things worse when I refused to get in the car with him. I was walking home from the beach, and Bob Mitchell stopped and offered me a ride.

"I'm sorry. I can't get in the car with you. Mommy says I can't get in cars with strangers."

When I got home, I could hear them talking in the kitchen.

"Imogene, we're getting married in a few weeks, and she still thinks I'm a stranger!"

Bob Mitchell sounded very unhappy. I knew I had to start calling him something besides "Mr. Mitchell" and came up with a plan. I would call him "Pop."

I had called Daddy "Pop" just once. Daddy was a stickler for proper grammar. When I called him "Pop," he glared at me with disapproval. "Pop," he said, "is soda, like Coca-Cola. Do not call me Pop. I am not a bottle of soda." He snapped his newspaper open in front of his face and left me standing there, blushing. I could feel the chill all the way across the room.

I decided I'd slip in "Pop" when I got the chance and see what Bob Mitchell did. I was at the end of my possibilities. If Bob Mitchell objected to being addressed as if he were a bottle of soda, I'd find out soon enough.

The next time Bob Mitchell came over, I said, "Hi, Pop," and waited for the explosion. His blue eyes filled with tears of happiness. He grabbed me and gave me a big hug.

"Imogene," he called to Mommy, "she called me Pop!"

If only all of the "step" problems were so easily solved.

No one had asked the kids their opinion about anything because we were just "the kids." Each one of us had lost a parent. The advice: Get over it. Pop's boys were moved from the home where they'd grown up and from the schools they'd attended to live in our house, miles away. My younger brother and I felt as if the Mitchells were invading *our* house. The advice: Get used to it.

On the morning of Mommy and Pop's wedding, I woke up to the sound of loud bangs. I heard Beau and Bill, Pop's teenage boys who would become my stepbrothers in a few hours, laughing like crazy. They were dropping lit cherry bombs into soup cans and throwing them out of the upstairs windows.

Mommy and Pop said their vows: "For better or worse, until death do us part," they pledged. They were so brave. They had no idea of the "worse" they were getting into.

Many explosions followed as the parents did their best to squeeze two families, two sets of furniture, and one grandmother inside a house that suddenly seemed too small. My worries about what to call my new stepfather were trivial compared to the tornado that was about to hit our home because the kids didn't "get over it" and we didn't "get used to it."

Each one of us had a hard time finding a place in the new living arrangement. We were jigsaw pieces that didn't fit, and some of us didn't want to fit. There was screaming and yelling, slamming of doors, and some physical fighting. I was the only girl and stayed out of the brawls, but I did my share of crying and yelling. I spent hours hiding out on a nearby beach, telling all my sorrows to my dog and wishing Daddy could come back.

Eventually, Pop's older boys graduated from high school, and only the three younger kids were left at home. Family life fell into a routine, and the fighting slowed to minor skirmishes.

Then, after years of marriage, much to everyone's surprise, including theirs, Mom and Pop had their own baby, a boy. "It's too good to be true," wrote stepbrother Bill, who was away in the Marines.

We had become a family. We had a brother in common, who belonged to all of us. We had lived through the "worse" and started in on the "better." Not the perfect. But definitely the better.

Throughout Mom and Pop's marriage, Pop walked the tightrope between making me feel like a "step" and taking Daddy's place. As Mom hoped, I grew to love Pop. After several years, I realized that, without thinking about it, I was calling him Dad.

When my husband and I had our first child, a girl, we named her Roberta, in honor of the man who had raised me and loved me as if I were his own. Mom and Dad were married for over twenty years until his death. She followed him a few years later.

Some people aren't as blessed as I am. I had not one, but two, wonderful dads.

~Josephine A. Fitzpatrick

78

Just a Few Big Lies

A half-truth is a whole lie.
~Jewish Proverb

y folks used to come from Baltimore to our home in New England to spend some time during the beautiful autumns. Once, they came for two whole weeks. That was when my husband, Bob, made a bet with me that I couldn't go twenty-four hours without lying to my parents.

"I'm glad you can stay two weeks," I said, as I hugged my mom. Lie.

Bob whispered, "You said you could stand five days max! You're lying already."

"You didn't say when the twenty-four hours started."

"Right now."

Actually, the lying began before I got married. Back then, when I had guts (which meant I did courageous things without obsessing about every conceivable thing that could go wrong), I was giving lectures at the local Cape Cod Community College. One lecture was called "Life After Divorce." Bob was enrolled. That's how we met.

Later on, when we were dating, I lied to my parents about my social life. Bob isn't Jewish. And having been raised in an Orthodox home, I wasn't even allowed to have non-Jewish girlfriends, much less suitors.

But lying used to be easy. When Bob found a carton of spoiled milk in my fridge, I said it was a Jewish tradition. "To commemorate the sour times the Jewish people had on their journey through the desert, we all keep rotten milk in our refrigerators."

When he asked about the blue spots on the rye bread, I said, "That's what makes certain food kosher — the ability to grow mold. Cheese is kosher. So is zucchini. The Hebrew prophets said we should always remember — with age comes new growth."

When Bob occasionally answered the phone when my mom would call, I'd say he was just some local guy who helped me around the house a lot, repairing things.

By the time we were engaged, I made the dreaded phone call home. "Mom," I said, with much throat clearing and nervous sighing, "Bob and I have sort of developed a serious relationship." When I told her we planned to marry, she laughed and said, "I knew that. Bring him home." My mother saw right through my lying. Imagine that.

And so, it is with great humiliation that I admit I lost the twenty-four-hour no-lying challenge when Bob's folks came to visit. We were married by then. Here's what happened.

They had this canine mutant named BooBoo. I'm not prejudiced against small Shih Tzu-type dogs, but there was only one way to describe BooBoo: greasy. He always kept his paws around my calves. When I feigned tenderness as I removed him, my hands got coated with oily yuck. It's easy to figure out how he got his name.

So when Bob's mother asked if we'd take BooBoo when they went on their cruise, what could I say? "He'll throw my feng shui out of whack, thus creating disharmony in my environment?" No. "The projectile vomiting I do when I'm around him is a dander allergy?" No. I said, "Sure, I'd love to." And that's when Bob shouted, "Gotcha!" which made everybody jump.

As my parents grew older and their life-shaping Jewish traditions enveloped them more, their pleasure in my happy mixed marriage grew as well. They pulled off a pretty remarkable transformation, if you ask me.

And so, before each one died, I felt great peace in knowing that my husband was *mishpocheh*, which meant family... not just in my heart, but in theirs.

And that is no lie.

~Saralee Perel

79

One More Day

*Until one has loved an animal a part of one's
soul remains unawakened.*
~Anatole France

xperience fostering retired racing dogs led my husband
and me to believe we could handle anything. Yet nothing
prepared us for what padded into our lives the day we
adopted Ray.

Steve and I had inquired about a sleek, handsome boy who sported
a black-and-white tuxedo coat. Retired due to injury, he had transferred
into foster care almost immediately. Within two short weeks of house
training, he pranced through our door.

Ray had no other place to go. Behind his sweet face lurked a dark
and damaged soul. An atypical Greyhound, Ray possessed an aggressive nature. Wide-eyed and fearful, his strong prey-drive kicked into
overdrive during his foster care with other pets, and he created havoc.
Desperate to find him a home and not deliver Ray to the farm, the
adoption agency rushed him to our door when we offered to adopt.
Our experience with Greyhounds and a home without children or
other animals made us perfect candidates, and we were his refuge of
last resort.

Ray pranced around our house. He tried to understand the enormous world he now lived in, a strange one compared to the confined
quarters he had known for so long. Adjustment would take time,
but his inexperience, and apparently ours as well, made coexistence

interesting.

Patience and training with any new pet is important, but with Ray, it was vital. He tested our limits and tried our patience in every way possible. He did not respond to commands, love, encouragement, or food. He had no idea what we expected of him. In fact, he had no idea that he was a pet, or that he even had a name. Like an alien from another planet, he had no concept of life in our world. He had known only the racetrack, so he sped around our back yard with a crazed look that shouted, "This is what you want from me — to race and to win — right?" And so a new and challenging journey began for all of us.

In a large, scary world, fear manifested in bursts of rage. Ray's hostility coupled with separation anxiety and antisocial behavior were a recipe for disaster. He literally threw himself at the window whenever anyone approached our home. In a canine frenzy, he scratched at windows and doors whenever we left the house. Concerned for his safety and the condition of our home, we crated him. But he resisted and attempted to bust free, so leaving our home became increasingly problematic. The stress we encountered as a result of the stress our dog endured overwhelmed us.

Then things got worse.

We had adopted Ray in the heart of the recession. Two weeks after welcoming him into our family, I lost my job, and then Steve lost his. Now three worried individuals paced anxiously through the sanctuary of our loving home. Our burdens consumed us. Steve and I no longer had any idea how to alleviate the mounting bills or threats to our sanity. Still, we focused on the positive. Time not working provided additional time to teach Ray about life in a house.

Eight weeks after adopting our dog, we hung our heads in defeat, ready to send him back. Ray had consumed our attention 24/7, showing minimal improvement and unabated anger. He attacked the window blinds for obstructing his view, the coffee table for daring to be in his way, and the baby gate for barring his entry. By the end of the second month with Ray, our frazzled nerves had stretched to the breaking point. We discussed alternatives and realized we had only one: returning Ray to the adoption agency, where he would most likely be put down.

"Do we call first thing in the morning or give him another week?" I whispered to Steve. His eyes filled with tears. He shrugged. The question tormented us. We decided to give Ray one more day and then make the call. We saw no other option. Ray was too aggressive to enroll in obedience training and too unpredictable to leave home alone. He'd shown slight improvement — at last, he knew his name — but little will to change, and his aggression persisted. The quality of life for all of us had deteriorated. Something had to give.

I knelt down beside Ray that night, hugging him tight. Tears stained my face as I whispered into his ear. "Please, Ray, please try harder. You must be good tomorrow, or we'll have to send you back. We want you to stay, but you have to want it, too!"

As if my words had struck a chord of meaning deep within him, the next morning Ray's attitude was transformed. Calm and mindful, he came when called and responded to commands. He still had a long way to go, but now exhibited a willingness to learn and behave. All that training had sunk in. Steve and I breathed easier each day that Ray improved. If he was willing to keep trying, we owed it to him, and to ourselves, to do the same.

Within a month, we had found work, and Crazy Ray no longer tore at doors, windows, and blinds when we left the house. We trusted him home alone, knowing no harm would befall him or our possessions.

Like training, socialization played a huge role in his development, and Ray evolved into a socialite. When he padded through the pet store door to attend a meet-and-greet, it was like Norm walking into a bar of welcoming cheers. Everyone would call out "Ray!"

Ray grinned at the smiling faces, and other dogs rushed forward, dragging their owners along to ask, "So, how's Mr. Personality today?" The group recognized the change in our dog, and pats on his back for all that he had accomplished felt like a tribute to all of us.

After retirement, Ray still needed a purpose in life, and he found it in guarding our home and being a loyal, loving companion. He also provided comic relief with his never-ending funny faces and attempts to pilfer food. In the process, he earned a few nicknames: Corned Beef Thief, Baklava Bandit, and Strawberry Stealer.

Sweet Baby Ray entered our lives at a time when we needed him most. We taught him how to thrive in our world, and he taught us how to focus our attention on something tangible and valuable, rather than on failure. We three became a family. Ray learned to open up and love, and with a huge heart, he loved us with all of it.

Despite a difficult beginning, Ray's time with us ended too soon. Losing him to illness at age seven tore a hole in our souls that still hurts, but we remain grateful for our time with him. Ray taught us a great deal about endurance — to never give up on ourselves or those we love — and to give new members of our family a chance to find their place.

~Cate Bronson

Counting to Five

It's never too late to have a happy childhood.
~Berkeley Breathed

Most people call their mom "#1" because she is their champion, support system, and all around cheerleader. But for me it's a bit different. My mom married young, had me young, and then things changed... and she earned the #1 moniker because of her place in the line-up of my father's wives. I ended up having a bounty of moms, each bringing her own personality and life to the family. They shared a common theme though: *You have a #1 mom, and I don't want to replace her.*

Mom #2 came into the picture very soon after #1 moved out. The funny thing is she knew us already and we also got two stepbrothers, which was a ton of fun. She was nice, friendly, and to be honest, just wanted to be a part of the family. She knew #1 and she knew the family, but of course that was the awkward part, too. She had been my father's secretary.

The whole Mom #2 experience was short-lived though. Her ex-husband came back into the picture very quickly, and their family of four got back together. One day, they boarded a plane and they were gone. In retrospect, #2 made a great decision because it didn't take long for my father to find #3.

She came into the picture not too long after #2 left, and I would call her "the placeholder." She was sweet and thoughtful. I recall her having a daughter before she met my dad… and we moved into their house. After a summer visit, I think that was the last time I saw her. She made a nice home, tried to blend in, but as I mentioned I call her the placeholder because she was just keeping things warm for #4.

Mom #4 was fabulous. She made it clear she was not replacing Mom #1 right away, but she was a great role model for me. I must share one thing; she was the divorce attorney for my father as he exited his marriage to #3. I know… but still. She had a good business career, we had great talks, and she gave me solid advice. She also had a kid, a quiet one but sweet. Mom #4 lasted a while. Holidays were fun with #4 as she made the house a home. She went out of her way to make us feel comfortable and was keenly aware she was #4 and we had seen a lot. I think what was so interesting about #4 was that she made us into a working family even though we were such a dysfunctional bunch. I would say she provided the perfect balance of parenting guidance and fun.

Things got complicated when my father's father took ill. This became a big part of my father's life. I didn't get to the hospital too much but when I did there was a nice doctor who took care of my PopPop. She seemed to have a good connection with my father, and you guessed it, not long after PopPop passed, that doctor became Mom #5.

I am not sure I even attended this wedding. I truly can't remember. But I still had Mom #1, and I didn't want to give up Mom #4, and I was out of the house anyway, so I didn't need to interact with #5. I know she's smart and highly educated, and she came with a couple of kids who I hardly know. I keep #5 at a distance and don't know too much about her. She has stayed longer than #4 though, so she seems to be doing well.

The only Mom I see is #1. And I still miss #4. I must admit that I did learn a lot from my father's five wives. They all tried, and they each brought a unique perspective on family, and #4 was a tremendous example of how to be a strong woman in business—a lesson that I hold very close to my heart.

Families are crazy and messy, but I try to find something positive in each person. I hang onto that. But I must admit I'm hoping that we don't see a #6.

~Sarah Slattery

Chapter 9

My Crazy Family

Family Fun

81

Flight of Fancy

At the height of laughter, the universe is flung into a
kaleidoscope of new possibilities.
~Jean Houston

While making plans for our annual trip to Charlotte, North Carolina, to visit our grown children, I received a call from our daughter, Bambi, who lives there. She had just had a visit from our son, Adam. "I want to give you a heads-up," she said. "Adam stopped by a while ago. He found an old, sky-blue, polyester suit at Goodwill and got this crazy idea. Adam thought it would be hilarious to wear it when he goes to pick you up at the airport. He was laughing pretty hard, but I think he said that the jacket is a tad too tight, and the pants are a bit too short. He'll be the goofy-looking guy holding up a sign that says 'OWENSBY' so you won't miss him when you deplane. He thinks it's going to be a hoot."

A plan suddenly began to form in my head. "I guess that means we should dress appropriately as well, so he won't miss us either."

After hanging up, I found my husband Wayne, told him about Adam's outfit and suggested we turn the tables on him by wearing wacky outfits as well. Wayne loved the idea.

Usually, when we travel, it's just Wayne and me. However, this time our middle son, Ryan, and his wife, Gillian, would be coming with us. We gave them a call, hoping they would want to join in the fun.

They were immediately on board. We discussed a variety of ideas for outrageous outfits, silly styles, and wacky wardrobes, and set a date for shopping.

Shopping day arrived. Armed with a list of thrift shops, we headed out. One store, in particular, had a humongous variety of clothing options. We found some splendid items to complement our new personas.

Wayne: "The Cheap Act."

Aptly titled, Wayne's gaudy outfit looked like he came straight from a swanky lounge. He found a mustard-yellow leisure suit. The pants were a tad too big, which we remedied by hiking them up to his chest and securing them into place with a large white belt. To complement the leisure theme, he found a yellow silk shirt missing several of the top buttons. The shirt simply screamed for cheap gold jewelry to hang down on his chest where the buttons were missing. They went great with the gold "John Hardy" platform-style shoes. The finishing touch was the way he fixed his hair with a nifty side part, complete with a comb-over. Perfect!

Ryan: "Jethro's Doppelganger."

Our son Ryan also discovered some fabulous duds. His outfit looked as if he had shopped in Jethro Bodine's closet from *The Beverly Hillbillies*. Like Adam's, his suit was also a tad too tight and a bit too short. No matter. The fact that the pants were short allowed ample opportunity for him to show off his cartoon-character stockings. A pair of cheap sunglasses finished off his getup nicely.

Gillian: "Nasty Barbie."

Gillian hit the clothing jackpot. She found an outfit that suited her persona perfectly. Her sparkle-plenty costume jewelry glittered and glowed. She would have stood out in Las Vegas. From her foot-high hairdo to her four-inch-spike heels, she looked altogether different from our innocently sweet and charming daughter-in-law.

Senia: "Old Hippie."

My outfit happened to fit my style nicely. Since I decided to become an old hippie, finding my clothes was easy and fun. I picked up a tie-dyed T-shirt, bell-bottom pants and, of course, extra-tall white platform shoes. My hairstyle was simple: I would simply not brush my hair that day. Beads added some authenticity, as did a pair of

groovy-looking glasses. I loved my look; it [...]
able. I secretly decided to keep those clot[...]
wardrobe to wear again.

So the big day finally arrived. Though [...]
some strange looks and giggles, we were de[...]
with the plan — if for no other reason than t[...]
Adam's face when we stepped off that plane. Th[...]
11, 2001, so there was no danger of being que[...] ...orities.

I'm usually a bit of a Nervous Nellie when it comes to flying, but on this trip we were having so much fun that I didn't worry at all. As expected, most of the folks on the plane gave us the curious once-over. A few averted their eyes, but some folks asked if we were part of a singing or acting group.

We explained what was going on. It didn't take too long before word spread through the entire passenger list. It made for lively conversation during the trip as others shared their dress-up stories. It was a fun flight. Before we landed, most of the folks on the plane (including the flight attendants) were looking forward to watching the expression on the face of the young man dressed up in the sky-blue, polyester suit holding the sign as we got off the plane.

We finally landed. The moment had arrived for us to walk out that door. We stepped out and spotted Adam immediately. Then he spotted us. The expression on his face was priceless.

"Adam!" I shouted from the ramp. "I'm so happy to see you!" I gave him a big hug. Folks who had not been on our plane must have wondered greatly about the oddly dressed group hugging and laughing.

Adam's a smart boy and had a pretty good idea about who let us in on his wardrobe plan. He wanted to get the last laugh, so he decided that the first order of business would be to run us by Bambi's workplace so we could see her right away.

Imagine the look of surprise on her face when she responded to her receptionist's call that her family was waiting for her in the lobby. She had thought Adam would be taking us directly home from the airport. Thankfully, she's a good sport.

All too soon, it was time to go home. As I was repacking my

ed to me that I had not seen my "flying outfit" since
. Where could the clothes have gone? After searching
e with no success, I decided to ask Bambi. I found her
stairs looking intently out the window.

"Hey, Bambi," I said as nonchalantly as I could, "you don't happen to know what happened to my flying clothes, do you?"

With a twinkle in her eye, Bambi said, "I know you pretty well, Mama, so…" She motioned me over.

I hurried to the window and watched with her as a garbage truck rumbled down the road. Sigh.

Okay, I think she really got the last laugh on that one.

~Senia J. Owensby

82

Madeline the Mannequin

I'd rather laugh with the sinners
than cry with the saints.
~Billy Joel

My tiny town was just like many other quiet villages dotting rural Connecticut, at least until the summer when sultry Madeline came to town. Nothing would ever be the same after she exposed what little soul she possessed — and other parts, too — for all the townsfolk who cared to see, and some who did not or wished they had not.

It all started when the remodeling of a department store's clothing department rendered obsolete all sorts of fixtures, wall partitions, and shelving. However, the most intriguing item was a life-sized female mannequin.

My cousin Richard, who is always on the lookout for good stuff, was cruising through the store parking lot when he spotted the mannequin hanging out of a dumpster. Unable to resist such a treasure, Richard rescued the fair maiden, brought her home and proudly presented her to his family. They were not impressed.

Undaunted, Richard named the mannequin Madeline and prominently displayed her in the corner of his garage. Initially, Richard's wife did not mind the other woman, but upon discovering Madeline adorned with some of her best clothes, she gave Richard the dreaded ultimatum husbands have heard for years: "Either she goes or I go!"

To keep his marriage intact, Richard had no choice. The problem was how to be rid of Madeline without hurting her imagined feelings. Richard's friends declined to adopt the fiberglass houseguest, and there were no takers at any of the local garage sales. Even the transfer station operator admitted to a lack of experience with strange ladies, especially their disposal.

Then Richard remembered that there would be a bachelor's party that very evening at the local firehouse and thought it would be a good idea to bring Madeline along—a privilege denied real-life females. Madeline was a perfect guest as she silently watched from her corner post. However, as the night wore on and spirits were lifted, Madeline was lifted, too. Someone who did not appreciate her persistent stare decided she needed to go for a swim in the brook behind the building.

As onlookers gathered in the pale moonlight to watch Madeline eerily bobbing in the water, Richard contemplated another rescue. But rather than navigate the steep gully to the rock-laden stream, he opted to wait until daylight.

On his way to the firehouse the next morning, Richard was surprised to see a small crowd gathered on the bridge over the brook. After realizing they were gawking at Madeline's body, he was also stunned to see a rookie police officer—who obviously had not verified that Madeline was not a real corpse—hastily cordoning off the area with yellow crime scene tape. Apparently, a prankster had shoved Madeline into a storm drain so only her legs stuck out, reminiscent of the Wicked Witch of the East after Dorothy's house fell on her in *The Wizard of Oz* movie.

Richard leapt over the tape, yelling "I'll save her!" and then yanked Madeline out of the pipe. He frantically wiped the mud from her face and pretended to administer mouth-to-mouth resuscitation.

Madeline played the lifeless victim fabulously, a part she was made for. After several labored breaths, Richard cried out, "She's alive!" and then heaved her skyward. The crowd gasped in disbelief as she arched high into the air. Almost before Madeline clattered to the ground, Richard was last seen hightailing it back to the firehouse. The police officer shook his head dejectedly at the heap of loose arms and legs, wondering how he would ever live down this one.

As for Madeline, she was never seen again, but it has been rumored that she is in someone's garage, patiently waiting to make another dramatic appearance.

~Arthur Wiknik, Jr.

83

Gone On to a Better Place

When people are laughing, they're
generally not killing each other.
~Alan Alda

My husband's family members all live within an hour's drive of each other, and one summer they decided to take a big, multi-generational vacation to the beach—despite the fact that getting together for even a quick coffee can often result in what I like to call "an unfortunate incident." But in theory, this trip would be a blissful assemblage of aunts, uncles, grandparents, cousins, siblings, parents and kids spending a week together in one big, laughter-filled house by the shore. And though any such venture will doubtless include a few bumps in the road, no one could have anticipated the bizarre occurrence that would form everyone's lasting memory of this familial voyage.

The morning my mother-in-law, Caroline, and father-in-law, Daniel, were about to hit the road for this trek, Daniel made a grim discovery in the back yard. Boogie, their elderly German Shepherd, had quietly passed away in the shade of his favorite weeping willow. Worried that this news would start the vacation off on the worst possible note, Daniel decided to keep Boogie's untimely demise to himself, ship Caroline off to the beach with their daughter Ellen, and then bury the dog by himself once everyone was out of town.

"I called Ellen to come pick you up and take you with her," he announced rather gruffly, preoccupied by the dark task ahead. "I've got some things I need to do today. I'll head down tomorrow and meet up with you at the rental house."

"What are you talking about?" Caroline asked, dismayed by this last-minute upheaval. "That's ridiculous!"

By now, Daniel, who could be a bit short-tempered, was starting to feel overwhelmed by the heat of the August day, melancholy over Boogie's death and general anxiety over the impending family get-together. The volatile combination caused Daniel to erupt, rather loudly, at his wife.

"For heaven's sake, Caroline, just DO WHAT I ASK!" he yelled. "Why can't you just GO and not make a big deal of it?"

Caroline snapped back at him, returning his elevated and angry tone. The spat continued for a few moments before Daniel caught himself and apologized.

"Please," he said quietly, placing a hand on her shoulder. "I really need you to do this, but I promise I'll be there tomorrow, and everything will be fine."

Ellen pulled up just then, so Caroline shrugged an "okay," got her luggage and left for the beach with her daughter.

As soon as they were gone, Daniel got to work on making Boogie's final arrangements. He gathered up a few of the dog's favorite toys, the old green blanket Boogie always slept on, and a half-chewed rawhide bone. Finding the shovel and pickax in the garage took a while, and by the time Daniel had everything he needed, it was mid-afternoon. Concerned about the oppressive heat and humidity, he decided to wait until after sundown to begin excavating Boogie's grave, and settled into his easy chair for a quick nap.

It was after 10:00 p.m. when the sound of pouring rain woke my father-in-law, who was stiff from his unexpectedly long sleep in the recliner. He felt groggy and disoriented, but the thought of poor Boogie alone in the storm compelled him to action. Daniel went outside, lovingly wrapped Boogie and his playthings in the blanket, and began digging the dog's final resting place. He chose a spot close to where the canine had died, but Daniel soon hit a large root and had to adjust his plan, shifting the perimeter of the hole away from the willow's trunk. It wasn't long before he came upon another unyielding patch, and then another. Both times, he had to realign the grave's border to circumvent the obstacles.

The heavy rain made it difficult for him to proceed in the darkness, so Daniel got an old camping lantern and set it atop a nearby fencepost. When he turned it on, the splash of yellow light revealed a jagged, sprawling pit beneath the willow's sheltering branches. Aided by the lantern, Daniel continued to dig, straightening and deepening the trench as he went. At last, he placed the green-wrapped bundle in the hole, said a few parting words, and then began re-filling the cavity with muddy earth.

Meanwhile, at the beach, the adults had finally gotten the children settled in and were enjoying a late-night comedy show. We were right in the middle of planning the next day's activities when Caroline's phone rang.

"Hello? Yes, this is Caroline," we heard her say, and then there was a lengthy pause while she listened to the caller.

"I'm sorry," Caroline said at last. "I have to put this on speaker so everybody can hear that." She hit the button, and then asked the person on the other end, "Would you mind repeating what you just said?"

"Sure, ma'am," a man's voice replied. "This is Officer Green of the Prince William County Police. I just got a call from one of your neighbors saying he heard shouting at your house earlier today. And then about an hour ago, his wife saw your husband outside in the rain digging a pretty big hole. Neither of them had seen you since the shouting earlier, and they say your husband was definitely burying something in the back yard. And, well…" the policeman hesitated a moment before continuing, "well, ma'am, we just wanted to make sure that 'something' wasn't you."

~Miriam Van Scott

84

A Cast of Five

The further you get away from yourself,
the more challenging it is. Not to be in
your comfort zone is great fun.
~Benedict Cumberbatch

Halloween. Not my favorite holiday. But one year, my son Mike and daughter-in-law Crescent decided they were going to have a party. A multi-generational, family-and-friends party for about forty people. Come one, come all. Bring your parents and your kids. Aunts, uncles and cousins… Everyone was welcome. There was only one requirement: Everyone had to be in costume. Everyone. No costume… no party. Stay home! And that meant everyone, including my husband Ebenezer — I mean Frank — had to dress up. I only call him Ebenezer because when he heard he had to wear a costume, he said, "Bah, humbug!"

What to wear? And how elaborate do we get? Crescent is the most creative of all of us, and she had just the solution. She decided that our immediate family would come as some of the cast members from *The Wizard of Oz* — family-themed costumes that would all go together!

Mike was the Tin Man. He wore a silver shirt, silver cloth pants, and silver gloves, and wrapped his shoes in tinfoil. He wore a huge silver funnel upside-down on his head, and he carried an oilcan just in case he had trouble moving. Very much in keeping with the Tin Man in the movie.

Crescent would be Dorothy. That was a no-brainer. She pulled her hair into two cute pigtails tied with ribbons and wore a white blouse with ruffles and a perky blue-and-white pinafore. She finished off her costume with white socks and glittery ruby red slippers. Very authentic.

Eli, our four-year-old grandson, was really into this costume thing. He couldn't decide whether he wanted to be Toto or the Scarecrow. The Scarecrow won out, and he made the cutest scarecrow ever, complete with straw sticking out of his floppy clothes, shoes, and floppy straw hat. Although not exactly true to the movie script, the Scarecrow carried a stuffed dog that he named Toto.

As for me, who else would I be but the Wicked Witch of the West? Perfect casting! I wore a black top, black pants, black pointy shoes, a black cape, a long black wig and a very tall, black, pointy witch's hat. To complete the ensemble, I wore long striped socks, just like the Wicked Witch did in the movie. And I put on lots and lots and lots of make-up. My lips were bright red, and my eyes were rimmed in black. My long false eyelashes were a thing of beauty. Fetching! And I got to cackle, cast spells and say, "I'll get you, my pretty," all evening in a rather witchy voice. Crescent and I wear the same shoe size, so I also kept trying to steal her ruby red slippers so I could get my powers back. I was not successful and just wound up melting in the corner.

So, our family was all set except for one person—the most difficult of all. What would Crescent decide to do with Ebenezer... I mean, Frank? He didn't want to wear weird clothes or a full-face rubber mask—too uncomfortable and confining to wear for the entire evening. He wasn't ready to cross-dress and come as Glinda, the Good Witch. And he was too big to be Toto or a Munchkin. He decided he didn't want to be the Wizard because he'd have to stand behind a curtain all night. What's the fun of that?

So, with very few other characters to choose from, Frank came as the Cowardly Lion. On his head, like a hat, was his mane—golden in color and curly—and his lion ears on top of his head. His mane came down the sides of his face, covering his own ears, and wrapped around his chin like a long beard — a full, curly, golden beard. Crescent found a tiny lion's mask that was just a little bigger than one of those funny clown noses, but this one looked like a lion's nose and open mouth, complete with teeth. It met his criteria for a small mask. He wore his own golden color shirt (to match his mane, of course) and jeans. We pinned a cute lion's tail to the back of his jeans to complete the costume. He looked amazing!

As we arrived at the party, we all had to walk through a graveyard that Mike had set up in front of the house. Spooky music was playing, mummies were hanging from the trees, and containers of dry ice were placed all around the yard, giving the whole place a very haunted feeling. People really went all out on their costumes. It was so much fun to see how creative and talented people could be, but we were the only people who came dressed as a group with a theme. Ironically, even though Frank's costume was minimal, no one recognized him behind his mane and mask! And he knew everyone at the party. People would come up to him, look into his lion's face and try to figure out who he was. They couldn't — until he talked. Then they recognized his voice. Man, he really got into playing the part and decided to only roar for the rest of the evening. He was loving it and milking it for all it was worth. He was even awarded the prize for best costume, and there was a lot of competition.

We had all kinds of scary and spooky foods: appetizers galore (including curly cheese straws that looked like crooked fingers); witches' brew (fruit punch) for the kids complete with black ice cubes and chunks of dry ice for that steamy effect; Bloody Marys with Devil's Eyeballs (green olives) on toothpicks or blood orange martinis for the older kids (adults); green goblin salad with toasted fingernails (almonds); intestines and monkey brains in blood (spaghetti and meatballs); garlic ghost toast; and spider leg, lizard tongue, diced tarantula, and haunted house ghost cookies, among other delicacies for dessert.

The party was a complete success. Naturally, we were the last to leave because we didn't want to miss anything. And Frank, the person who used to be known as Ebenezer — the one who complained the most and the loudest about going to a Halloween party and having to go in costume — had the best time. Ever. We even have the pictures to prove it!

~Barbara LoMonaco

85

Road-Trip Souvenir

If you carry your childhood with
you, you never become older.
~Tom Stoppard

It was our annual summer road trip and my two brothers and I were stowed away in the third seat of the station wagon. Our various pieces of luggage, fishing poles and blankets were stuffed strategically between my parents and us. It made the perfect buffer zone. The only way this seating arrangement changed was if one of us acted up. The culprit would be summoned to the front of the car with little chance of parole until the next gas station.

As we drove through Michigan, it started to pour. I was sitting up front, having been given a time-out for less than illustrious behavior. The windshield wipers couldn't keep up and my father was having trouble seeing. "I think we made a wrong turn," he said. We had not seen a single car in almost an hour. Looking out the rain-splattered windows, all we could see were miles and miles of old barbed-wire fences and posts that surrounded tiny dots of farms and houses off in the distance. Spotting a farmer up ahead, Dad pulled over and asked for directions.

"Follow this all the way to the fork, go left and drive to the end. You'll see the signs back to the highway," he assured us. The rain continued, but I could feel my parents' relief at knowing we were no longer lost in the middle of nowhere.

"Stop the car! Stop the car!" my mom shouted suddenly. Dad pulled over, and he and my mom, with umbrellas in hand, stepped down into the gutter and up onto the edge of a farmer's field by the fence.

They talked beside a tall fencepost for a few minutes, and then came back to the car. Shaking off their umbrellas, Dad said, "Well, all they can say is 'no.'" Then we drove to the first farm lane and turned in.

The lane was solid mud from the rain, with huge potholes. Nearby branches slapped each side of the car hard, like thick chamois cloths in an automatic car wash. We stopped at the top of the hill by an old redbrick farmhouse and big barn. Dad walked to the front door and knocked. An older man in dark pants, white shirt and suspenders opened the door. The man listened as Dad talked and pointed to something way down the lane. After a few minutes, the man scratched his head, looked down the lane and then back at my dad. Bursting into a big grin, he shook Dad's hand vigorously.

"Good show," whispered my mom. Dad got back in the car with a pleased smile and said, "Let's just hope it fits."

We heard a horn toot beside us. The man and his two sons pulled up beside us in an old blue pickup truck. "Follow me," he said. Back down the lane we went. When we reached the fence line, his sons jumped out of the truck and grabbed a couple of shovels from the back. My brothers and I watched them dig out what we thought was an old fencepost. Curiosity overcame us. We all got out of the car and ran over to take a look. This was no ordinary fencepost. It was a lot taller and wider. The colours were faint, and the wood post was cracked and weather-beaten. But when we looked really close, we could see three faint carved-out faces atop strange animal-like bodies.

This was not a fencepost. It was a totem pole, a real totem pole.

With one final pull, the farmer's sons and my dad managed to wrestle the totem pole from the ground. The farmer and my mom wrapped it up in an old blanket, and we all helped carry it to our car. Dad and the farmer carefully navigated this long, heavy wood pole through the back window, over the luggage and into the front seat. It touched the radio at one end, with about one foot hanging out the back window.

We waved goodbye to the farmer and his sons, and off we went. I was still up front with my parents in the penalty box, but I didn't mind. Miraculously, the rain rolled back into the sky, and the sun came out about a mile later, which no doubt pleased my brothers. With the tail end of the totem pole sticking out the back window, I'm sure it was a little wet and windy back there.

"It'll make a great conversation piece," Dad said.

"What a wonderful memory from our trip," Mom added.

Squished between my parents and the totem pole, I noticed one of the faces peeking out from a gap in the blanket. Reaching over, I smiled and gave it a hug. Like a rescue dog, these three faint totem characters had no clue where they were going or what lay ahead. But one thing was for sure: They never had to sit out in the rain again. We'd seen to that.

"I bet that farmer thinks we're out of our minds," Dad laughed. "He'll be telling that story for years to come, about that crazy Canadian family who knocked on his door in the middle of a rainstorm to buy that old, beat-up fencepost with all the faces."

Over fifty years later, it's a story I still love to tell. And every time I walk past those three faces stacked one upon another in our home, it always makes me smile.

~Cheryl E. Uhrig

86

My Carnival Summers

*There is a garden in every childhood, an enchanted
place where colors are brighter, the air softer, and the
morning more fragrant than ever again.*
~Elizabeth Lawrence

Growing up around carnivals was my childhood dream,
eating hot dogs, cotton candy, and chocolate ice cream.
My dad owned a stage show so we traveled around,
setting up colorful scenery on the outskirts of towns.
He had a magician who pulled a skunk from his hat.
There were dogs in pink tutus and limber acrobats.
There was Tarzan the chimp, who performed on high wires.
Blue overalls and suspenders were Tarzan's attire.
Tarzan rode a red bike, which he taught me to ride,
as I rode through the fairgrounds with him by my side.
I have a small mole on my neck that he was fascinated by.
We would cling to the bars of the Ferris wheel as it touched the sky.
Soon my carnival days as a child would end,
but not the fond memories of Tarzan my friend.
Years later, a small trailer pulled into our driveway.
It was Tarzan and his owners who came for a visit that day.
Tarzan looked at my family and then looked back at me.

He pulled back my collar to touch that mole gently.
That was a time in my life that I will always remember,
those carnival summers with my dad from June through September.

~Nora Beason

87

A Cruel Joke

Family time is the best time.
~Carmelo Anthony

"Mom, how soon do we eat?"

"Yeah, Mom, when do we eat?"

"John, Jerry," my mother replied, "the turkey isn't done yet."

I persisted, asking, "How much longer 'til it's done?"

"Well, let's see," my mother returned, stepping to the stove. "Boys, come here."

"Yes, Ma'am."

Mom bent over in front of the stove and flipped on the oven's light. "Look inside at the turkey," she said.

I knelt down, cupped my hands at my temples, and peered through the glass in the oven's door. My younger brother did the same.

Then Mom asked, "Do you see that little, white, plastic thingy stuck in the turkey?"

"Yes, Ma'am."

"Well, when that thing pops up, the turkey is done."

"Okay," I replied. Then I removed my face from the glass, asking, "Mom, how does it know?"

Standing erect, Mom laughed. "I don't know," she answered. "It just does."

Jerry and I looked at each other and shrugged.

Mom flipped off the oven light and added, "Now why don't you two go play and come back later to check on the turkey."

"Okay, Mom," Jerry replied.

We scampered across the kitchen's linoleum and disappeared into the family room. We didn't even notice our dad get up from the dining-room table and stride into the kitchen after our departure. Dad never went into the kitchen.

Fifteen minutes later, my mother yelled, "John! Jerry!"

"Yeah, Mom?"

"It's time to check the turkey again!"

Two young boys came tearing back into the kitchen.

As my dad leaned back against the refrigerator and watched, Mom bent over in front of the stove once more and flipped on the oven light. "Check the little, white, plastic thingy," she instructed.

Again, I knelt down, cupped my hands at my temples, and looked through the oven door's glass. Jerry followed suit. Then two boys fell back upon the linoleum with mouths wide open.

"Mom," I began, "didn't you see the little, white, plastic thingy pop up?"

"Yeah, Mom," Jerry added. "You shrunk the turkey!"

Immediately, my dad busted up laughing.

Then Mom grabbed an oven mitt and opened the oven door. She reached inside and pulled out a Cornish game hen that Dad had brought home.

Then Dad removed a turkey that was perfectly done but hidden in a kitchen cabinet.

Later, we feasted on roast turkey, mashed potatoes, bread stuffing, fresh vegetables — and one Cornish game hen.

~John M. Scanlan

88

Oleo Run

Children must be taught how to
think, not what to think.
~Margaret Mead

erhaps when people hear the words "oleo run," they think of a 5K race — a foot race. The oleo run in my life was a race all right — but not a foot race; it was more of a road race.

I grew up in the Middle West — some say there is a difference between Midwest and Middle West. Let me be clear: It wasn't either coast or the Gulf of Mexico. It was in the middle of the country. I would rather not be any more specific.

The people my parents associated with in my childhood were rock-solid folks. They took their families to church every Sunday, and they placed a huge value on education and honest hard work. They considered themselves reliable, dependable, trustworthy, level headed and stable Americans. Not given to political outbursts, they thought through what they heard and moved very slowly toward change. It took quite a bit to get their ire up. But one didn't want to get their ire up.

In the state where we lived, and some adjoining states, the agriculture lobby had succeeded in getting a law passed proclaiming that butter was better than oleomargarine (oleo). If oleomargarine was to be sold, it must be uncolored. Back in those days, uncolored oleo looked like dull, almost dirty, lard. However, oleomargarine was so much cheaper than butter. Like us, all my parents' friends had big families, making this a serious financial issue. So, as a concession to the harsh no-color oleomargarine mandate, the butter law "allowed" that the oleo could be packaged with a dime-sized, orange-looking blob of food coloring in one corner.

To make our oleomargarine colored, we would push and squeeze the food-coloring blob while it was still in the sealed package until we got the coloring throughout the oleo evenly or until the package burst. It was a great way to amuse hungry children before dinner. If the oleo was softened sufficiently, we could use our kitchen mixer and achieve marginally tolerable-looking oleo. Still, on all accounts, it was disgusting. Lots of parents would just spread lard on their children's bread and sprinkle it with sugar.

But my parents and other families were not that easily put off. They could eat their bread bare, but the idea of a monopoly — a dictated product — was too much. And the cost of that monopoly angered them deeply.

When the parents thought the children weren't listening, they devised a plan: the oleo run. Geographically, we were located more than 100 miles from any state that sold colored oleomargarine. So to make the oleo run pay for itself — actually, make a profit — my father, an accountant, pushed some numbers. Each load had to be a certain size, so many pounds. The oleo runs would also have to take place at certain intervals to factor in things like steady supply, change of supplier and summer heat.

Here's how it worked: For each oleo run, one father in the oleo consortium drove to the prearranged store in another state with his pickup or station wagon, paid cash for the oleo and headed right home after calling on a pay phone to report that the "transaction" had taken place. I guess they were worried that someone would see a strange vehicle with an out-of-state license plate loading boxes out the back door of a store. His wife would pack him a lunch to take and a thermos of black coffee. With a full tank of gas, he could get pretty far before taking a gas-and-restroom break. It was an all-day affair, what with small-town speed limits (they didn't want the constable to take notice), and it usually happened on a Saturday. There were no interstates, so they didn't have the advantage of speed or anonymity.

When that father came back late Saturday afternoon, the oleo would be distributed quickly and quietly among the four to six families who paid for it before the oleo run. Of course, buying that much colored oleo meant they got it wholesale. The extra oleo was stored in someone's freezer or out in a shed in the winter.

Other town folks would hear that an oleo run had taken place (probably at church the next day) and ask to buy as much colored oleo as was allowed without being greedy about it. Remember, these solid citizens were willing to share. But, of course, the additional oleo was sold at retail. Soon, it would be gone. No one could be accused of having more than they needed for personal use in their possession. It was like a contraband cooperative. The extra oleo that sold at retail paid for the gas and oleo-run expenses.

My parents and my friends' parents were very secretive, but little by little we kids learned of their plans. There were multiple suppliers in several states in different directions, so they didn't buy from the same supplier each time, and the same dad didn't drive all the time. Every family had to bear equal risk. That way, it allowed the small-town grocers to amass oleomargarine over a longer period of time and avoid suspicion. Also, family station wagons became a preferred mode of transportation: throw a blanket over the load, and it just looked like someone was moving. Small community grocers were eager to be as accommodating as possible because these cash sales affected their bottom line several times a year. It was like a tourist trade for the towns in states bordering ours.

Sometimes, we would go visit "family" in other states, or they would come to our place for the holidays and bring a few pounds of colored oleo. Of course, their purchases were haphazard and often unnecessarily expensive. Fortunately, we had a steady supply of colored oleomargarine all during those dark years thanks to the oleo runs.

In due time, the law requiring oleomargarine to be sold uncolored was repealed. But the damage was done. My parents and their friends went back to being law-abiding citizens. But it was not until adulthood that we "kids" started to speak of these things. Historically, we knew that none of our family, generations back, had been involved in any kind of evil or protest. But then we would find out that lots of families drove to other states and bought colored oleomargarine whenever they could.

People always wonder why the children of the 1960s protested. I say they learned it from their parents.

~Anna Anderson

Hot Dog and Bun Conspiracy

Everyone loves a conspiracy.
~Dan Brown, The Da Vinci Code

My extended family has always put a high value on discussing things. Not so much the weather or snowfall, the family next door or sports scores, but conversations about stuff we are passionate about. After Sunday dinners, the great-aunts and great-uncles with assorted spouses discussed stuff around the dinner table for hours. There are no lawyers in my family, just folks who could, if pressed into service, discuss and argue either side of a point. I can't say these were elegant or graceful conversations, but they were passionate and intense.

To my knowledge, there were only a couple of rules of engagement: no cursing or calling people names. Everyone got a chance to speak. They couldn't interrupt when someone was talking, but knowing my kin, there might have been intermittent side conversations. Probably the most important rule was that when they got up from the table, the conversation was finished, and the debating was over. There was no holding grudges. Perhaps this is just common civility. But they all knew there would be another time to take up the same topic again.

Although none of these conversations, arguments or debates about politics or poverty, economics or religion, world affairs or taxes ever reached the ears of the Supreme Court or foreign leaders, I believe they affected the way my family has lived — how they viewed the world, as well as their personal integrity and spending habits.

As would be expected, these conversations continued into my generation among my siblings. My sister got the family heirloom — the table used for those first discussions — so the tradition continues. But I believe my brother has carried on the tradition with the most intensity.

As a kid, he would bring up topics that perplexed him, things like social justice, economic policy, why some places required us to collect taxes at our lemonade stand, why all religions didn't get along, and why migrant children didn't go to school. Much to my parents' credit, they were able to provide a satisfactory conversation and answers for his questions.

However, my parents almost always got themselves in trouble when he brought up hot dog and bun issues. It is a conspiracy, he told them, and pressed for answers. One of the other siblings mentioned other mismatches of items: shampoo and conditioner, salt and pepper, peanut butter and jelly. There was a discussion about how the other items depended on consumer use and weren't a deliberate fraud by any companies and manufacturers.

He was satisfied with the discussion — except for the hot dog and bun conspiracy. "The bakers know how many hot dogs are in a package, and the wiener makers know how many buns are in a package," he told my parents. "There are children starving in China who could eat what we throw away because of this conspiracy." The "children starving in China" line was one my parents used on us to get us to eat our vegetables, but now he was using it against them.

My mother didn't give up. "There are lots of ways to look at that," she told him. "You can do the math: buy two packages of wieners at twelve each and three packages of buns at eight each. That gives you twenty-four sets of buns and wieners that you can eat and put in the freezer what you don't use. There is no waste." Our family continued these assorted discussions all through our high-school years. Mom would throw in quotes from Shakespeare and Dickens with a sprinkling from Psalms and Proverbs just for another point of view.

What might seem to outsiders as generations of hot air has taken on a life of its own among my siblings. They work with homeless people and high school dropouts, developmentally disabled adults and physically challenged kids, as well as others who are marginalized or on the fringe of society. There are no answers to these great questions of the universe that are discussed by generations of my family, but there is great satisfaction in involvement.

But we try not to bring up the hot dog and bun conspiracy question because it seems like we still can't do anything about it.

~Ela Oakland

The Family Vacation: A Cautionary Tale

*I think togetherness is a very important
ingredient to family life.*
~Barbara Bush

riends raised eyebrows. My own sister sounded a note of caution. But we bulldozed our way beyond those presumably wiser heads, determined to go with the plan proposed by our irrepressible daughter Amy, the fun-lover/sybarite/optimist in the clan.

We'd do it. We'd gather on a summer weekend in the Berkshires in New York State for our own version of *Little House on the Prairie* family bonding. Except this time, the house would be the "villa" that Amy had discovered on her rambles through the area in previous searches for a summer share for her Manhattan pals.

Amy was rhapsodic once she'd zoomed in on a weekend opening on the villa's roster. On this hallowed weekend, it would be just the fifteen of us. That boiled down to one set of original-issue parents, our three daughters and sons-in-law, and seven assorted grandchildren, several under the age of five — the new generation.

Never mind the number of phone calls, strategy sessions, social and work commitments standing as obstacles. Schedules were altered and re-altered, and when the family weekend was ultimately etched in stone, woe unto anyone who tampered with it.

Which is how it came to pass that on an unbearably hot Saturday, my husband and I drove through a town with one traffic light, one tavern, and a few scattered ramshackle houses.

The villa in question came into view once we'd traveled down a dirt road, past crumbling stone gates. The place looked like something in an old Agatha Christie novel: a sprawling, mysterious, gloomy mass of stone that had definitely seen better days.

The massive front door actually creaked. So did the steps. There was a huge bell at the back side of the place that sounded a piercing gong to announce — well, our first thought was — a murder.

The place had that quality known as "character" in abundance, with its sweeping hallways, grand balcony, faded period furniture. But here is what it lacked:

> Any suggestion of air conditioning
> A kitchen that contained anything created after the Great Depression
> A logical floor plan for eating or sleeping
> A bathroom a mother would call "decent"

It was going to be a long weekend...

On that first day of our togetherness, the temperature hovered at 97 degrees. The humidity was record-breaking.

Carly, then fourteen months old, exquisitely expressed what the rest of us were feeling as we settled in for the siege. She howled for five straight hours. And while we're a family that loves its babies, Carly was not nominated for the "Best Vacation-Sharer" award that day and evening.

Nor was Danny, the redheaded demon who decided to play with the lock on the downstairs bathroom door, causing each of his grandparents to spend desperate minutes coaxing out a four-year-old miniature Houdini.

The outdoor barbecue that night was a gastronomic success for us — and for the insect world that Amy had failed to mention in her raves about this summer place. The insect repellent was definitely somewhere in the villa… its exact whereabouts, however, could not be determined.

No matter. Who minded being bitten alive when there was still the giddy prospect of assigning six bedrooms — some habitable, some not — to fifteen heat-crazed, itching mortals?

Carly said it best with her ongoing protest. This was, her shrieks suggested, a lousy idea.

We all ran true to form on this family vacation.

Jill, the orderly, organized oldest sister, tried unsuccessfully to impose a schedule. Her husband, a scientist, watched us all carefully. He was working on some sort of chart, attempting a rotating bathroom schedule. Never mind its fate.

Nancy, the baby of our family and a psychologist, was our unofficial peacemaker, settling minor and major squabbles. Her husband, a delightful fellow whose appealing charm allows him to get away with a lot, spent much of his time on the hammock. The rallying cry, "Where's Mike?" went out endlessly when there were chores to be done. The answer always was the same: "Napping!"

We attempted to lead a hike just to break the tension but received loud protests of "Too hot!"

Amy, the family's cheerleader/camp counselor/coach wanted to start a color war — a summer-camp style competition. Her husband, a gentle psychoanalyst, pondered whether his wife was having a "regressional experience."

It turned out that the pool that graced our villa had beautiful tile and a grand design, but also was inhabited by a few snakes and a dead mouse. Alfred Hitchcock himself couldn't have set it up better for shock and revulsion.

Emily, generally a spunky kid, was positive that there was a murderer behind one of the creaky upstairs doors. She bunked in with us. Who knew that adorable little girls could snore like stevedores?

Then there were also those pesky issues of control: while we still carried the title of parents, we were clearly no longer in charge of these totally independent, some might even say pig-headed, adults.

Like it or not, our advice about how to get a balky child to bed or how much ice cream is too much ice cream for a two-year-old child generally went unheeded.

Ditto for our piercing views about the use of sunscreen, the appropriate hour for dinner and whether proper nouns should be considered in fierce *Scrabble* games.

By the middle of Day Two, it was clear that at least two of us were going to jump ship. "We may leave early," my husband and I told Amy, the Chief of Operations for this idyllic little family odyssey.

That led us into a — shall we say "spirited" discussion of Mom and Dad's past crimes and misdemeanors, our unwillingness to be adventurous, and while we're at it, the time we'd refused to go white-water-rafting because of our tricky backs, wimps that we were.

Ah, forgiveness and family harmony...

Okay, we did bail out after the second day of our scheduled three-day family weekend. We did it with heads held as high as the mercury soared that Sunday. Our bodies and spirits had reached the boiling point, what with dead mice, snakes, and replays of ancient family psychodramas as our impetus.

But we didn't regard it as a total loss.

On the (limited) plus side of the ledger, we had, after all, laughed a lot during this blazing, daunting weekend. We swam in a lake with various grandkids on our shoulders, delighting in the notion that history was repeating itself a generation later. We had eaten sweet corn and the kind of greasy hamburgers that need to be enjoyed every now and then.

Most of all, we had added one more experience to the bulging family annals in this new, oxymoronic "adult children" stage of life.

But this time we learned the eternal verity about life with these adult children: Even though once upon a time, we changed their diapers and tied their shoes, they're in charge now.

For better and for worse.

~Sally Friedman

91

A Very Mary Pat Christmas

Christmas is not as much about opening our
presents as opening our hearts.
~Janice Maeditere

The doorbell rang and I waved thanks to the deliveryman as he walked away fifty pounds lighter. I sighed when I saw the familiar, looping handwriting on the colossal box.

Every December was the same.

"Greg, Mom's gifts are here. I need you to lug this inside, please!"

Greg moaned. "Another Mary Pat Christmas."

I rolled my eyes, remembering the conversation I'd had with Mom only a few weeks earlier.

"Mom, please don't send a million presents this year. We always end up throwing most of it away, and you can't afford it."

"You throw most of it away?" Her voiced dripped with hurt.

I backtracked. "Well, what I mean is that we just don't have a use for most of the stuff, Mom. And besides, how much do you spend? The shipping alone has to be astronomical. You and I both know you can't afford it. Please just… don't this year."

"But it's fun for me, baby. I love being able to spoil you all like that."

"You'd spoil us if you'd make something for us. Make a stuffed animal for the kids, or a pillow, or send us some banana bread. We don't need all that junk."

"Junk?" Drip. Drip. Drip.

Greg heaved the box inside and dragged it over to the tree. I grabbed the scissors and sliced through the tape, revealing a mountain of presents, each wrapped in shiny, stiff paper and tied with colorful coils of ribbon.

"Can you believe her?" I complained.

Ever the steady voice, Greg replied, "I know it's frustrating for you, Shan. But it makes her happy."

"But she can't afford it!"

"I know... but you can't make her stop."

"I know." I grabbed a gallon-sized garbage bag from the pantry. "You wanna try to knock this out before the kids wake from their naps?"

"Sure."

We knew better than to wait to open the gifts until Christmas morning. With two little kids, it made no sense to lengthen opening time by an hour. Especially when most of the gifts wouldn't be of interest to them, anyway.

The first thing I opened was a toothbrush. No enclosed container, no packaging... just a single toothbrush in a plastic baggie. I dangled it in the air for Greg to see.

We both burst out laughing, then tossed the contaminated tooth-brush into the garbage bag.

Next, it was Greg's turn. He was shocked when he pulled out a pair of Beats earbuds.

"Shan, these are really nice earbuds. Oh, wait a minute..." Looking closer, we noticed the packaging had Chinese characters on it. "They're knockoffs," he said.

"Well, maybe they still work well?" I asked.

I plugged them into my phone but couldn't even bring them close to my head. The crackling would've deafened me.

Slowly, the garbage bag began to fill with a random assortment of items no one could ever use. Pens engraved with the name "Paul" (no Paul in our family), broken sunglasses, knitted leg warmers, every item from the Avon catalog, and a single, large marshmallow in another plastic bag. At one point we opened a gaudy, gold "family tree" necklace that looked like old-style rapper bling. I couldn't help but laugh when Greg slung it around his neck and broke out into "Funky Cold Medina." But it wasn't just that one necklace. Because Mom bought in bulk, we soon opened a second family tree necklace. And a third. By the time we'd opened our fifth identical necklace, we were rolling on the floor, holding our sides.

Finally, we came to the last present. It was enormous.

"You want the honor?" Greg asked.

"Let's open it together."

We ripped the paper, revealing a box with a lion's head on it. Looking closer, we realized it was a plastic fountain, to be mounted on the wall. Immediately, I called my siblings.

"Did you guys open your gifts from Mom?"

"Yeah… you?"

Suddenly we were all laughing. Each of us had received the fountain, the earbuds, Paul's pens, leg warmers… even the toothbrushes and marshmallows.

As we collected the items that we thought we could use or donate, Greg pulled aside a pair of adult-sized slippers that looked like dinosaur feet and said, "Keep or donate? They're way too big for the kids."

I considered them. "Let's keep 'em," I said. "They might like them someday."

Wiping our tears, we cleaned up before the kids awoke.

We didn't know it then, but that would be the last box we ever opened from Mom. Less than four months later, Mom passed away suddenly from a stroke.

At the funeral, my siblings gathered in a hotel room and talked about our Mary Pat Christmases. We laughed about how we all should've invested in Avon. How she had once given my brother and his family piles of presents when they visited her in Florida from Brazil, where they lived at the time. Not only could they not use all the gifts, but they had no way of getting everything home — so they ended up abandoning most of it at the airport. Laughter flooded the room as we shared our treasured memories, one silly gift at a time.

Suddenly, they didn't feel so silly. They felt priceless.

Right then and there, we decided that the best way to honor Mom each year would be to continue the tradition of a Mary Pat Christmas. We would take a ten-dollar budget, someone's name, and a limited amount of time in Walmart to shop for things Mom would've picked.

Somewhere, Mom was laughing in approval.

When we returned home, I was unpacking when I heard a little voice behind me.

"Aaaaaaarrrrrr!"

"Hmmm?" I said, not turning around.

"AAAAARRRRR! Look at me, Mama!"

I turned to see my four-year-old boy, hands clawed, teeth bared. And on his feet, a pair of adult-sized dinosaur slippers.

I began to cry as my baby T-Rex stomped away.

"Merry Christmas, Mom," I whispered. "Merry Christmas."

~Shannon Stocker

Chapter 10

My Crazy Family

Now I Get It

92

The Deli Fella

I would maintain that thanks are the highest
form of thought, and that gratitude
is happiness doubled by wonder.
~Gilbert K. Chesterton

I spent the spring of 1995 watching him worsen. I watched the pussy willows out the window of the rest home ripen from green buds to furry little animals. I watched his body waste away and waited for a sign our hearts would soften. I began composing a speech in my mind.

Here lies Harold, born and raised in a delicatessen. Amazing he lived this long, the way he ate — the way he cooked. He never met a vegetable he couldn't render unrecognizable. Cabbage marinated to a mystery. Carrots pickled to oblivion. I never knew how food was really meant to taste 'til I went away to college. I never knew how love was meant to feel 'til he welcomed me home.

But he never had, and I never went.

I had deified my handsome daddy when I was little. Then when he outshouted my mother and demeaned my dreams, I defied him and stayed far away — until my sister called for help.

He'd opted for his third triple bypass, and the new hog's valve was hiccuping in his heart. As soon as he got home from the hospital, he knew something wasn't kosher. The organ was chugging arrhythmically along; the rest of his body couldn't keep up. It was like being dragged behind a horse. He wanted it to end.

"Not 'cause I'm some brave guy," he said. "I just can't see any other way out."

There wasn't. Yet he and his stubborn life force fought any evidence of failing.

"This isn't normal," he'd bellow.

"This is normal… for dying," the hospice worker assured us.

Hospice care made it clear that Dad's descent was irreversible. This was forcing me to rethink every action. Compassion was running neck and neck with bitterness in my psyche. I wanted compassion to win.

"Dad?"

He surfaced slowly from a fitful sleep, struggling to understand where he was and who the hell I was. Pointless "Get Well" balloons were hovering near the ceiling. Finally, he focused on my face.

"Oh, it's you. You still here?"

"I'm going to your old friend Manny's sandwich shop. Can I get you something?"

"Yeah," he brightened a watt or two. "Get me a ham sandwich, thick-sliced, on rye, with three slices of Swiss cheese, Gulden's mustard and garlic pickles."

"Sure," I said, grabbing my coat to go.

"And… thank you," he said fervently.

He'd not said "thank you" to me since I'd grown up and away from his entitlement—and never in this way. He was trying, too. This was more than sandwich gratitude, and I was determined to take nourishment from any crumb he offered.

"Well, you are very welcome."

Driving through the old neighborhood, I put a more positive spin on his eulogy.

How this man could concoct. How this man could create. My dad invented "matzoh-rella marinara," and my sister and I were his "garlic girls," chopping it for hours on end to make batches of his sauce. Our hands stunk so much that even the fishermen's daughters stayed away. We'd spoon layers of that marinara over thick slices of mozzarella on matzohs. And we topped the "matzoh-pizzas" with slices of lamb sausage from the Greeks. On Sundays, neighbors would bring their ethnic dishes over, and Dad would celebrate all the differences in tastes. He was a true "Jewmanist."

Manny made the sandwich and helped me carry an optimistic eight cans of Ensure to the car. He was seventy-three, like Dad, but still fit and feisty.

"He won't drink that crap," Manny said.

"It's the only thing that stays down," I said. "He needs to keep up his strength."

The "for what?" in his eyes made me sad.

For us to love each other! I knew inside.

When I brought him back the sandwich, with romantic notions of atonement on my mind, his drugs were wearing off. He opened his eyes. I opened the bag. He opened the sandwich. He summoned his strength. He raised a furious face to mine.

"Hey! I asked you for the ham thick-sliced!" he growled.

Hurt resurfaced and darkened his obituary.

Dad inherited his overeating from Grandpa, dead at sixty-two, and his fat happy cooking from Grandma, dead at sixty. Aunts, uncles, cousins — one whole branch of his family was wiped out by heart disease. The Holocaust didn't help, but it was ultimately the cholesterol that did them in.

The hospice helper took me into a hallway where dogwood blossoms danced outside the windows. She carried a clipboard with his history.

"It won't be long," she said. "His heart will give out soon. You should call your family."

"There's nobody left to come. He always ate too much and made himself sick and mad. He drove my mother to divorce, and me and my sister away."

"But he didn't make himself sick," she said.

"What do you mean? He ate like there was no tomorrow."

"There almost wasn't," she said. "It says here Harold got rheumatic fever in the Air Force outbreak in 1943. Those poor guys all suffered severe heart damage. They were doomed. He must've had a strong will to live this long."

My father had been a victim of his sick ventricles, and so had we all. He'd lived a diminished life in constant fear and pain. And we hadn't known. He'd been expecting this last moment all these years.

Returning to his room, I knew I'd better make the most of it.

There I saw the shell of Harold in hell, lying in his last bed. My resistance liquidated in sympathy. The rock in my belly was melting. Now I'd have to feel the loss of the first love of my life, darn it. I covered his hand with mine. He felt my empathy, opened his eyes, softened his focus, and said, "You know what, kid? I can be a jerk, too."

I wasn't sure if it was Dad, the drugs or dementia talking, but that sounded oddly like an apology. An apology and a thank-you in the space of an hour? I knew it wouldn't be long now.

"I… love you, Daddy," I quavered like his little girl who'd gone so far from him, who'd just this moment gotten back.

"Hey. I always loved you, kid," he whispered. "Even when you were mad at me, I always loved you."

He left his scarred and defective body behind soon after. I wondered how big the presence of his absence would stay in my mind. Still pretty big.

And in 1995, on a ridiculously beautiful spring day at the New Haven Jewish Cemetery, I eulogized.

Dad loved to picnic on this gravesite, given free for his service in World War II. "Hey! It's a lovely little piece of property," *he'd say.* "Why wait till I'm dead to enjoy it?"

He knew loss young as his whole big deli family left him behind. Their section of this cemetery is so crowded, you've got to get in line and take a number to get in.

He was funny and feisty and always hungry. Food and laughter were the currencies of love my father offered most freely. Our hungers weren't quelled, but he gave us big appetites for life.

~Melanie Chartoff

93

My Two Grandmas

Grandmothers always have time to
talk and make you feel special.
~Catherine Pulsifer

I'd known these two women for my whole life, but I'd never seen them in the same room. Both were my grandmothers, one by blood and one by marriage. They'd married the same man — my grandfather. He'd divorced one of them and then married the other. He'd passed away four years earlier.

My two grandmothers hated one another. Even though the man they'd fought over was gone, they still despised each other. For my entire life, we'd celebrated holidays with them separately because they'd insisted on it. Even after my grandfather had died, they still refused to be in one another's presence.

Until today.

Today, the three of us were meeting for lunch to discuss the one thing we all shared: divorce.

I was going through one, and it was positively excruciating. When Grandma-by-blood heard that my husband had left me, she'd called Grandma-by-marriage for the first time ever.

"We have to help Sarah," she said. "She's my granddaughter, and she's your, well, I guess when you married my husband, she became your step-granddaughter."

Grandma-by-marriage said, "I married her grandfather — your ex-husband — before she was even born. She's my granddaughter, too."

"Well, that's all semantics," Grandma-by-blood said. "Anyway, I've been through a divorce, and my husband was your second husband because you were divorced from your first husband, so we both know what she's going through."

"Yes, I married your ex-husband eight years after you and he split up," Grandma-by-marriage reminded her. "Your divorce had nothing to do with me."

"Yes, and you were married to him longer than I was anyway, but he never had any kids with you," Grandma-by-blood said. "A real marriage produces children."

"But he didn't divorce me," Grandma-by-marriage said. "We were married until the day he died. He never left me."

"Which brings me back to the reason why I called you for the first time ever in my life," Grandma-by-blood said. "My granddaughter needs us. Both of us."

So we went to lunch. It was strange to see these two septuagenarians in the same room after all those years. It felt strange, especially when I remembered that they only did it because they wanted to help me.

"How are you doing, honey?" Grandma-by-blood asked, reaching for my hand.

Before I could answer, Grandma-by-marriage grabbed my other hand. "Yeah, sweetie, tell us how you're doing," she said.

"I'm all right, I guess," I said. "It's hard. Divorce sucks."

"Oh, you're right about that," Grandma-by-blood said. "When your grandfather and I split up — you know, so he could marry her," she nodded at Grandma-by-marriage and continued, "I felt like my heart was ripping out of my chest."

"He did not divorce you to marry me," Grandma-by-marriage snapped. "I didn't even know him then." She shook her head, suddenly seeming to remember that she was supposed to be helping me. She patted my hand. "So does it feel like your heart is ripping out of your chest?"

I shrugged. "Yeah, kind of. I have good days and bad days."

"What kind of day is today?" Grandma-by-blood asked. Before I could answer, she said, "I'd say it's an historic one. You know, because me and her," she nodded at Grandma-by-marriage again, "are here together in one place just for you because we love you, and you need us."

"I sure appreciate that," I said. "It means a lot to me."

"I would think so," Grandma-by-blood said. "Because me and her," another nod, "haven't always gotten along that well."

"Yes, I think my mom might have mentioned that once or twice," I said.

"Well, you know, it's on account of your grandfather," Grandma-by-blood said. "He caused a rift in the family when he divorced me to marry her." Again, she nodded at Grandma-by-marriage.

Before Grandma-by-marriage could jump in, I jumped up, thankful that the restaurant had a buffet. "I'm going to get some food now," I said.

As I ate, my two grandmas continued to pretend to talk about me, all while taking jabs at each other. Grandma-by-blood nodded at Grandma-by-marriage about fifty more times, I think to avoid saying Grandma-by-marriage's actual name. Grandma-by-marriage defended herself and her relationship with my grandfather in the calmest possible way, gritting her dentures until I feared they would grind into dust.

When Grandma-by-blood asked me if I thought my husband was seeing another woman — while nodding like a bobblehead at Grandma-by-marriage — I knew I'd had all I could take of their wise counsel.

I grabbed their hands and said, "This has been lovely. I appreciate you putting aside your differences on my behalf."

Grandma-by-blood squeezed my hand. "It wasn't so hard. I'm not sure why we waited so long." She looked at Grandma-by-marriage and smiled tentatively. "Do you want to do Christmas together this year?"

Grandma-by-marriage nodded. "I think that would be wonderful for the kids."

"Well, they're my kids," Grandma-by-blood said. "They're only your step-kids."

I sighed. "Grandma, I speak for my mother, her siblings, and all of your grandchildren when I say that we belong to both of you. And Christmas as a family sounds terrific."

And, oddly enough, it was terrific. As the years went on, my two grandmas actually became friends, and their problems in the past were finally forgotten.

Most of the time, when a couple gets divorced, it tears apart a family. But my divorce brought together two of the most amazing women I've ever known.

~Sarah Foster

94

Threads that Bind

Call it a clan, call it a network, call it a tribe,
call it a family: Whatever you call it,
whoever you are, you need one.
~Jane Howard

Our parents had a saying: "We want you kids to grow away, not go away." But when the time came to test that sentiment for the first time, it was harder than they imagined. The summer of 1969, my parents watched their oldest child grow away. Our big brother left, clean-cut, with a brand-new knapsack, fresh jeans and a good pair of hiking boots. His plan was to hitchhike across Canada. Beyond that, there were no plans.

Now it was just the four of us: my parents, my younger brother and me. I was fine with it. It did not change my summer plans of camp and hanging out with friends. Mom and Dad did not talk about my brother's absence much, but his postcards were welcome arrivals.

Mid-July, my aunt who lived in Winnipeg called. My brother had dropped in for a couple days to visit. My mom was ecstatic. She wanted details. "Is he okay? Is he getting enough to eat? Did he say what his plans are?" As summer drew to a close, there was still no news. Then, late August, my brother called to say he would be home that Friday. Like the return of the prodigal son, Mom sprang into action. Steaks were bought, and potatoes were scrubbed. Favourite snacks and desserts were made. Our family had much to celebrate.

On Friday, my brother walked in the back door like he had done a thousand times before. Visibly taller now, he had long, stringy hair and a big beard. His jeans were tattered and faded. His hiking boots had been traded for a pair of well-worn leather sandals. Over his T-shirt he wore a scruffy, colourful sleeveless vest with frayed edges. "It's called a serape," he told us proudly. Our brother was immediately embraced with a rush of hugs and tears. After we chatted for a bit, Mom tactfully said we'd help him take his knapsack and clothes down to the laundry room. She suggested he "get settled in and cleaned up. Supper's at six."

Down in the laundry room, I helped Mom load the washer. But when it came to my brother's serape, Mom paused. Holding it up to the window, she took a good look at it, including its length and inseams. Moments later, she was on the phone to Dad. My father worked in a shoe factory. They often sold odd bolts of materials used to make slippers and linings. She asked if they had any colourful material with a bold, horizontal pattern. Shortly, three bolts of material arrived, and Mom went to work. Using the now freshly washed serape for a pattern, Mom measured, cut and sewed for the next couple hours.

At 6:00, the four of us gathered on the back porch and waited excitedly for my brother to join us. It was the first time in months we'd all be together. The barbeque was on, and the coffee table was filled with my brother's favourite foods. The moment he walked out, we jumped up and shouted, "Welcome home!" Welcome home, indeed. For there he stood in his newly washed serape, and there we stood in our bright new serapes. Taking this all in, my brother paused for a minute, and then he nodded with a wry grin and said, "Yep, I'm home."

Our family talked well into the night. We each shared our summers. Our brother told us about his many adventures, the people he met and the places he visited across Canada. Occasionally, my mom joined in, but mostly she sat back and enjoyed. Her family, at that moment in time, was home, safe and together. Years later, I realized that matching serapes was my mom's way of reconnecting our family. It was her way of showing we were all made from the same fabric. After that summer, my parents knew it was just a matter of time before their children would all grow away. Letting go is never easy. But we were forever grateful that our brother took the first step to blaze that difficult path for all of us.

Our bright, bold serapes are long gone. What remains are the endless threads of love with which they were made.

~Cheryl E. Uhrig

95

Outspoken and Outright Outrageous

*The day two girls or women can genuinely be friends
to each other, we will see then no war, camouflaged
or open, between the wife and her
mother-in-law in any house.*
~Anuj Somany

They could make an entire TV show with my mother-in-law, Agnes, as the main character. She was born in South Fork, Alabama, graduated at the top of her class of twelve, and has truly made her mark on this world.

She wasn't sure I should marry her son. In fact, I'll say it like it was. I wasn't her first choice. I wasn't even in the running! Yet, Marty and I did marry, and we made our home on the opposite side of the United States.

Marty was quite content with living in California, keeping his mom at a distance. I, on the other hand, wanted our future children to have two sets of grandparents who were involved in their lives.

Before we got married, I tried to look past his mom taking my seat at our rehearsal dinner. I even pretended not to hear her when she said, "I just don't understand why God is takin' Marty away from me and givin' him to you" — right as we left for our honeymoon! I fought the temptation to get mad. Instead, I thought about the wonderful man she had mothered and wanted somehow to reach her heart.

At first, we began with weekly phone calls. They were expensive back then, but I believed it was money well spent. Week after week, we called "home," with Marty and I each on a line. Eventually, we invited her out for a visit, paying for her plane ticket. Sometime within that first year, I won her over. She was now proud to have me as a daughter-in-law. But this did not change the fact that Agnes was outspoken — and at times outright outrageous.

Years went by, and we learned to live with the unexpected from her. But my husband and I, and eventually our three children, were smothered in love. We made it a policy to laugh our way through the shock over the crazy things she would say and do.

I'll never forget the cold December day when Agnes and I took my three kids, ages six and under, to the mall to see Santa. We were there for several hours, window-shopping, picking up a few presents, and eating lunch. Then the kids sat on Santa's lap, whispering in his ear exactly what they wanted for Christmas. By the time we were finally ready to leave, I'm sure we'd have worn out even the best of shoppers.

Just as we got in the van with the three tired kids, a downpour hit — and the whining began. The kids had been angels all day. Not a single reminder to behave while at the mall, even after they had seen Santa and given him their Christmas list.

"Jason," I said now, "quit kicking the back of Jenna's seat, please."

And then, "Jenna, quit screaming! Now the baby is crying."

And again, "Jason, I've asked you more than once! Stop it!"

I could barely think as the noise and commotion took over the van. It seemed the more I asked the kids to sit quietly, the louder they got. Even the rain now pelting the windows didn't drown out their dissatisfaction.

Finally, I'd had it. "If you guys don't stop when I count to three, I'm going to stop the van and come back there! Okay, one, two, three!"

But they still totally ignored me!

Furious, I turned down a side street and parked the car. In the pouring rain, I got out of the van and walked around the front. When

I got to the passenger's window, I saw my mother-in-law sitting there perplexed.

Our eyes met. And just as I reached to open the slider door, my mother-in-law made the move — locking me out of my own van!

Total hysteria broke out in the van. Crying and complaining suddenly turned into laughter and cheers for Grandma. I, on the other hand, stood in the rain staring at Agnes. With her head bowed in prayer-like fashion, she was actually shaking from laughter!

The longer I stood there in the pouring rain, the wetter I became. Without any sign of laughter or thinking this was funny, I walked back around the van and stood at my door. With the kids finally voting to let me in, Agnes unlocked it.

The kids were silent as I crawled into the van. Water was still dripping off my hair when I drove into the garage. Then I got out of the van, leaving everyone still strapped in, and walked inside.

There, my husband met me in the hall.

"Wow! What happened to you?"

Gritting my teeth, I growled, "Your mother!"

Yeah, his mother! But then I began to think about her.

She was the one who flew in to help me when my children were hospitalized, prayed for my family daily, called me with recipes and made me laugh more than most. She had truly become my friend. And today she had purposely tried to take the heat off the moment, not letting anything ruin an otherwise great day by, yes, again doing the outrageous.

I shouldn't have expected less. Thanks, Agnes!

~Janet Lynn Mitchell

96

Bio-Dad

Understanding comes through communication, and
through understanding we find the way to peace.
~Ralph C. Smedley

y wife spent her first thirty-two years on this planet believing that her biological father was the town drunk, who was usually passed out in the ditch next to the local gas station. Her friends and neighbors walked by him on Sundays, clucking their tongues and shaking their heads to show their disgust. As a child, she was guilty by association, shamed by an invisible bond that could never be broken.

He wasn't a part of my wife's life growing up. Her mother said that he left, abandoning both of them when she was only a baby. But they lived in a small town, so he was always there — just out of reach, but too close for comfort.

When she and I first started dating in our early twenties, we spent hours staying up late at her brother and sister-in-law's place. We drank beer and tossed around the kind of stories coaxed out by bottles of Yuengling and the moonlight. Late one night, we were stringing together the pieces of their broken childhoods, and her brother mentioned that he wasn't so sure the town drunk was truly her father. He threw around some wild theories of potential candidates who used to hang around with their mother back in the 1980s. It all seemed a little far-fetched at the time, so we had a good laugh and moved on.

Nine years full of jobs, apartments, friends, weddings, and funerals passed in a blur. Then our son was born. We experienced all the joy and pain of those first few months as new parents. And again, in the wee hours of the morning, over cups of black coffee and bottles of thawing breast milk, the question of Bio-Dad bubbled back up to the surface. After all those years, was it possible that her brother was right? We finally decided that there had been enough uncertainty. We wanted to know the absolute truth — if not for us, then for our son. So, we hatched a plan.

"Why not just walk up and ask the guy outright?" I asked. "Or I could do it for you."

"No, we're not talking to him. Besides, his brain has been pickling in alcohol for forty years — he's not exactly a reliable source." *Good point,* I thought.

We knew that over the years, the town drunk had married, then divorced, and had a grown son who still lived locally. If a DNA test showed that they were half-siblings, then we could finally put an end to our decade-long, half-drunk, sleep-deprived sleuthing. After some gentle prodding, the potential half-brother kindly provided us with a single swab soaked in DNA from his inner cheek. We sent it off to be tested and waited.

A week later, a thin white envelope with a slick logo showed up in the mail — the results! She held it in her hand, took a deep breath, and ripped it open.

"Probability of relatedness: .000001%"

She stared at me, eyes filling with tears, and all I could do was hug her. After a few minutes, we pulled ourselves together and spotted our son, already halfway over the baby gate. I grabbed him and cradled him on my hip.

"So… what now?" I asked.

We were both thinking the same thing: How could we possibly track down even half of the potential Bio-Dads? All we had was a list of sketchy nicknames compiled from her brother's foggy childhood memories.

She took a deep breath. "Now, I talk to my mother."

The next day, she took her mom for a drive and asked her point-blank just what the hell was going on. She theorized that if they were both trapped in a moving car, there was no escaping the question. I spent the morning pacing around our house, waiting for an update.

Finally, I heard the back door open and ran into the kitchen.

"James Sweetland," she said.

"Wait, what? Who's that?" I stammered.

"Bio-Dad," she answered.

I stood there, slack-jawed, and a million questions erupted in my brain: "Your mom lied for over thirty years? Why? How do we know it's the truth this time? Who the hell is James Sweetland? What if he's somehow worse than the town drunk? How do we find him? Wait… do we even want to find him?"

We spent the rest of the day re-hashing the talk with her mom, Internet stalking James Sweetland, and trying to figure out what to do next. That night, she called Amy, one of her best friends from high school, and told her the news. Out of nowhere, I watched her face turn white.

"Yes, I'm sure that's his name. Why?" she asked into the phone.

Within an hour, Amy was at our front door with a stack of old family photos. She sat on the couch, fingers shaking, and pulled out a worn Polaroid.

"That's my Uncle Jimmy. He was married to my biological aunt. They got divorced when I was in middle school."

Amy pulled out another picture of a large group of people, all smiling for the camera, giving each other bunny ears.

"This is my high school graduation party. Remember? Sadie, that's you." She pointed to my wife's smiling face.

"And that over there is Uncle Jimmy. Jimmy Sweetland."

The three of us stared at each other. Not only did we believe James Sweetland was my wife's biological father, but he also happened to be her best friend's former uncle by marriage — and my wife had met him before.

We opened a bottle of wine.

After some booze-fueled Google searching and a phone call to

Amy's aunt, we discovered that James Sweetland lived only a few towns over. He held down a full-time job, had no criminal record, and was most likely not an alcoholic.

The hunt for Bio-Dad had taken a seriously unexpected turn.

Amy agreed to reach out to him via e-mail and take his temperature regarding the whole "you might have a daughter" situation. James wrote back to Amy the same day and agreed to meet Sadie as soon as possible. All my wife wanted was a DNA test so she could finally know the truth. They went out to dinner together that week, and they did a cheek swab before the appetizers.

The results almost didn't even matter — they were two peas in a pod from day one. They talked on the phone and texted during the day, stitching together a patchwork quilt of her childhood and his adulthood. After a few weeks, the DNA tests confirmed what we already knew: James Sweetland was my wife's biological father.

When we started on the journey of finding him, we assumed that it would be a long road with a dark ending. I do still mourn the stolen parts of my wife's childhood; the years she and her dad missed having together can never be replaced. At the same time, I'm so happy that they have the chance to build their relationship as adults. Best of all? Our now four-year-old son has another grandfather. He will never even remember a time when "Poppy" wasn't around to hand out toy cars from his jacket pockets on weekend visits.

~Virginia B. Harmon

Marry Her Off!

Family is a treasure chest with more
than a mountain of gold.
~Author Unknown

For years, I avoided dating like the plague. I was the type of person to give 110% in love and life and I decided not to date around casually. I reasoned that my heart was too fragile, and I was busy traveling the world. I also never found anyone interesting enough to bring home.

This just wouldn't do for my big Italian family. After one of my younger sisters married early, the family started looking to me. Why wasn't I even in a relationship? Better yet, what could they do to change that?

Dad was the first in the family to break the silence. On one of our father/daughter coffee dates, Dad got straight to the point. "Have you been seeing anyone?" This had become routine questioning in an effort to help me find a man. I had crafted a reply that seemed to satisfy my family's curiosity, but this time was different.

With furrowed brow, he followed it up with, "Well, if you are waiting for my permission to date, you know you have it. How are you going to meet anyone if you don't date around?"

"Thanks, Dad, but that's not what's going on here," I said. As I tried to explain that I was happily single right now, something dawned on me.

Perhaps more than marrying me off, my dad was looking for

Now I Get It | 351

reinforcements in a son-in-law. Our estrogen-dominated family was getting the best of him. While he had two sons, he also had three vocal daughters who were much like their mother in various ways. I'm sure the thought of another couple of sons-in-law was his only hope.

Next it was Mom who had a hard time understanding why I hadn't met the right one. So she reasoned her way through my singleness.

"You know, some people like the same gender," she said casually to me one day. "Not everyone likes the opposite sex. Don't worry, we will love whomever you bring home, no matter what."

At first, I didn't get it. Then I realized she thought I was a closet lesbian. After I reassured her that I do in fact like men, she was relentless in trying to set me up.

Mom just couldn't resist the cute cashier at Costco. "My daughter is single," she would say to him in front of me. "She loves to travel, and she…." Her voice would fade as I walked away inconspicuously with my sisters. Then she would find us and say, "He's a babe alert. Don't you think? What about him?"

In her defense, Mom loved my dad very much. She had shared that love with five children, and she just wanted me to find the same kind of happiness that she found in life. Her desire for more grandbabies was also a motivation, I'm sure.

The most epic moment was when my brother called me with urgent news.

"Sis, I just want you to know that Mom and your sister are setting up an eHarmony account for you," John said. "It's not cool that you have no idea what they're doing."

I laughed out loud.

"Wait, what?" I said. I could hardly believe it. "Are you kidding me right now?"

"No, I just left her house, and they're checking out your matches," he said. Later, I found out both my sisters were there with Mom.

"I really don't think she's going to like what we're doing," my other sister said. Somehow, her voice was drowned out in the excitement.

To this day, I have no idea what they put on my profile page. Matches were chosen by eHarmony based on my profile. What information did they include? Which pictures did they use?

I could hardly believe my potential love life was now unfolding in their hands.

At my brother's suggestion, I called them back and played a prank. I pretended that I had a dream they were at my sister's house, and they had set up an eHarmony profile. For a quick minute, they were fooled. But it didn't last long.

Once they figured out that my brother had let me in on their little secret, they pleaded shamelessly with me.

"Come on, Jenny, what's the harm?" said my mom. "This guy's profile says he lives in Huntington Beach, and his passion is Jesus!"

Who were these people? Oh, yes, my crazy but very well meaning family.

Mom knew I loved the beach, and at the time I wasn't living too far from there. She knew that my faith was important to me. I think she was hoping her words would seal the deal. Sorry, Mom. I just wasn't ready.

A few years prior to this incident, I was engaged to a good man but for various reasons I had reservations about my decision. Although I hadn't told anyone at that point, my brother made it very clear that he wasn't at all impressed and didn't think I would go through with the engagement. He told me flat-out, "You won't marry him." And, for various reasons, I actually didn't.

Looking back now, I'm thankful for all of my family's love and support, even if it was shown in different ways. They tried to figure out why I was still single. Deep down, they worried about me. They wanted to see me happy and in love.

Today, I'm happily married to a man I met on a dating site, and my brother approves. He let our wedding guests know at the reception, too. In front of hundreds gathered for the day, my brother's toast to the new couple went something like this. "This guy is way better than the one you almost married. I approve of him."

Well, thanks, Brother. Your opinion matters to me.

Behind these uncomfortably funny and sometimes crazy family incidents is a lot of love. In the end, our families keep us grounded.

Sometimes, they go about doing things for us in a way that we don't understand, but it helps us see there's more than one way of doing things. We can't choose our blood relations, but we can choose to see their better intentions.

~Jen P. Simmons

98

An Alarming Situation

*Go placidly amid the noise and haste, and remember
what peace there may be in silence.*
~Max Ehrmann

When we marry someone, we become family, which means that we agree to take on all of the other person's quirks and idiosyncrasies. Before I married my husband, Roger, I knew he had difficulty hearing. I was already trained to walk on his left side. I knew that if we were outside, and a lawnmower or a chainsaw was running, he would ask, "Where is that coming from?" while looking in the wrong direction.

But I didn't realize how bad the problem really was until we got married. When he was facing people, he could read their lips and expressions. But when he went to bed and put his good ear down on the pillow, a bulldozer could crash through the wall right next to his head, and he would snooze away, never having heard a thing! Meanwhile, I have always been a light sleeper, waking up at real — and imagined — bumps in the night.

When I moved into Roger's house I made a big discovery. Alarms were going off in the house at all hours!

The first time I heard the alarms going off in the middle of the night, I kept thinking there must be a faulty smoke alarm. Every time I jumped out of bed to find the alarm, there was no smoke, and the alarm stopped after a few minutes.

But after testing the smoke alarms and replacing their batteries, I realized that there must be old travel alarm clocks stashed in forgotten corners around the house. Some of them must have been going off dutifully for years. Since Roger couldn't hear them, he was blissfully unaware of the racket they were making, but they were driving me crazy.

I kept a notepad and a pen on the nightstand, and I made a checklist that went something like this: 12:17, 1:35, 2:15, 3:18, 4:42. Those were the times I knew the alarms went off each and every night.

I made it my mission to track down these alarms, one by one, and shut them off for good. I would jump out of bed and stagger around, disoriented from being jerked from sleep, yet desperate to find the alarm, as I would have only a few minutes to locate it before it turned itself off again.

Before we would go to sleep at night, I would announce, "2:15 a.m. I'm going to get that one tonight," much to the amusement of my new husband, who couldn't hear the alarms at all.

It took me several weeks, but hunt them down I did. One alarm was in the bottom drawer of an old desk, underneath stacks of papers, colored pencils, photographs, and other memorabilia.

Another one was stuffed in a duffel bag in the back corner of a hall closet behind shoes, umbrellas, and a deflated basketball.

One by one, I tracked down the alarms and turned them off. Problem solved.

I adapted in other ways, too. I would set an alarm for the time Roger needed to get up, and when the alarm sounded, I would turn it off and wake him up by gently touching his shoulder. When I needed to go out of town for work, I bought him an alarm that strapped to his leg and vibrated to wake him up.

Then the bat moved in. It seemed to be trapped in the wall right above the headboard of our bed. I couldn't sleep for all the noise it was making.

At first, when Roger said he couldn't hear it, I thought he was messing with me. "It's right here!" I wailed, pointing at the exact spot in the wall where the bat was fluttering, scratching, and chittering away.

Finally, I realized that he really couldn't hear it. The bat noises were high-pitched, and he had lost that range of hearing.

After eighteen years of marriage, Roger recently got hearing aids. I can't believe the difference it has made. When he first started wearing the hearing aids, he was startled by each new noise.

"What's that?" he'd ask, and I would tell him: That's the icemaker in the refrigerator; those are the sparrows in the bush outside the kitchen window; that's the beep that means the oven has reached 350 degrees.

"The oven does that every time it heats up?" he asked in disbelief.

"Yes," I assured him.

Once Roger could hear again, I, too, made a surprising discovery. In the intervening years of not being able to get his attention unless he was looking directly at me, and saying things five times in a row in order to be heard, I had developed some bad habits. I had gotten used to saying pretty much anything I wanted to, knowing that he would never hear me! Sarcastic comments and snide remarks were coming out of my mouth left and right — only now, Roger would ask, "What did you say?" I knew I had to knock it off quickly, so I started shutting down the *yeahs, rights,* and *whatever you says,* just like I hunted down and switched off those forgotten alarm clocks all those years ago.

~Gwen Hart

99

My Mom the Worrier

*If I have done anything in life worth attention, I feel
sure that I inherited the disposition from my mother.*
~Booker T. Washington

My mom's a worrier — an all-the-time, worry-about-all-things worrier. But she especially worries about my sisters and me. Nothing changed when we grew into adults. In fact, I don't think she really noticed.

I'm the baby of the family, the youngest of three girls. Mom stayed home until I was about nine, when she went back to work part-time.

I was a radio, TV and film major in college. When I graduated, I did a short stint in Boston, where I worked at a local music video station. Mom called every day. That's right, every day. Don't get me wrong. Whenever anything happened, I would call her. I once banged my head on the corner of a fuse box at work and needed stitches. Before I got in the car with my colleague to go to the hospital, I called Mom.

I moved to L.A. to pursue my dream. Mom still called long-distance every day. In those days, we had to wait until 8:00 p.m. when the rates went down. And I still called her. There was the time I was living in a studio apartment in Sherman Oaks, and I couldn't find my checkbook. I called Mom. Yes, I called my mom on Long Island and asked her to help me find my checkbook. She said, "Did you look under the couch?" And, I kid you not, that's where it was!

Maybe that was why she worried about me so much. But the time she called the police on me was a bit much. I was living in Hermosa Beach in the 1990s before cell phones. My roommate didn't pay the phone bill, and the phone was cut off. I knew where my checkbook was, I didn't need stitches, so there was no reason to call home. I didn't call for five days. I was in my bedroom when I heard a very loud, self-assured knock at the door — more like a pounding than a knock. It scared the pants off me. I opened the door, and two very tall, uniformed police officers were there.

"Dana Klosner?" one of them belted out.

"Yes," I cowered.

"Call your mother!" he said.

"What?" I quivered.

"She hasn't heard from you in days, and she's worried. Call your mother!"

"Okay," I said, still not really sure what was going on.

"Have a nice day," the other one said. And off they went.

I went downstairs to a pay phone to call collect. After all, I didn't want to go to jail.

Then there was the time I was in an airport coming home from a long trip, and I was catching a connecting plane back to New York. My plane was canceled, and I was trying to figure out how to find a hotel, when I heard an announcement.

"Dana Klosner, pick up a yellow courtesy phone."

All I could think was, *No, it can't be.*

I went to a counter and found a yellow phone. I picked up the phone and said, "Mom?"

She said, "I had to let you know, there's a big storm here, and your plane has been canceled!" She always knew how to track me down!

When I drove across the country from New York to Los Angeles, Mom wouldn't let me go alone; she made my older sister go with me. It was a great trip, but every night, from every hotel, we called Mom. After all, it was both of us on that trip.

I was living in L.A. for a few years when I went up to San Francisco to meet a friend. We did a crazy road trip, driving up and back to Seattle in one weekend. And, of course, every night I called Mom. My friend, who grew up as a foster child, couldn't believe I would do that, or that she would even want me to.

"I have to," I told him. "She worries."

And when she worried, I felt bad. That same friend moved to New York City. I was home from L.A., and I went into the city to see my friend. I didn't make it home from the city until about 2:00 a.m. It turned out that Mom called my friend over and over to see where I was, and my sister told me Mom was crying. How could I not feel guilty about that? At that point, I was used to living on my own and not checking in with anybody.

The tables turned when I got married. My husband was a Naval Officer. After a few years, he was stationed in D.C., and we moved to Maryland. We already had a little boy, and while we were in Maryland, we had a baby girl. My parents love their grandchildren; they already had four by my sisters in New York. So Mom and Dad would make the drive down to Maryland every few months to see the grandchildren. As they would get in their car to trek back to Long Island, I would tell them to call me as soon as they got home, and I would worry for the five hours it would take them to get there.

Another time, I was in New York with my kids visiting, Mom and Dad were out, and it was snowing. They were out too long, so I called the police non-emergency line to make sure there were no accidents. My parents couldn't believe I did that.

Now, my family and I are back on Long Island. My son is in school five hours away, and I make him text me when he takes the bus back to school.

My daughter took a trip to London on her own when she was sixteen to stay with her friend and her family. She would text two or three times a day. Then her friend's dad took the girls on a trip to Paris, and I didn't hear from her all day. I was "this close" to calling the American embassy. I was ready to get on a plane and go find her.

When I finally heard from her, she said, "Oh, sorry, Mom. My phone was on airplane mode!"

At that moment, I understood.

~Dana Klosner-Wehner

100

The Head

Love is what's in the room with you at Christmas
if you stop opening presents and listen.
~Author unknown, attributed to a
7-year-old named Bobby

unt Betty opened the gift, threw back her head and laughed so hard she snorted. This made the rest of us crack up, too. Then she showed us the Christmas present from Aunt Marcia that had elicited her guffaws.

It was a head — a hideous, plastic doll head. Creamy pink skin, creepy round eyes, and a rug of awful yellow-orange hair. No body, just an oddly square-shaped head, with tissues protruding from the top. Apparently, it was a tissue-box cover. A handwritten note from Aunt Marcia, taped onto it, said: "For your boudoir." She had tucked it in with other, actually nice, gifts for Aunt Betty's new house.

The story of the world's gaudiest tissue-box cover had begun more than twenty years earlier, in the early 1970s. Neighbors had asked then-teenaged Aunt Marcia to watch their dog — The Killer Chihuahua, as Marcia and her older siblings called him. The four siblings (my mom being the oldest) had shared a great laugh when Marcia came home with her beyond-tacky, dog-sitting thank-you gift. Then she tossed it in the back of a closet.

When Aunt Marcia resurrected that crazy-old-tissue-box-head as a holiday gag gift years later, it could have been the end of it. But, no, not in our family. The Head — as we officially named it — took on a wild and wacky life of its own.

My mom's side of the family was large, so every year we picked names from a hat — each of us getting a Christmas gift only for the person we picked. The year after The Head made its first appearance, Aunt Betty decided to carry on the joke. She gifted it to Aunt Elaine. The next Christmas, Aunt Elaine upped the ante, gifting it to our family angel-collector, Grandma — with handmade wings and halo attached.

Now, it was ON.

We each began to plot and plan when we received The Head. How could we make it even more outrageous than last year? We cringed as we waited to see who last year's giftee had picked from the hat. Someone was going to get The Head each December 25th.

The Head became an executive one year, complete with shirt and tie, and business cards in its tissue hole. Another year it was a railroad engineer, with striped denim hat and red bandana. It once wore an old-fashioned golf hat, with a red pompom.

One time, jokester Uncle John tucked a cackling Halloween noisemaker into The Head — then wrapped it in a box identical to four other boxes stacked on top of one another. All of Christmas day, before gift-opening time, he would walk by the stack and give it a whack, making it cackle and shake. We all knew The Head was in one of those boxes, but which one, and who was getting it? Torture.

Another year, Grandpa had The Head. Well, Grandma thought it would be hilarious to hide it in the shower, so when my family came to stay overnight on Christmas Eve, one of us would open the shower curtain to a surprise — like a scene from a horror movie. It was me, and Grandma giggled like a schoolgirl at my startled scream.

The kooky tradition of The Head went on for over a decade, and Grandma even recorded in a notebook, with her flawless handwriting, who got it and how it was dressed every Christmas. Our ritual faded out as the family stretched, scattered and aged, and we grandkids started families of our own.

Earlier this year, when I decided to write about this crazy past tradition, I e-mailed family members and asked them to share their favorite memories of it. We had a hilarious e-mail chain and some good laughs reminiscing — which was particularly poignant given my grandparents are gone now.

Then Aunt Marcia decided it was time to tell me the "One Secret of The Head," as she called it.

The back story: In the mid-1990s, I'd gotten engaged to my college boyfriend of five years — a young man the whole family had gotten to know. The week before wedding invitations were to be mailed, he abruptly called off the wedding and relationship with no explanation. At the time, I was shattered (though, in hindsight, thankful I dodged that bullet). It was my first heartbreak, and it was a doozy. The family came together to console and support me, which I will never forget.

But there was something I didn't know. That year, Grandma had The Head. In a huge box, she arranged my mother's wedding dress (which was a 1960s mini dress that would never fit me, as I'm several inches taller than her). Grandma inserted The Head into the wedding dress and sewed a flowing veil to match. She planned to give me this most-elaborate presentation for Christmas, before my early spring wedding. But when my engagement was broken in late fall, she called on my aunts to help her scramble and disassemble her masterpiece. They remade The Head as something else for another family member.

I had no idea until Aunt Marcia revealed the Secret, now decades later. Learning about it, tears welled up in my eyes. I could imagine Grandma working so hard on that wacky-but-touching gift for me. And I can just see her and my aunts frantically taking it apart and remaking it to spare my young, crushed feelings.

Reflecting now on that family secret — and our whole zany holiday ritual of The Head — I see my maternal family in a new light. I appreciate even more the silliness, humor and jokes of that raucous group of relatives. And I also realize that, beneath it all, is a spirit of creativity, graciousness and, most importantly, true family love.

~Megan Pincus Kajitani

My Dysfunctional Family

Family means no one gets left behind or forgotten.
~David Ogden Stiers

When I look at my family,
I see a mixture of souls and personalities
That don't fit together at all.
I see my father — the hard worker
And car fanatic
Who was seemingly always missing
Yet somehow always there.
I see my mother — her kind heart and loving spirit
Working full-time and taking care of four kids
And still getting supper on the table
Before Daddy got home from work.
I see my eldest brother,
Strong, stubborn, never lukewarm.
I see my other brother
Following the oldest's footsteps unintentionally.
I see my sister,
Short, sassy, clever.
I see myself — a mess.
I wonder if they see me the way I do.
I wonder if they see themselves the way I do.

I wonder if other families seem as dysfunctional as ours.
I wonder if others see our dysfunction.
I wonder if we even see our dysfunction.
When I look at my family,
I wonder how we have made it this far.
But I never once wonder what life would be like
With a different family.
When I see my family,
I look past all of the dysfunction and fights
And clashing personalities.
All I see is love.
When I look at my family,
I thank God that He put us together.
And I wouldn't have it
Any
Other
Way.

~Adrienne Sladek

Meet Our Contributors

Kristi Adams is a travel writer who has written about llamas in Europe, the trials of using German GPS, adventure caves, and more. She lives in Germany with her husband and a curmudgeonly rescue cat and is a proud seven-time contributor to the *Chicken Soup for the Soul* series. Read more of her work at www.kristiadamsmedia.com.

Anna Anderson no longer lives in the Midwest. She enjoys butter on everything and never eats oleomargarine of any sort: colored or uncolored.

Nora Beason loves writing and has self-published four books. She enjoys researching an historical event, then writing a story around it. Nora has six more thrilling fiction books that she hopes someday will be published and is currently writing a book on an eighteen-year-old female private investigator and her adventures.

Freelance writer **Florence Calderone Blake** has had over 2,250 stories published in newspapers, magazines, and anthologies. Her memoir has been read on six continents.

Kathy Boecher is a retired granny who spent her life encouraging young people as a drama instructor and public speaking coach. She continues to freelance as a director for children's theater and loves to write her Christian daily blog. She is living the dream with her artist husband of fifty-three years.

Jan Bono's specialty is humorous personal experience. She has published five collections, two poetry chapbooks, nine one-act plays, a dinner theater play, and has written for magazines ranging from *Guideposts* to *Woman's World*. Jan is currently writing a mystery series set on the southwest Washington coast. Learn more at www.JanBonoBooks.com.

Laura L. Bradford treasures her family, no matter how crazy they may appear. Having spent thirty-six years as a family caregiver, she's seen how a little craziness can bring laughter, even to the hardest of days. Now a grandmother to three young children, she's looking forward to many more years of craziness and laughter.

Christy Breedlove is a Texas girl but now calls Georgia home. She and her husband have two children and an evil dog. She published her first book, *When Lightning Strikes*, in 2017. She enjoys geocaching, knitting, and annoying her children. Visit her at www.christybreedlovewrites.com.

Cynthia Briggs celebrates her love of cooking and writing through her cookbooks and lighthearted tales of country living in the 70s and 80s. She writes for newspapers, magazines, and publishers. When she's not writing, Briggs enjoys teaching and coaching budding authors. E-mail her at books@porkchopandapplesauce.net.

D.E. Brigham grew up on a dairy farm in Litchfield, NY. He currently lives and writes in Eastern Tennessee, where he enjoys pickleball, kayaking, bridge, and hiking in the Smoky Mountains. E-mail him at davidebrigham@gmail.com.

Cate Bronson is an accountant turned author of speculative fiction and nonfiction. She is also a Writer's Digest awarded writer in mainstream fiction, and contributor to magazines and anthologies. In her spare time, Cate lounges with her husband and Greyhounds in Florida, and helps retired racing dogs find loving homes.

Melanie Chartoff is an actor/writer/director/charisma coach residing in L.A. A contributor to *Funny Times*, *Huffington Post*, *Jewish Journal*, *Better After Fifty*, she readies an essays compilation, *Got Medicare, Got Menopause, Got Married* for publishing, she voices characters on Cartoon Network's *OK, K.O!* and on the *Rugrats*.

JoAnne Check graduated from Kutztown University and lives in North Carolina. She's authored six books of historical fiction as well as contributions to the *Chicken Soup for the Soul* series. Currently, she is working on the novel *Mad Mattie*. She also loves art, travel, gardening, and camping in the great outdoors. Visit her at www.joannecheck.com.

Mara A. Cohen, Ph.D. is a writer, public speaker, civic activist and mother working on a memoir about family and resilience. Her essays have appeared in numerous literary publications, scholarly journals, and general news outlets. Her greatest joy is spending time with friends and family. Read more of her work at maracohen.com.

Veronica I. Coldiron is a singer/songwriter from Columbus, GA. She has several music CDs and works of short-fiction published and is proudest of being a good wife and mom. Her new full-length suspense thriller, *Nightworld Shadows*, will soon be available online.

Cj Cole lives between the Chesapeake Bay and the Atlantic on the eastern shore of Virginia. She has been a radio personality on the shore for fourteen years and was a weekly advice/opinion columnist for twelve years.

Joy Cook is a freelance writer, substitute teacher, and mother of four. Her story, "Family Meeting," was included in *Chicken Soup for the Soul: The Power of Gratitude*. Joy's busy life often leads to plenty of craziness and her kids often joke, "Well, here goes our crazy family again!" They enjoy finding the perfection amid craziness.

Gwen Cooper received her B.A. in English and Secondary Education in 2007 and completed the Publishing Institute at Denver University in 2009. In her free time, she enjoys krav maga, traveling, and spending time with her husband and Bloodhound in the beautiful Rocky Mountains. Follow her on Twitter @Gwen_Cooper10.

Laura Dailey-Pelle received her master's degree in Health Care Administration from Central Michigan University. She works for a health system in southeastern Michigan as the Director of Radiation Oncology. Laura enjoys walking, reading, writing, and spending time with her family.

Pamela Dawes-Tambornino lives with her husband, two rescue dogs and four cats in the country. After thirty years, she recently retired from teaching English Composition at the college level.

Karen Ekstrom is a frequent contributor to the *Chicken Soup for the Soul* series. She and her husband David have five children, a dog, and three cats. They live on a Texas cattle ranch; all of which gives her lots of entertaining tales for her quirky, offbeat blog www.FlunkingFamily. com. E-mail her at kcekstrom@yahoo.com.

A forty-four-year veteran of the CIA's Special Operations Group and of Israel's Mossad, **John Elliott** holds a Bachelor of Science degree in business, an MBA, and a Juris Doctorate law degree. Fluent in several languages, he was also involved in law enforcement both in the United States and with Interpol in France.

Madeline Evans received her Bachelor of Arts in English in 2016 from Texas A&M University as well as her Master of Education a year later. Madeline teaches middle school English Language Arts in Southeast Texas, and she plans to continue pursuing her passion for writing.

David Fingerman is a retired court clerk who now devotes his time to writing. He lives in Minneapolis and finds Zen in shoveling snow. He's sure one day a relative will write a story in a book about crazy families and it will be about him.

Josephine A. Fitzpatrick is a retired attorney, wife, mother, and grandmother. She loves to write. Josephine co-facilitates a memoir writing class at Cal State University, Long Beach. She has been published in the *Chicken Soup for the Soul* series, *Creative Nonfiction*, and two anthologies.

Marianne Fosnow lives in Fort Mill, SC. When she doesn't have her nose in a book, she enjoys photography and jigsaw puzzles. She's very proud to be a contributor to the *Chicken Soup for the Soul* series!

Sarah Foster is a wife, mother, and writer. She is also a daughter, granddaughter, and sister. She loves her quirky, crazy, wonderful family with all her heart.

Surrounded by pets, farm animals, and gorgeous countryside, **Vera Frances** is a retired banker who enjoys frequenting the nearby mountains for fly fishing, hiking, and painting. She is a nature enthusiast by day and writer by night.

Sally Friedman has been writing personal essays for four decades. A graduate of the University of Pennsylvania, she has contributed to numerous publications including *The New York Times*, *Huffington Post*, *Ladies Home Journal*, *Family Circle* and other regional newspapers and magazines.

Becky G. grew up in the Midwest in a large family full of love and made the typical dysfunctional family moments ones that brought laughter and good memories. When you live your life from the heart, you cherish each individual for the way they are despite all their quirks, as taught to her by her momma, Cathy.

Pamela Gilsenan has five adult children and assorted grandchildren. She lives in the Colorado Rocky Mountains. Thanksgiving is her favorite holiday.

Marsha Henry Goff is an author, editor, journalist, and former newspaper humor columnist. She lives with her husband in the home they built on a rural Kansas hill. She has two sons, four grandchildren and is rich in family and friends who provide her with great copy.

Jase Graves is a college English instructor and a nationally syndicated humor columnist. He is a lifelong resident of East Texas and a Texas A&M Aggie. His hobbies include spending time with his wife and three daughters and sleeping as late as possible. E-mail him at susanjase@ sbcglobal.net.

Virginia B. Harmon lives in beautiful rural Vermont with her wife and son. She is a construction Project Manager by day, and enjoys playing ice hockey, roller derby, and wielding power tools in her spare time.

Rob Harshman was a secondary school teacher for over forty years and has traveled widely around the world. He lives in Mississauga with his wife and spends much time with his family, especially his three grandchildren. Rob enjoys gardening and photography while he continues to write short stories for publication.

Gwen Hart teaches writing at Buena Vista University in Storm Lake, IA. Her poetry, short fiction, and essays have appeared in numerous literary journals and anthologies. Her second poetry collection, *The Empress of Kisses*, won the *Texas Review Press* X.J. Kennedy Poetry Prize.

Erika Hoffman received her B.A and her M.A.T. from Duke University. She used to teach teens; now she teaches retired folks for OLLI at Duke. Erika's nonfiction narratives, essays, and travel articles have been published in magazines, ezines, and anthologies. She has authored books about her 2015 trip to Cuba; they're available as ebooks.

Gina Farella Howley received her Master's in Special Education from Northern Illinois University in 1991. She has been a teacher, tutor, and freelance writer. Most importantly, with husband John, she manages the craziness produced by her three sons Martin (thirteen), Joe (eleven), and Tim (nine). She enjoys beaches, books, chocolate and wine.

C. Joy lives in the Midwest, nestled among cornfields and cows. Mother to five children, grandmother to three, she enjoys gardening, reading, knitting, and traveling.

Megan Pincus Kajitani is a writer, editor, and educator. Her writing has appeared in several anthologies, including three other *Chicken Soup for the Soul* books, and publications such as *The Chronicle of Higher Education*, *Mothering* magazine, and *Huffington Post*. As Meeg Pincus, she also writes nonfiction for children.

Dana Klosner-Wehner's first foray into writing was selling a script to NBC-TV. She began her freelance journalism career after her kids were born because she wanted to spend mega-amounts of time with them, like her mom did with her. Her work has appeared in major newspapers and magazines. Learn more at www.Danaklosner.com.

April Knight is an author and an artist and never misses an opportunity to walk in the woods, go on a picnic or ride an elephant. She believes life is short and our happiest days, our greatest love and our biggest adventures could all still be ahead of us.

Jeanne Kraus is a retired elementary educator who taught in Florida for over forty years. She now lives in Tennessee and continues to write short stories and poems for anthologies. She has been published in other *Chicken Soup for the Soul* books and is an author of three children's books and a Boomer Humor book for women.

Dale Kueter wrote for Iowa newspapers for forty-one years. He grew up on an Iowa farm and graduated with a degree in journalism from the University of Iowa in 1958. Kueter is the author of three books. He and his wife are the parents of five daughters and have fourteen grandchildren. They live in Cedar Rapids, IA.

Joyce Laird is a freelance writer living in Southern California. Her features have been published in a wide range of consumer magazines and she is a regular contributor to *Woman's World* magazine and the *Chicken Soup for the Soul* series. Joyce is also a member of Mystery Writers of America.

Cathi LaMarche is an essayist, novelist, and writing coach whose work has appeared in nearly three-dozen anthologies. When not immersed in the written word, she stays busy reading, cooking, gardening, and walking her three beloved Collies.

With the passing of her mother, **Cindy Legorreta** has fulfilled one task — that of caregiver. Now she intends to keep a promise made. She will begin her "second life," post retirement, and relocate with hubby, Ric, to his home city of New Orleans. There Cindy plans to focus her energies — guiding and mentoring NOLA youth at risk.

Barbara LoMonaco has worked for Chicken Soup for the Soul as an editor since 1998. She has co-authored two *Chicken Soup for the Soul* book titles and has had stories published in numerous other titles. Barbara is a graduate of the University of Southern California and has a teaching credential.

Sarah Lyons is a writer and stay-at-home mom to her six children, including three-year-old triplets. She enjoys cooking, reading, and spending time outdoors with her family. They live in a suburb of Kansas City.

Christie Collins Lypka is a Southern Girl — born and bred. She has been writing short stories since she was four years old. She is currently working on her first book, *Into the Abyss*. She resides in Michigan with her Yankee husband, Mike.

Betty Maloney is a multi-award-winning painter and artist. A widow, she is surrounded by wonderful grandchildren and Boston Terriers.

Mike McCrobie is a retired high school teacher from Oswego, NY. He writes a column for his local newspaper, *The Palladium-Times*, and has self published *Our Oswego*, a collection of columns about his home town. His children (Matt, Sarah, Brian, and Eric) along with wife Sally have provided plenty of "crazy family" memories.

Bronwyn McIntyre is a writer on a mission to make every story more fun and more human. In her spare time, she walks dogs and drinks coffee in alarming quantities. You can check out her other works at jollywriter.com.

Rosemary McLaughlin has loved stories and storytelling since she was a little girl — writing plays for her friends to perform. After thirty-five years as an English teacher and reading her students' writing, she is now retired and doing her own writing and enjoying her family. She is proud to be part of the *Chicken Soup for the Soul* series. E-mail her at Rosemarymclaugh@gmail.com.

Janet Lynn Mitchell is an author, speaker, wife, mother, grandmother, and friend. Her passion is to communicate God's love to others. Whether writing, speaking or hanging out, she hopes to encourage others. Her latest book, *A Voice Once Silenced*, is soon to be released.

Ela Oakland loves hot dogs. When there are too many buns she makes croutons and feeds the crumbs to the birds.

Senia J. Owensby has always loved to write. Her passion for writing has produced a broad variety of literature, including several books and an assortment of articles for numerous publications. She's married to the love of her life and is also a mother and grandmother. Read her blog posts at finishingwellinlife.com.

Lucia Paul is an award-winning humor writer whose work has been published in anthologies including *That's Paris: Life, Love and Sarcasm in the City of Light*; *Motherhood May Cause Drowsiness: Funny Stories by Sleepy Moms*; *It's Really 10 Months Special Delivery* and *Laugh Out Loud: 40 Women Humorists Celebrate Then and Now*.

Saralee Perel is an award-winning nationally syndicated columnist. She may be reached at sperel@saraleeperel.com or via her website at www.SaraleePerel.com.

Kay Conner Pliszka is a retired high school teacher and an award-winning author with over thirty-five stories and articles in books, magazines, and newspapers. This marks her twenty-fourth entry in *Chicken Soup for the Soul* books. E-mail Kay for humorous or spiritual presentations at kmpliszka@comcast.net.

Connie K. Pombo is an inspirational author, speaker, and freelance writer. She is a frequent contributor to the *Chicken Soup for the Soul* series and other anthologies. When not speaking, writing or traveling, Connie enjoys spending time with her three grandchildren. Contact her at www.conniepombo.com.

This is **Mark Rickerby's** twentieth story published in the *Chicken Soup for the Soul* series. He's the co-creator/head writer of *Big Sky*, an upcoming western series, writer for Six Rivers Entertainment, co-author of his father's memoir, *The Other Belfast: An Irish Youth*, and lyricist/singer of fifteen songs for *Great Big World*, a CD for his daughters, Marli and Emma.

Heather Rodin is an award-winning writer, speaker, and author of two books. She serves as Executive Director of Hope Grows Haiti, a mission she and her husband, Gord, founded in 2007. With six married children and twelve grandchildren, her life bursts with blessings. E-mail her at hrodin@hopegrows.ca.

Martha Roggli taught elementary school for twenty-five years before retiring four years ago. She now spends her time taking Jazzercise classes, long naps, and writing. She advises anyone who enjoys writing to find a group. The people will become your inspiration, mentors, and best critics.

Bill Rouhana is the CEO of Chicken Soup for the Soul. He is married to Amy Newmark, the Publisher and Editor-in-Chief of Chicken Soup for the Soul. They like to tell stories about each other. Their four children think they are equally crazy.

Chana R. Rubinstein is a stay-at-home mom of five children. She loves to write in her spare time. Poetry is the most fun, but she is also currently working on her third novel and has written several children's books.

John M. Scanlan is a 1983 graduate of the United States Naval Academy and retired from the Marine Corps as a Lieutenant Colonel aviator. He currently resides on Hilton Head Island, SC, and is pursuing a second career as a writer. E-mail John at ping1@hargray.com.

Helen A. Scieszka is a former ad executive, psychologist, professor, church pastoral associate, and marriage and family life director; also a published author of three novels and in *Chicken Soup for the Soul* books. She loves reading, travel, music, photography, art, sports, and family genealogy. Learn more at drhelenscieszka.com.

Troy Seate's storytelling runs the gamut from Horror Novel Reviews Best Short Fiction Award to the *Chicken Soup for the Soul* series. His memoirs and essays report fact while his fiction incorporates realism, fantasy, or humor featuring the quirkiest of characters.

Jen P. Simmons is a wife and a new mom who works full-time for an outdoor clothing company. Jen enjoys a good cuppa, being with family, writing short stories, gardening, the great outdoors, and triathlons. She hopes to write content that inspires others to embrace this life motto: live well, laugh often, and love much.

Debbie Sistare, a retired RN and Ordained Minister, has a BSN and a Master's in Religious Psychology. Her thirty-year nursing career included flight nursing, hospital nursing, nursing instructor, hospital supervisor and private counselor. Her 1st fiction novel, *In Search of the Key of David: The Symbol of Knowledge*, debuts in 2018.

Adrienne Sladek is a small-town girl from Fruitland, MO, who always looks for peace in the craziness of life. She loves her family and her dog Brutus more than anything, is a baker by profession, and a lover of all things pumpkin. However, most importantly, she is a forgiven child of a loving God.

Reverend James L. Snyder is an award-winning author whose writings have appeared in more than eighty periodicals including *Guideposts*. *In Pursuit of God: The Life of A.W. Tozer*, Snyder's first book, won the Reader's Choice Award in 1992 from *Christianity Today*. Snyder has authored and edited thirty books altogether.

Suzette Martinez Standring is a syndicated spirituality columnist with GateHouse Media/More Content Now. She is a recipient of the 2017 Will Rogers Humanitarian Award from the National Society of Newspaper Columnists. E-mail her at suzmar@comcast.net or visit www.readsuzette.com. In God all things are possible.

Jan Kendall St.Cyr is a wife, mother of four and grandmother of six. Always an avid reader, journal writer, and writer of a monthly column in her hometown paper, Jan uses the experiences of her family as fodder for her many stories.

Shannon Stocker is a coma survivor and RSD/CRPS advocate. Shannon has previously written for the *Chicken Soup for the Soul* series, writes picture books, blogs, is a musician, and is currently writing her memoir. Her world revolves around Greg, Cassidy, and Tye. Follow her crazy life at shannonstocker.com and on twitter @iwriteforkidz.

B.J. Taylor harbors a secret smile every time her brother calls to recount another family caper. She's an award-winning author whose work has appeared in *Guideposts*, many *Chicken Soup for the Soul* books, and numerous other publications. You can reach her at www.bjtaylor.com and check out her dog blog at www.bjtaylor.com/blog.

Dawn Turzio is an award-winning writer whose work has been featured in many publications including *The New York Times*, *MSN Lifestyle*, *Yahoo! News*, and *Salon,* which can be found at www.dawnturzio.com.

Cheryl E. Uhrig is an author, illustrator, cartoonist and painter. Cheryl's stories and artwork appear in children's books, magazines, and in local galleries. She lives in Newmarket, Ontario with her family.

Miriam Van Scott is an author and photographer whose credits include children's books, magazine articles, television productions, website content and reference books. Her latest titles include *Song of Old: An Advent Calendar for the Spirit* and the *Shakespeare Goes Pop* series. Learn more at miriamvanscott.com.

Originally from Seattle, **Barbara Walker** is a physical therapist, wife, mother, and grandmother living in the Atlanta, GA area. When she's not helping her patients walk again, she enjoys reading alone, hiking with her husband, playing with her grandchildren and laughing with everyone.

David Warren is the vice president of Lutz Blades and resides in Kettering, OH, with his wife Angela and daughter Marissa. David loves traveling, music, and writing. He is the author of two children's books and has stories in various magazines. He survived full cardiac arrest and this is his sixth story published in the *Chicken Soup for the Soul* series.

S.E. White is an author, blogger, and mom to three tiny destroyers. The kids assist in the writing process by asking when dinner is — every fifteen minutes. Her work can be found on sites like *HerViewFromHome*, *Mamalode*, *Parent.co* and *Pregnant Chicken*.

Arthur Wiknik, Jr. served in Vietnam with the 101st Airborne Division and has appeared on the History Channel and the Military Channel. This is the eighth *Chicken Soup for the Soul* book he has been published in. Arthur frequently shares his military experiences at schools and civic organizations. Learn more at www.namsense.com.

Jenny Wilson is a writer, wife, and mother. She is blessed with a wonderful family that pulls together when one member is in need. They're quirky, but loving, and she counts them among her greatest blessings.

Following a career in Nuclear Medicine, **Melissa Wootan** is joyfully exploring her creative side. She enjoys writing and is a regular guest on *San Antonio Living*, an hour-long lifestyle-show on San Antonio's NBC affiliate, where she shares all of her best DIY and decorating tips. Contact her at www.facebook.com/chicvintique.

Hannah Yoder is a misplaced Tennessean wandering the foreign lands of Southern Ohio. She is a full-time crazy horse lady, part-time trainer of off-the-track Thoroughbreds, and a part-time freelance writer.

Jerry Zezima writes a nationally syndicated humor column for his hometown paper, the *Stamford Advocate,* in Connecticut. He is the author of three books. He lives on Long Island, NY with his wife, Sue. They have two daughters, three grandchildren and many creditors. Mr. Zezima has no interesting hobbies.

Meet Amy Newmark

Amy Newmark is the bestselling author, editor-in-chief, and publisher of the *Chicken Soup for the Soul* book series. Since 2008, she has published more than 150 new books, most of them national bestsellers in the U.S. and Canada, more than doubling the number of Chicken Soup for the Soul titles in print today. She is also the author of *Simply Happy*, a crash course in Chicken Soup for the Soul advice and wisdom that is filled with easy-to-implement, practical tips for enjoying a better life.

Amy is credited with revitalizing the Chicken Soup for the Soul brand, which has been a publishing industry phenomenon since the first book came out in 1993. By compiling inspirational and aspirational true stories curated from ordinary people who have had extraordinary experiences, Amy has kept the twenty-five-year-old Chicken Soup for the Soul brand fresh and relevant.

Amy graduated *magna cum laude* from Harvard University where she majored in Portuguese and minored in French. She then embarked on a three-decade career as a Wall Street analyst, a hedge fund manager, and a corporate executive in the technology field. She is a Chartered Financial Analyst.

Her return to literary pursuits was inevitable, as her honors thesis in college involved traveling throughout Brazil's impoverished northeast region, collecting stories from regular people. She is delighted to have

come full circle in her writing career — from collecting stories "from the people" in Brazil as a twenty-year-old to, three decades later, collecting stories "from the people" for Chicken Soup for the Soul.

When Amy and her husband Bill, the CEO of Chicken Soup for the Soul, are not working, they are visiting their four grown children and their first grandchild.

Follow Amy on Twitter @amynewmark. Listen to her free podcast, The Chicken Soup for the Soul Podcast, at www.chickensoup.podbean. com, or find it at Apple Podcasts, Google Play, the Podcasts app on iPhone, or using your favorite podcast app on other devices.

Thank You

We had so much fun reading and editing these stories about all those eccentric, wacky, quirky, and very lovable family members. We all have them, and it's wonderful sharing them with each other. We are grateful to all our story contributors and fans, who shared thousands of stories about family members. Barbara LoMonaco, Elaine Kimbler, and Susan Heim read all the stories that were submitted and narrowed down the list to a few hundred finalists that ended up filling this collection.

Susan Heim did the preliminary round of editing and Associate Publisher D'ette Corona continued to be Amy's right-hand woman in creating the final manuscript and working with all our wonderful writers. Barbara LoMonaco and Kristiana Pastir, along with outside proofreader Elaine Kimbler, jumped in at the end to proof, proof, proof. And yes, there will always be typos anyway, so feel free to let us know about them at webmaster@chickensoupforthesoul.com and we will correct them in future printings.

The whole publishing team deserves a hand, including Senior Director of Marketing Maureen Peltier, Senior Director of Production Victor Cataldo, executive assistant Mary Fisher, editor Ronelle Frankel, and graphic designer Daniel Zaccari, who turned our manuscript into this beautiful book.

Sharing Happiness, Inspiration, and Hope

eal people sharing real stories, every day, all over the world. In 2007, *USA Today* named *Chicken Soup for the Soul* one of the five most memorable books in the last quarter-century. With over 100 million books sold to date in the U.S. and Canada alone, more than 250 titles in print, and translations into nearly fifty languages, "chicken soup for the soul®" is one of the world's best-known phrases.

Today, twenty-five years after we first began sharing happiness, inspiration and hope through our books, we continue to delight our readers with new titles, but have also evolved beyond the bookstore with super premium pet food, television shows, podcasts, positive journalism from aplus.com, movies and TV shows on the Popcornflix app, and licensed products, all revolving around true stories, as we continue "changing the world one story at a time®." Thanks for reading!

Chicken Soup for the Soul

Share with Us

We all have had Chicken Soup for the Soul moments in our lives. If you would like to share your story or poem with millions of people around the world, go to chickensoup.com and click on "Submit Your Story." You may be able to help another reader and become a published author at the same time. Some of our past contributors have launched writing and speaking careers from the publication of their stories in our books!

We only accept story submissions via our website. They are no longer accepted via mail or fax. Visit our website, www.chickensoup.com, and click on Submit Your Story for our writing guidelines and a list of topics we are working on.

To contact us regarding other matters, please send us an e-mail through webmaster@chickensoupforthesoul.com, or fax or write us at:

Chicken Soup for the Soul
P.O. Box 700
Cos Cob, CT 06807-0700
Fax: 203-861-7194

One more note from your friends at Chicken Soup for the Soul: Occasionally, we receive an unsolicited book manuscript from one of our readers, and we would like to respectfully inform you that we do not accept unsolicited manuscripts and we must discard the ones that appear.

Chicken Soup for the Soul

for the Soul

All in the Family

101 Incredible
Stories about Our
Funny, Quirky,
Lovable &
"Dysfunctional"
Families

Jack Canfield,
Mark Victor Hansen, Amy Newmark
and Susan M. Heim

Paperback: 978-1-935096-39-9
eBook: 978-1-61159-144-6

and wacky relatives

Chicken Soup for the Soul

Changing lives one story at a time ®
www.chickensoup.com